The Heart of the Creator

Manny Mpock

ISBN 978-1-68570-319-6 (paperback)
ISBN 978-1-68570-320-2 (digital)

Christian Faith Publishing
832 Park Avenue
Meadville, PA 16335
www.christianfaithpublishing.com

Printed in the United States of America

Contents

Introduction

Accept it or not, man is the greatest creation in the universe—a masterpiece with a mental capacity and ability whose potential the modern man has barely tapped into. This is a special gift bestowed on man to reflect his creator's ability. Looking at the current state of humanity, it is quite sad to see just how much the perceived value of man has deteriorated.

His known accomplishments to date are impressive with improving understanding and application of the laws of nature. Some of these aspects of understanding have contributed to improved life expectancy, comfort, travel, agriculture, entertainment, and some other areas of the quality of life. On the other hand, the same understanding has led to the creation of some of the deadliest killing techniques and machines yet seen in day-to-day living and triggers for unending violence in society. He is now very proficient in the development of weapons of mass destruction in warfare and engaged in very nefarious scientific undertakings with very disturbing and unpleasant outcomes.

However, man appears to be living with the proverbial "elephant in the room" problem. He seems to be shying away from honestly engaging and confronting life's greatest challenge—the question of why humans die and must die.

The bulk of human efforts appear to be a struggle to delay the inevitable death caused by disease, natural disasters, murderers, age, animal, and human predators. Some humans have gone as far as stating that under certain circumstances, they would rather kill themselves to escape humiliation in this life and rather face the consequences in the "hereafter" or whatever exists after this relatively short life.

Is there really a "hereafter" or, clearly put, life beyond the grave? And if so, in what form is it? It is known that a dead body rots, and so logically, if there is life beyond the grave, it will take a different form than the current earthly form—or does it? And what is that form? Why has a human's lifespan shrunken to about a tenth of what it is claimed to have been in the past?

Why is humanity here on this floating sphere called Earth? Why is there evil, and why is there the good we see? Who or what is responsible for good and evil? Is there a spirit dimension to life, and if there is, what is the implication?

Even trees can live for thousands of years if undisturbed. Mountains and minerals from which human bodies are made can exist indefinitely, but not man. Was man really meant to be born, sometimes toil through life in peril, and then just die off and fade away into oblivion?

Could man have been created as an eagle to soar in the skies, but along the way, something happened, whereby he resigned himself to live with a chicken mentality and just accept what appears to be his fate—someone's dinner in the food chain?

Is there any way to find out the *truth* about life of a man in a very simple but verifiable way without religious crackling? Can man honestly and verifiably overcome death outside of religion? Is man's apparent fate reversible and restoration to his intended glory possible? Is Jerusalem a cup of trembling and a realistic peace possible in the Middle East between Israel and its neighbors?

There is someone who says *yes* and claims to have a trail of high-powered neon signs spanning thousands of years starting from a distant point of time to the very origins of humanity's past until now and into the future, clearly mapped out. He is willing and ready to continuously disclose his creation blueprints and to accept a global challenge to his claim, and here is what he dares to say:

> I have a very transparent and verifiable global
> track record, therefore, remember the former

things of the past, for I am the Creator, and there is no other; I am the Creator of everything that is, and there is none like me. I had declared the end from the beginning, and from ancient times things that were to happen, many have, and the others not yet, until the appointed time that I stated. My counsel will always stand, and I will do all my pleasure. Indeed, what I have spoken, I will also bring to pass. What I have purposed, I will also do, and no one can change it, no one.

Even from the beginning I have declared things easily verifiable by you; before they came to pass, I proclaimed them to you, so you would know it is no coincidence or an accident. For I know the plans I have for my creation even in your current state, plans to prosper you and not to harm you, plans to give you hope and a future and an expected end. I am willing to listen and reason together with you. No one can explain me, except by revelation and that is why I have made myself accessible; I will reveal myself to anyone who truly seeks me just as I have done to my servants in the past.

He therefore claims to be an interactive Creator, though shrouded in invisibility, can—when he chooses—manifest himself visibly in intelligible ways easily understandable by humans. He is willing to engage anyone who seeks the truth with no mediators needed, just a one-on-one interaction with anyone on earth because it means that much to him. He offers an open invitation for anyone to challenge every word and claim he has ever uttered and hold him to it and see if his claim of being the Creator is true or not, and he has said a lot—a whole lot.

Does the world have climate issues, sickness and diseases, famines, other global-size problems, and death? Is this a golden opportunity for the world to call this self-declared Creator out to the mat and call his bluff? What an opportunity for a showdown that could change the world! As he has declared, everything starts with him and will end with him exactly as he has stated. If he cannot back his claims, the whole world should castigate him since he has left himself wide open for verification. What has humanity to lose in getting the truth?

Humanity may be pleasantly surprised to find out that its worst problem in existence has an amazingly simple solution—so simple that even a fool cannot go wrong. If the Creator is therefore real, he can speak, hear, interact; and if what he claims is true, this makes the exercise quite simple indeed.

As he indicated—and just to emphasize the simplicity, what he has to say is so simple to understand and verify that even a fool cannot go wrong—being the Creator who has done a lot to reveal himself, let us follow the neon-lit trail from the knowable beginning and see where and what they lead to as stated by him.

Chapter 1

The End of Mortality

The dreadful journey—separation

Don the oracle of Wall Street had just completed one of his most ingeniously crafted corporate acquisitions, which further solidified him as one of the all-time great darlings of shareholders of his portfolio of companies. He enjoyed the power and prestige that came with his wealth, and his counsel was greatly sought in the business circles at the highest levels and even by nations. He had more personal wealth than many good-sized nations, and he was not shy in making that known. Statements from him could drive the global stock markets in different directions, and the successive string of huge profits for his shareholders bore testimony to his financial wizardry.

Clearing off his glass of champagne, he leaned back, relaxed in his seat, and drifted off into a light sleep as the thrill of the success was already wearing off even though it had just been a few hours since the closure of the deal. As he playfully toggled thoughts through his mind, he saw certain scenes that caught his attention. His lack of genuine joy in normal-life issues and a certain level of coldness seemed to have eclipsed his heart. Even his laughter had no mirth to it, and he felt so empty for a man who had no lack in the world and was capable of personally bankrolling a nation. He could get anything he wanted from anywhere in the world, and he had a dozen medical specialists watching his health like a man on life support though he was in perfect health and did not even have allergies to anything known—he was a picture of perfect health.

Don was being driven by limousine to his next company meeting when suddenly the freeway erupted into a mixture of loud noises ranging from shrill blaring horns to screeching tires and a series of explosions. A projectile that looked like the fuselage of an airplane made a direct hit on Don's automobile, killing him and the driver on impact; they did not even see it coming. It was an eight-seater plane which had lost power and control, and desperately trying an unsuccessful landing on the freeway, the only open space available, the uncontrollable plane plunged like a rock, resulting in it crashing into the freeway, causing multiple-vehicle fires and casualties.

As Don looked up, he saw that he was engulfed by the shadow of death. He could not see the face of death, nor did he have any desire whatsoever; he just knew it, and it was like nothing he had ever imagined death to be. Strangely enough, Don found himself emerging, or what he realized was his real self, leaving his physical fleshly body. Though he was fully intact and unhurt, the lifeless body he was leaving behind looked like a slowly smoldering shell of flesh crushed between metal frames.

He could hear, see, smell and did not feel inhibited initially, but he was trapped within the gates of death. The last things he saw before he was totally eclipsed by the shadows were a set of fire engines driving to the accident scene from both sides of the freeway, his corpse and the driver's, and then he was fully engulfed and then whisked into its dark passageway where he floated along effortlessly, as he was conveyed by the powerful, invisible but mortal force of death. He was, however, all alone and engulfed in unnerving silence. He knew the driver was dead too, but where was he? Far down the passageway, he could see light rays, and that provided some comfort because everything was happening so fast, and he had absolutely no control of anything.

He was gently discharged unto a magnificent platform that looked like a one-thousand-star equivalent of an ultraplush airport or train terminal. Happy to be out of the terrifying power of the grip of death's shadow, he was awestruck by the grandeur of the majestic structure. Inside the beautiful greenish-blue glasslike walls was the biggest jumbotron he had ever laid eyes on. It was dead quiet, and he had never experienced that kind of silence. On the platform was an attendant, a very formidable humanlike being but with a grave countenance that looked like that of a loving religious minister about to bury a loved congregant with an uncertain future.

This was getting unsettling because it all looked like something he had heard about before. The beauty and elegance of the architecture and construction of the terminal was just breathtaking, and nothing on earth even came close. The landscape was out of this world, and the vibrancy of colors was quite spectacular. As a matter of fact, he knew what this meant. One thing became obvious to Don—he was in a timeless dimension—and though it looked incredibly beautiful and peaceful in his surrounding, a fiery tornado was beginning to brew inside him. Under different circumstances, this was one place he would pay any price to visit or just travel through, but no, not at this time. He knew he did not want to be here, and he was beginning to develop the shakes—the very bad shakes of an alcoholic.

He quickly glanced at the edge of the platform and saw what looked like an autonomous driven tram awaiting a passenger. The attendant then politely but sorrowfully asked Don if he could be of service. Don knew he was dead though he never felt more alive. His reflexes were sharp, and his brain and perception were out of this world and never better. He knew this was not good, and for once in his adult life, he was helpless and very afraid. The whole landscape was spectacularly dazzling, but he did not care for it, faced with what he knew was his fate.

Mustering some courage, he asked the attendant what the jumbotron was for and where the tram was going, even though he already knew the answer.

"The jumbotron will provide answers to your questions. The transport will take you to your temporary accommodation until later when you will be taken to your final residence," he graciously and very politely replied.

Don glanced down at the tram's optically glowing rails descending into the bowels of the eerily quiet and enormous low mountainlike structure through a foreboding pitch-black opening. The low mountain stretched out for miles into the horizon, indicating it could easily have stretched out about the distance of a quarter of Earth in length. He could not even imagine a cavity that gigantic and he knew he was not mistaken about the faint guttural sounds emanating from deep down under and a cold shudder ran down his back, adding to his shakes.

As he looked at the attendant, he asked, "Is there anything I can do to not go down there?"

Replying, the attendant said, "It is appointed unto man once to die and after that judgment. He will have to give an account of how he lived his life in relation to his fellow humans and to the Creator. The jumbotron has a record of your whole life—like every human born on earth—and you are welcome to view it. On judgment day, the rest of the humans also being judged will have a chance to view your life with you. You already know that."

With that, Don jumped at the opportunity—anything to delay his trip. He knew without a shadow of doubt about his fate and where he was heading. The lounge door opened automatically, and he walked in and slumped into an amazingly comfortable and plush couch that smelled like the best blend of rose flower petals. He did not need to vocalize his questions because his thoughts were transparent to the jumbotron.

His life started flashing before his eyes starting at the age of accountability, and for the first time, he knew exactly at what age he knew and fully understood right from wrong with an understanding of its true implications. His life unfolded like the most exquisite five-dimensional movie—just as in real life. He could see his exact locations from his life, hear his words, see his deeds, thoughts, and motives in every single moment of his life, in every graphic detail. He scrolled through his memory effortlessly for all the great deeds he had done while alive, but he screamed as he saw his motives for the best top fifty of his best life's deeds.

He could not find anything worth hanging unto, and it got worse as he went down the list because even he himself was profoundly disgusted by most of what he saw. He knew deep inside that he was doomed, and his very existence and great deeds were like filthy rags even to him looking at his life. He did not need anyone to tell him what was right or wrong because his own conscience bore screaming witness to truth, and that was quite frightening.

He knew quite well how much he had intentionally and directly contributed to the ravages of economic exploitation of the helpless, bigotry, failure to address threats to the health of his fellowmen when he knew he should have, human trafficking, destruction of the environment by many of the products his companies manufactured, and the nefarious human genetic engineering research he had secretly funded with massive profits. He did all this because he could, and he enjoyed wielding the power he had especially when there was potential for massive profit margins, and it brought him the notoriety he craved for. What had mattered to him in life and business was whether there was profit to be made at any cost; it was just business.

As if this was not bad enough, in the fifth dimension offered by the jumbotron, he could very clearly and graphically see how his life negatively impacted every other person on earth and how he had directly and indirectly contributed to the horror of atrocities and violence in society. Without realizing it, he found himself screaming in horror as he gaped at the jumbotron, knowing everything he saw was accurate and captured in vivid color. Even though he had been conscious of that in life, his immediate desires clouded his judgment, and he just brushed off the thoughts whenever they came up.

As if what he had already seen was not bad enough, his heart sank further when he saw the myriad of opportunities he had had of chances to discuss life issues, like life after death and the existence of a Creator and the possibility of some kind of accountability of his social and moral decisions while alive and at the inevitable end of human life. He even saw how often he had been directed at acknowledging the existence of a creator and establishing a relationship with him. He saw the numerous times when he actually pondered the evidence to support his existence. It was clear as night and day at how much effort had been made to lead him to the Creator and he was shocked and he knew he could not use the excuse that he did not know. He wished he had such an excuse. In life, he had been too

13

sharp mentally to overlook evidence by chance; it had been a conscious decision based on his acute logical processing ability.

Afraid to see more, he bolted out of his seat, sweating and trembling very badly, and headed straight for the tram; but then, he stopped. Looking at the attendant who had a very grave and sympathetic expression on his face, he asked if he could be allowed to see his funeral service. The attendant was granted permission by the Creator, to which he motioned to the jumbotron, and the funeral service came into play.

He saw his friends, business partners, and dignitaries from around the globe in expensive dark suits and endless array of beautiful wreaths and flower bouquets. The motorcade to the cemetery was over a mile long. It was a funeral service befitting a great prince, one he would have liked had it not been that he knew his fate. Shaking his head in disgust, "What a waste," he sneered while honestly wishing that none of them would end up with his fate though he knew better.

He listened to the two-faced preacher who heaped praises and accolades on his life's accomplishments, the same one who was more spirited in preaching for a financial contribution to his institution than the more important things about life such as what happens after death—at least as he now saw it. Oh, how he wished he could warn his equally foolish friends and partners who all believed that only the weak and poor needed a god or Creator. Their conviction was that these weaklings could not make it in life, and so they used their imaginary pies in the sky after they died as a crutch to maintain their sanity while trudging through life. Boy, was he ever so wrong!

The eulogy was even more disgusting as it was full of lies and stupid exaggerations about his work ethics and him being a self-made man and generous to a fault with his great philanthropic undertakings. He wished he could reach out and punch the preacher in the mouth when he said with confidence that his death had transferred him to a better place. Why did religious people not tell people the truth or at least point them to where they could find it? Did most of them really know the truth? Looking back, truth was a lot simpler than humanity made it to be.

Oh, how could he have been so blind and foolish to go along with the belief that life and the universe were just accidents! Well, believing this made him acceptable in the upper echelons of society. Most of his colleagues disdained those who believed in a Creator because they were a circle of self-made men with lots of power, and taking orders from a Creator made them look weak and foolish.

He was more alive in death than he had ever been, and now, having rejected any relationship with the Creator, he was doomed because he could not undo the impact of his life to humanity. With one final look, he glanced at his grave in the cemetery, and on the tombstone was written, "REST IN PEACE."

"Hogwash to the fool who ever came up with senseless profanity like that for the dead," he swore.

He bolted out of the lounge, wailing in despair as he plunged into the tram, sobbing helplessly. He was dazed and very afraid as it chugged down into the dark cavern at the very greatly appreciated speed of a slow funeral procession. As it descended into the bowels, he thought he could hear echoes of some long distant moans and groans with unmistakable undertones of dejection, just like people possessed by their own painful thoughts in solitary confinement. He judged that the sounds were quite distant in nature, miles away, as he could not see anyone; it was so dark and ugly compared to the beauty just outside, and he was all alone and isolated, reminiscent of his penthouse in his concrete, steel, and glass jungle.

He gnashed his teeth like a possessed lunatic as the tram sank deeper and deeper; oh, how he wished someone would reach out to his family and friends and warn them of the reality of life beyond the grave and the absolute stupidity that things just materialized from nothing. It again occurred to him that he was enveloped in the same shroud of the shadow of death and he could feel the weight of the darkness and the smell of death was awful.

All the jokes and mockery of those who believed in life after death, heaven and hell now haunted him because the joke was now on him. How he wished he had just one more minute of life to take back and make amends with the Creator. If people thought life was complex, they needed to step into eternity.

Covered in tears and overwhelming grief, he did not notice the tram stop and the door open. He was ushered out into a solitary holding cell, and dazed by his tears, he heard the door slam shut; and as he tumbled into a chair, through the thick darkness, he saw the faint glow of words written on the doorposts which read,

> ETERNITY MEANS NO END, AND THIS FATE WAS NEEDLESSLY CHOSEN BY THE OCCUPIER.

Upon reading this, he wailed even louder, and the last thing he heard was the tram chugging away to the surface, probably for another transport. The regret was worse than hot coals. Looking back into life, nothing was worth coming here for; he would gladly give all he had in his previous life in exchange for escaping this dreadful place.

He once believed he was among the few who owned the world and could do as they pleased, for who could stop or touch the ultrarich? Now he realized that humans were indeed living in a world created by someone else, who had graciously given it to man. Now he was desperately afraid of and not wanting to meet that someone because he had insulted the giver and abused everything he had been given and had failed to contribute to society as he knew he should have. He needed no court or jury because his conscience and his whole life shown by the jumbotron said it all—"guilty as charged."

He tried calling out for mercy, help, or someone to talk to, begging the departing tram not to leave him there, but only an eerie silence echoed back; the place was practically lifeless and dark, similar to a barren planet in Earth's solar system except shrouded in darkness. Oh, how dreadful!

Without realizing it, he had been gnashing his full set of teeth, and the sound jolted him to reality as he could now see life more clearly. Why had he been so blind and stupid? None of the things he had chased in life was worth even a lick. How could he have embraced the lie that life was just an accident even with the evidence provided by DNA, RNA, how organized and structured life on earth was, with its self-sustaining design. He realized that all the billions of dollars he had toiled for and amassed, not a penny accompanied him into death, not even the suit on his charred remains. He had done all that for nothing and destroyed many lives for absolutely nothing including his.

He shuddered at the key takeaway from reviewing his life in the jumbotron. The worst thing he had done in his whole life, for which he fully knew, was that he had chosen to side with his fellow friends, associates, himself, and man as a whole against the Creator of the universe. He had falsely castigated the one who created him in front of his adoring fans, and he saw how many times he swore and used the f-word as a prefix to the Redeemer and the Creator and disparaged them to look intelligent and superior in the eyes of people. He saw how empowering that had been to him as his ego grew larger than life to the point where he believed he alone determined his own destiny.

There was a word he was even afraid to use to describe his attitude—*pride*, that was the word. It had gotten the best of him, and looking at it, he was no better than the devil. He had always known deep inside him that there had to be a Creator, but he wanted a relationship on his own terms, not on the terms of the Creator. His terms were selfish and hurt other people but stoked his ego, and it felt good at the time. He saw that he did not care for the Creator's ways because the Creator cared deeply about people, not him, and that was his problem.

How tragic, for now he was a captive of his own thoughts, and it burned deep inside! The thought of his final residence added more grief on him, and he was confident he knew where and why he deserved it; yes, he did not like it at all, but he knew he deserved it, and maybe even worse. He was now more acutely aware of knowledge; he was an eternal creature and could not just be burned off into oblivion or destroyed into nonexistence even as some religious teachers had taught.

It hurt him more because every decision he made in life was intentional, and he had indeed been granted enough revelations and opportunities to understand and relate to the Creator. He knew he was guilty and could not blame anyone—especially not even the

Creator. He realized that in his life, he had rejected love for the Creator and, therefore, people, rejected the offer of redemption from the Redeemer in favor of the vanity of love for money, self-gratification at any cost, and fame.

Caping his misery was another thing he had seen in his funeral, just how quickly his colleagues and partners had dumped even the very thoughts of him just hours after his death—like a diseased, hot, and burnt potato. His position was filled within hours of his death, and full allegiance was given to his successor within a day of his death and even by his supposedly adoring personal assistant and other office personnel. As soon as the new guy guaranteed their jobs with added pay and bonuses, his personal effects from his office were moved into storage even before his funeral. There was no regard at all or concern for him as a person; he had just been a disposable money-generation machine—apparently, the only thing his shareholders cared about. Oh, how it hurt, it hurt so badly, and he had turned his back on the one who truly loved and cared about him as a person—a living soul. It was gut-wrenching to see that in the eyes of humanity, he was just another statistic in the undesirable column.

Like fire in his bones was the regret of his choice for ending up as a fool! Now it was clear that it was too late; and he wept, shaking all over, and there was neither a comforter nor a sound from another soul but just the pain and anguish.

The journey home

Dimitri was raised as a tough and cold-blooded executioner for the mob, and he was surrounded by so much power and money that he was easily transformed into an ultimate narcissist. He was raised up in wealth and was very well educated in science and grew up under hardcore teachings where science, natural laws, and the state rules were all that was needed for the good life.

He was a very handsome young man and a hardened killer who worked with the special execution and disposal unit of one of the most feared mobs in his country. He was almost untouchable because he was only known by reputation and name but not in person, and he enjoyed the power his name and position wielded. He started believing that he had the power of life and death, and he could kill or keep alive as he pleased. This, combined with his relative youth, his acutely analytic mind, great intelligence, resourcefulness, and insatiable ambitions, made him very deadly. He introduced the concept of sending small caskets to targets to either accept requested terms from the mob or have their remains processed by the undertaker. No one had ever failed to comply and lived to see the next day of their lives, not even the upper echelons in government, especially since the government was a frequent client.

It had been exactly two months since he was diagnosed with an abdominal terminal cancer. He had asked for what it would take to cure him, and after examination by about a dozen of the best specialists known anywhere, he was told he was incurable, and it had nothing to do with money. He was given a maximum of six months to live, and two months had already gone by.

He had never known fear until now. In the past, he always got what he wanted; but for the first time in his life, he had a problem money and power could not buy, and his mortality hit him. The gradual pain gained traction, and he could see that his strength was slowly ebbing away.

Feeling like a mortally wounded creature, he was uncertain on how to spend the rest of the days he had left in life, and it got him thinking about death in a real sense. None of his relatives had yet died, and this was strange and somewhat perplexing.

Lost in his thoughts one day, sitting at the park to look for some solitude, he was approached by one of the most harmless-looking young men Dimitri had ever met. He had the most sympathetic eyes, and his demeanor was that of joy, kindness, and love impersonated. He slid into the bench and sat down next to Dimitri with a very affectionate and disarming aura about him, and he introduced himself as Vladimir. Dimitri's analytic mind determined this was a very harmless individual, and he was clearly not a killer.

There was a very elusive group that promoted the existence of a Creator in the country and the state considered it a subversive group and it was to be stamped out. The leader was known as Vladimir, and no one outside of the group knew him.

Looking at Dimitri, he said, "Brother Dimitri, I have been specially sent with a message and an invitation for you. I have been commissioned to introduce you to the Creator of the heavens and the earth, who sits outside of the laws of science and nature." Without giving him a chance to respond, he continued, "The Creator loves you, and he is giving you a chance to know him and a chance to spend life with him after you die—if you so choose. As a sign to you, the terminal cancer that your physicians have diagnosed you with will depart your body today, and you will not die from it regardless of whether you choose to accept the Creator's call or not. Within the hour, that dull pain radiating in your abdominal cavity will cease, and you will know it."

Dimitri was startled because no one outside of the immediate medical experts knew about his condition, and all the physicians were sworn to secrecy or face death.

Dimitri did not even know what to say as he sat there, stunned. Vladimir gently laid his hand on Dimitri's arm and quietly prayed for him, asking the Creator to heal him and that his eyes be opened to the truth about the Creator and life. He then reached into his jacket, pulled out a well-worn book, handed it to Dimitri, and asked him to study it, for it contained information about the Creator; and in turn, he was to let those he could in the community know that there is indeed a Creator.

Vladimir looked tenderly at him, put his hand on his shoulder, rose; and as he was leaving, he said, "Brother Dimitri, you are a chosen vessel, and if you are willing, the Creator will empower you to lead many to him through you." And with that, he gingerly walked into the street corner and into the crowd, never to be seen again.

Within a few moments, while still trying to process what just happened, Dimitri felt a warm glow spread around his abdomen, exterminating the cancerous cells, and the warmth seemed to crack the shell around his heart. Gently grabbing his belly, somehow, he knew he was being healed and something was happening to him that he could not explain.

Dimitri had been caught off guard, and everything had happened so fast that he had not had enough time to react one way or the other. It was like a very fast tornado that had ripped and shredded everything he had ever known in a one two punch that left him flat on his back.

Within the hour, Dimitri's pain from his cancer had vanished, and all repeated medical tests even months after turned out negative. The tumor had vanished, and his strength and vitality had returned. No science could explain this. Some of the doctors who had diagnosed him tried to explain it away as an unusual coincidence, but he was too afraid to tell them what really happened. He knew the truth, and he had imaging slides of the tumor as proof that it was not a misdiagnosis as some had claimed.

He devoured the book the young man had given him and saw things in it that he had never known, and it explained the mysterious power that had healed him supernaturally in the simplest of terms. He could not prove or explain it but knew without a shadow of a doubt that it was as real as the nose on his face. He had to start by accepting it by faith as a revelation or go insane because he knew how it happened, and the pictures of the tumor at multiple stages of its development were in his possession. He knew that if he were to tell what had happened the way it did, none could understand or believe him, and they would think he was a lunatic.

Based on what he found in the book, he came to grips with the fact that he was an evil person who deserved a certain fate if he died in his current state. He was at a loss as to why the Creator had chosen to show him such mercy, considering how evil he now saw that he had been to this point. He accepted the fact that he had been given a choice and healed unconditionally, an option that was totally contradictory to the way he had operated.

He had asked for three weeks off from work to ponder over things, which was granted because his condition was understood at the highest powers in office. He knew he was too smart to not acknowledge the fact that he was outclassed by the Creator who had been responsible for healing him the way he did. After having read the book Vladimir gave him multiple times over, he decided that he needed to ask for something equally impossible from the Creator directly as he had seen others do in the book. He just needed confirmation because it was a life-and-painful-death decision from his perspective; well, a different kind of death—the kind he had been used to dishing out. It had to be something that did not require a third party, just the Creator and him in the privacy of his home.

He had never knelt before anyone in his life, but he knew that it was a symbol of humility. He knew that because many a people had knelt before him behind mirrored glass to have their lives spared. His first prayer had been to thank the Creator for healing him, the second to accept the call, and now the third was for the Creator to send him the "anointing." He wanted this to happen in a way he would know, like what happened to the first group of people to whom he had done the same, because he had read that he needed that to be able to carry out the assignment given him. He therefore set an appointed time with the Creator for the next day at exactly 3:00 p.m. his local time.

Locked in his house alone, he knelt by his bed at exactly 2:59 p.m. local time, and as he was repeating his request, at exactly 3:00 p.m., what felt like a bolt of lightning passed down his head into his body and stayed there for a full minute. He could hear himself joyfully singing in a language he could not understand for over a half hour, and singing is something he had never done before nor cared to do. Dimitri knew then that this was the confirmation that there was a Creator whom he could talk to in prayer, the one who truly had the power of life and death in his hands. He got up a changed man and then asked the Creator to give him a heart, the power to be merciful to others, to refrain from his old practices of evil, the power to truly love and be brave in carrying forward the commission given him.

Dimitri's life changed forever because he left the mob, killed no more, and pursued a lifestyle that was the very opposite of what he had been doing. He believed the Creator indeed, and he lived the rest of his life to expand one of the most powerful underground and elusive ministries that led many in his nation and beyond to the knowledge of the Creator. The greatest thing of all was the fact that the Creator kept his promises, and that made walking with him incredibly easy. He had learned that the Creator did not need anyone fighting for him, and if one trusted him and stood on his word, he never failed.

This was the first time he knew anyone who kept his word even against all odds and did not give assignments that were impossible to do. Dimitri knew power well that was laced with death threats, but the Creator's power was different. There were no death threats; it was so pure and so good and made the Creator appear like a weakling in normal human perspective. Now he understood what it meant to be meek, and he could only define it as unlimited power under complete control and unprovokable. There was nothing like this in his sphere of existence.

He still could not understand why the Creator would choose a despicable person like him as a messenger instead of letting him perish for the evil he had perpetrated during his career and life for that matter. The strength he saw in the tenderness of Vladimir and even the compassion were guiding posts for his understanding of the Creator's influence on people. His life was enriched even more with a wife. She was one of the most loving human beings he had ever met. She helped to teach him a lot in his love walk. What a life!

Thirty-five years later, surrounded by loved ones who had come to know the Creator through his work, he spoke to them as he knew the time had come for his departure. He never knew the knowledge of the Creator and interaction with him would be so amazingly gratifying. Life had been tough but more rewarding in seeing people come into the knowledge of the Creator of the heavens and the earth. He saw the Creator perform miracles through him and divine power manifested in ways that made him wonder why entire nations sidelined the Creator of all things. His love was unexplainable and his ways far higher than that of men's ways, and so were his thoughts. Based on all that he had seen through to this point in his life, he believed love is really what the world needed—yes, the love of the Creator propagated through men.

With a look of gratitude and humility, he encouraged those members of his ministry who were present and asked them to keep the faith and keep up the work. With that exhortation, he raised his feet to the bed; and with a look of gratitude and contentment, he breathed his last with a very gratified expression on his face, dying an extremely happy man who looked ever so handsome and relaxed in death.

As the gates of death cast its shadow around him, his spirit disengaged from his body and floated upward. As he looked around him, he saw his brethren weeping around his shell of a body on the bed. As the gates closed, he drifted into a chute and passageway and was guided through effortlessly through the ugly darkness of death. Far out, he could see the beautiful rays of tantalizing light down in a distance. Eventually, he emerged from an opening into the presence of a remarkable and startling reception. The first thing he became immediately aware of was the sense of timelessness; this was eternity and there was absolutely no sense of time and he was more alive than he had ever been and was even more handsome than he had ever imagined possible.

There were celestial fireworks and a jubilating angelic host lining his path to a glistening and flaming golden chariot. The angelic host also included a security detail, and instinctively, he knew this was for him and he broke into tears of joy and ecstasy. The love emanating from those around him was infectious, and it could be felt. Nothing had prepared him for this, and it had never crossed his mind or his wildest imagination in all that he had ever read or heard. He knew this was the pathway to the Creator's dwelling place.

He was surrounded by intense beauty, and everything was just so transparently lively, lovely, and very inclusive. He cherished the company, and he knew he was cherished in great abandon. For the first time in his life, he felt loved by those visible to him as he had ever wished—a thousand times more than the love of a loving and proud grandmother. He knew his precious wife, the one person he loved in this world above any other, had loved him greatly and would have given him her heart if he needed it to stay alive without giving it a second thought, but her love for him fell miserably short and just as much as his fell even shorter in comparison to what he was experiencing.

He just wished the whole world could have just a one-minute taste of this loving splendor—just one minute, and it would change the world. The whole human race talks about love but does not understand the very meaning of it and how it really feels in eternity in the presence of the Creator. Oh, how he wished the world will embrace the Creator of the heavens and the earth and depart from the foolish practices of false religions, cults, and the madness of atheism which all contribute to the perpetration of cruelty, hate, and violence.

He was led with jubilation into the chariot where he climbed in and, holding the armrests, stood and broke into a song of joy and thanksgiving, backed by voices and instruments that were out of this world. The joy was a billion times in magnitude compared to the most joyous occasion he ever saw on earth. He knew he was heading home to join his other brothers, sisters and meet his Creator who eagerly awaited his arrival at the entrance of his home.

As he looked upward, emblazed in the sky in rainbow coloring of exquisite quality, he saw lettering that said,

ETERNITY MEANS NO END, AND WELCOME HOME, DIMITRI MY SON!

As he looked up covered in tears of joy, he could still not understand or explain why the Creator would accept an evil dead dog like him, why he was given such a privilege for absolutely free, knowing the kind of life he had led before his encounter with Vladimir. Why would his Creator pay such a hideous price at the redemption instead of just casting him aside like the rubbish blob he really was? This was love and joy like he never knew possible; oh, what amazing grace indeed! This is life! Even the music was so delightful, the kind played in the happiest occasions in life though a thousand times better and the dancing was just infectious and oh, what love!

As the chariot rose higher, the convertible design allowed him to soak in the view in all of its glory. Suddenly, up ahead of him in the distance was what looked like a gigantic diamond with a brilliance so awesome there are no human words to accurately describe it. It is true what he read about. Its size was like that of the full moon when viewed from Earth. It was a city—a city like nothing known to man, which is the dwelling place the Creator had gone back to prepare for those who choose to live with him in eternity.

It could only be summarily described as a physical place suspended high in the heavens like a satellite planet that was glowing, and its brilliance was like that of a very precious jewel, like a jasper, clear as crystal. As he drew closer, he could see that it had a great high wall, designed more for beauty to accentuate the indescribable architecture, and the wall had twelve gates.

The city was laid out like a square, as long as it is wide, measuring 1,400 miles, or 2,200 kilometers, in length, width, and height. The wall of the city was a work of art with nothing like it because it was made of jasper, and the city of pure gold as pure as glass. The foundations of the city walls were decorated with every kind of precious stone. The first foundation was jasper, the second sapphire, the third agate, the fourth emerald, the fifth onyx, the sixth ruby, the seventh chrysolite, the eighth beryl, the ninth topaz, the tenth turquoise, the eleventh jacinth, and the twelfth amethyst. There were twelve gates to get into the city, and each gate was made of a single pearl of exquisite beauty and splendor. The great boulevard of the city is of gold as pure as transparent glass. This city was to descend from its creation point eventually and was meant to be suspended above the earth at the appropriate time, just as the moon is, to serve as the residence of the redeemed from the earth, allowing for travel between the earth residents and those in this eternal city.

What a place, one reserved for the redeemed, and what a reception was in store for Dimitri as he travelled home to a great fanfare, a treat the Creator reserved for every one of his redeemed children going home. Dimitri sang and danced with his company all the way home.

Chapter 2

Meet the Creator

Excerpts of the celestial throne room precreation conference

FATHER. I would like us to undertake a special project, a father's gift
to his beloved Son—a creation for you and by you, living creatures with an unprecedented procreative ability to populate
their habitation, then the grand prize and our pride and joy—
and I know you love him already, the human. Him you will
create in our image and our Spirit as part of his constitution.
This means that he will be given a mind with unprecedented
and almost unlimited creative abilities using the tools you create
for him and a unique domain to thrive in. Whatever he sets his
mind to do, he will be able, in time, within his realm. With his
wife, we would give man the ability to procreate and populate
his habitation, just like the other living creatures you will be
creating. I look forward to seeing the children running around
in everlasting bliss and ecstatic joy, enveloped in our love. He
will be an eternal being like us with freedom and all the privileges he can handle. Yes, a unique free spirit, a little lower than
the angels in some respects, but with dominion over the habitation you create for them. He will be our regent for that domain.

SPIRIT. The Father understands the responsibility associated with
such freedom to a living creature since this implies that he will
have a soul, spirit, and a body, and he is being offered the gift of
free will in a communal setting!

FATHER. Yes, free will will he have. Like you and the Son, he will choose his own eternal destiny and that of his progeny. Every created angel has free will, and man will too. To every single procreated offspring, you and the Son will inculcate spiritual and physical gifts complementary to the others so that they will be productive and contribute to the society in all areas and enterprises in life that make their lives and that of others very gratifyingly pleasant and fulfilling. We shall give him a mind with an eternally unlimited desire to want to learn, explore, and dig deep from our inexhaustible eternal resources. This will give them a reason to look forward to each new day, since they shall live in a timed frame of existence that will stretch into eternity.

The Son understood the scope of the job and weighed the enormity and scale of the project. Even for an infinite being living in eternity, this was extremely huge and exciting, quite unique and significantly different from the creation of the angels, now being personal and nothing like it before.

SON, *with euphoric delight and great anticipation.* In that, you mean unlike us, who are Spirit, his home will have to be self-sustaining to support that physical body.

FATHER. Absolutely correct in every sense. Behold, the blueprints! His physical body will be made with the same elements of his environment, which he will be able to relate to, and each element will be made of a unity particle that will be a composite of subparticles, all of which will lend themselves to his use. The particle will be a microcosm of his surrounding and all animate and inanimate things. It will be a magnificent, eternal, and renewable tool for his use, and my son, because it is your gift, you will be the builder and sustainer of all that you create.

SON. Father, free will and almost unlimited mental ability and resources come with risks and responsibilities. Freedom of choice has consequences especially in a multiparty social and communal interaction. I can see the tremendous amount of thought and love involved in this magnificent project. However, I see a potential problem.

FATHER. I was waiting for you to bring it up, and you are right. Man will be given the freedom to obey or disobey our directives. If he chooses to reject our guidance, to his own hurt, I will graciously uncouple our Spirit from him if that turns out to be his choice. Secondly, I will choose in certain circumstances not to know the outcome of certain things until after they have transpired. Yes, he will be created and have our spiritual constitution analogous to his physical DNA. Our Spirit will be withdrawn if he chooses absolute autonomy and not want us as part of his constitution, whereby he decides to stray out of the boundaries we establish for him.

SON. That will be death—spiritual death and subsequently a physical death, seeing he will be mortal! Without our Spirit, man would be responsible for his own decisions, a dangerous prospect when those decisions affect others. The potential of becoming depraved will result in ultimate mandatory and necessary separation from us.

FATHER. We have never and will never force ourselves on anyone; that will not be love. We do not want robots. We want children created to be free in what is good for them and those around them and the environment they live in.

SPIRIT. This will work perfectly if man chooses to stay and live knowing only the good as guided by the Spirit. In the design, it is obvious you are making provision for a salvage job should he make the dreaded self-destructive choice.

FATHER. Yes, and I will leave that choice up to him and I will let him understand the responsibility and consequences that accompany choices in the knowledge of good and evil especially when others are involved in the mix. As I indicated, I will in certain cases choose not to see or know the outcome of some of the events until they have happened, and we shall never violate man's freedom to choose.

SON. The risk of negative possibilities is so high that we need to provide an insurance policy, a redemption plan, for the sake of love and justice. Seeing this is a gargantuan project of love, I am offering myself for the redemption price should man's decision be self-destructive. I see you want man to have a second chance should he err. The Spirit and I absolutely agree with the plan. I know and understand the price, and yes, I offer myself as the ransom to pay for his redemption should it be needed. However, who will determine the exact nature of the penalty?

FATHER. Excellent! Offer accepted, my son, for you will create and sustain him, his habitation, and his surrounding universe. Just remember, your love and kindness are also subject to acceptance or rejection by man. Regarding the question on the penalty, that will be determined by man himself in cahoots with other participants, who will become evident to you eventually.

SPIRIT. Father, as you put it yourself, love is only tested when you must truly love those who hate you. The love, life, joy, and sonship offered man is unprecedented, and it will be disappointing but understandable if he fails to appreciate it. But as you have instructed, your love is unconditional within the bounds you have established.

FATHER. True, it is easy to love those who love you, but the father's love, our love, transcends rejection. True love is very costly. It has a very high price tag indeed, and the kingdom is established on love, justice, mercy, kindness, goodness, grace, and free will! We never will violate an individual's free will, and that is why your kingdom is good.

SPIRIT. From the outline in the blueprints and accompanying time-table, it will take six human domain days of human time to complete the job. It would be interesting to see things from a referenced timeline and might take a little while to get used to it.

FATHER. That is correct, and it is tied to his environment, for which he will need some reference points for his activities. Also, after you create the atom, it will be your creation gift to man. What he will learn to do with it through eternity will be limitless. We have creation to do. Let's roll.

With this, the very Creator of the heavens and the earth, the Redeemer, was offered as the price to reinstate man, should he err, before the foundation of the earth was laid down to ensure that man did not have to be destroyed in case he fell but, rather, be simply restored at his own free will at no cost to him.

Creation of earth and the heavens

Prior to creating the earth, the Son created the basic atom then used it as the fundamental building block of the physical matrices to lay the astronomical complex and ethereal marvel known as the foundation of the earth. He arranged this structure, formed as a collection of majestic masses of rocks and gaseous balls with cores of various densities as their locations required, into galactic clusters. All were weighted out with great precision though being too innumerable to number by mortals but designed for weight and beauty with each having a distinct identity and name. Though defying even angelic capacity and understanding, they were not only structured for function and beauty as the foundation of the earth but to display the unfathomable greatness, power, and the essence of the majesty of the Creator with a full allure for timeless study, exploration, and enjoyment. Even more importantly, the invisible Creator wanted to leave his signature for all of creation to behold, understand, and remember him by.

The markers for these structures were stretched and positioned as an unrolled scroll. Earth's galaxy was located in its unique galactic cluster, which was fashioned into a spiral with a slot made for Earth's solar system. The distances between the galaxies and their associated stars were designed to provide the gravitational anchor and support to balance and protect the planned earth. This also provided the appropriate gravitational forces to accommodate, support it and its planned occupants, and allow for a great view of the celestial beauty of other galaxies, which NASA and other international space agencies are utilizing.

During the laying of this foundation, all was kept shrouded in darkness. Then he moved Earth's solar system into place with its related planets; but its star, like all the others in Earth's foundation, was not ignited but rather kept shrouded in darkness in its marker form.

The created earth was without form and void but covered in abundance of water, an unusual liquid with properties unlike other liquids to be created after. The immense power of the Spirit hovering over the earth in the formative process triggered mountain-sized tsunami waves on the water, making the created earth look like a gigantic spherical cauldron with ferocious geysers.

Following the blueprints, the Creator created light to provide illumination as part of the creation process, and the earth was awash with brilliant light stretching across the visible horizon of the earth. The explosion of light in the darkness was breathtaking, and it obliterated the darkness. He then contained the light, allowing a demarcation between the darkness and the light, thereby allowing light and darkness to be seen next to each other. The lighted part he called day, and the dark he called night, and these were to alternate on a fixed rotation defined as a day and the time tied to the eventual rotational speed of Earth relative to its star, our sun, or the satellites around Earth.

He then separated the waters covering Earth's crust into three parts—one part assuaged under Earth's crust into unfathomable-sized fountains and cisterns around the globe of Earth, the other lifted into the firmament and heavens as water-laden clouds and leaving just enough on Earth's crust to create rivers, lakes, seas, and oceans, leaving plenty of dry land. The seas and oceans were specially mineralized for part of the function for which they were created for cleaning and sustaining Earth's water cycle.

A moon was sized and put in place to perpetually generate just the right amount of attractive force on Earth to later control the tidal motion of the seas, among other planned functions like a time marker.

Minor adjustments were made to the position of Earth relative to the other planets in its solar system for additional comfort to the future occupants. A gaseous protective canopy was put around it as well as a magnetic field running along the south and the north poles.

Between the protective canopy on its upper atmosphere and the solid earth was the gaseous mixture complex maintained in this region comprising of elements needed to support all planned cellular living organisms on earth and the mechanism to automatically sustain them, including the Creator's crown jewel, man.

As a signature from the ultimate Creator, the Father had a surprise of epic and unimaginable proportions. On the day the stars were created, at the Creator's command, there was an ignition that activated them, shaking the universe. All the trillions upon trillions of stars in the billions upon billions of galaxies, some of Earth's foundation markers, specifically the stars, exploded spontaneously into trillions upon trillions of self-sustaining thermonuclear reactors with the heat and light blasting into interstellar space. It was like flipping on a light switch to light up space, and the reverberating shock and electromagnetic waves are still felt today in the intergalactic entropic resonance with some still travelling to reach Earth from the more distant stars.

The size of the universe, as punctuated by the galaxies, was just too much to grasp even for the majestic angels, and they were beside themselves in absolute awe, delight, adoration, and worshiped in reverence of the majesty of the Creator. The sheer sizes and power of the black holes indicated the awesomeness of the created galaxies and the unlimited power of the Creator.

Simultaneously, the entire galactic systems were set in motion of rotating and revolving planets and stars, including Earth's, joining the ballet of optical wonders still gyrating across the empty space of the universe. The heavenly host of angels watched as the synchronized and harmonious motion of these indescribable giants graced space with their tantalizing optical waves. They were showcasing the Creator's majesty with predetermined revolutionary and rotational velocities that staggered even the heavenly angels as they watched in great wonder. Every planet and star in these galaxies had been weighted and sized perfectly for their locations, and some galaxies clocked travel velocities of about six hundred kilometers per second, an awesome and even terrifying marvel. As frightening as those velocities were, they were designed not to be felt by the future occupants of Earth by the carefully computed gravitational force.

As the angelic host watched, it appeared as though there was no end to the optical display as the astronomical distances between the galaxies and stars were beyond even the angelic view limits. They could not wait to see why the Father was going into such extreme lengths to create such an elaborate and intricate structure anchored by an entire universe. Each star and planet in the universe was named and delicately weighted, and from the Creator's habitation, they looked like the display of fireworks humans are used to.

With Earth's solar system fully in place with its accompanying planets and their moons, Earth was tilted on its axis, and its revolution, having been initiated, resulted in the creation of measurable time and predictable seasons. From space, Earth exhibited such beauty with its mesmerizing crystalline deep-blue hue so much so that it is the envy of the entire universe. It floated there like a beautiful and exquisite jewel with nothing like it in the universe, let alone its solar system, which comprised mostly of very barren and hostile planet habitats unfit to support and sustain human life but protective to Earth.

To add to Earth's allure and beauty, land and aquatic plants, great and small beasts on earth and water, airborne animals and birds were all created for beauty and serve in the sustenance of Earth in its marvelously created and significantly buffered ecosystem.

Around Earth, in its upper atmosphere, the Creator deployed a protective canopy against potentially harmful solar radiation reaching Earth's surface and implemented a self-sustaining design like natural fertilization with lightning and rain, ocean waves cleansing action, water cycle and autonomous carbon dioxide/oxygen generation, culminating in Earth's self-sufficiency in distinctive design and adaptation characteristics in Earth moving, flying, and aquatic creatures.

The mystery of life

The earth seemed clearly designed and created to be inhabited with an ecosystem meant to sustain life using single cellular as well as multicellular organisms and inanimate elements autonomously and perpetually.

When the relatively lower forms of life were created, their inanimate matrices were spontaneously triggered into life by the Spirit from the single-celled to the multicellular great beasts and plants. Each of these cellular life forms had a mysterious genetic code in every cell simply described as a DNA and/or RNA unique to the species with no possibility of natural genetic mixing across species. These were responsible for the sustenance and propagation of these organisms. This life trigger was incomprehensible to the angels because they are created as spirits and have no physical bodies and, therefore, were understandably amazed.

Using the same atoms in the soil of Earth, he created man, a multicellular composite of somatic and nerve cells. This time, the life essence trigger was different. The Spirit breathed life into the human—a human spirit different from the spirit of the animals. A living soul was made from an inanimate mass of atoms on Earth's crust encased in a physical body. The Creator then breathed his own Spirit into the man to couple with the man's spirit, resulting in a creature that knew only good for as long as the Spirit of the Creator was in him.

The Creator, taking man to a vantage point, in a moment of time, showed him all of the magnificently created world with all the teeming variety and species of life forms. Though filled with amazement, he did not find the other creatures necessarily compatible or particularly desirable for his personal company; this had been anticipated by the Creator. He then put the man into a very deep sleep, took a rib off his side, and went to work in creating the female version of the man, and the finished product was a marvel to behold. The Creator looked at the work, and like the rest of the creation, she was built for function and beauty just like the man.

The woman was a very gorgeous and magnificent creature to look at. She looked relatively tender compared to the man but somewhat mysterious. Mentally, she was identical to the man, and they complemented each other perfectly, with each providing traits that the other lacked for the specific tasks they were created for. It was clear that they were designed to function as a team because neither of them appeared to have had the complete package, and the Creator did this to make their companionship the most enjoyable.

Just like the man, in a moment of time, she was shown all of the earthly creation and then led to the man. Looking at her, the man turned to look in the direction of the sound of the Creator as if to say, "Awesome job, Lord." He knew she was a part of him, and he liked and understood what he saw and spontaneously loved her very dearly as much as he liked her. They walked toward each other with their mutual affections literally worn on their sleeves in childlike abandon, love unfeigned and pure. He knew she was created with a part of him, and none of the other magnificent creatures came close to his desire for companionship as the woman did, and the feeling was evidently mutual.

The first wedding ceremony

The man turned to the direction of the voice of the Creator, questioningly whispering to him if he could keep her, to which the Creator said it was entirely up to her. With both their consent stated, the Creator decided he needed to perform a marriage ceremony so he could have her as his wife and him as her husband. The Creator called him Adam.

This first wedding ceremony performed by the Creator, the Son as the best man, and the Spirit executed and energized the eternal bond, and he blessed them and asked that they be fruitful and multiply to replenish the earth and to enjoy each other. This was the Creator's masterpiece and he was very happy and pleased with the product and the love and joy was thick as molasses and quite contagious. This ended the creation process.

The wedding present

For a wedding present, the Creator gave the man sovereignty over all his earthly creation and the legal and spiritual authority over the earth, for him to rule and subdue on behalf of the Creator; he was subject only to the Creator and no one else. He was given ownership of the whole earth and its content to enjoy as he pleased and to create whatever he so desired with the components found in it. He was also given a specially created, climate-controlled, lush, and self-manicuring garden which he was to tend. It was loaded with every fruit tree and food crop, and it was just plain beautiful to behold. This garden was designed for function and exquisite beauty and to serve as a starter home for him to modify, build, and upgrade to his taste.

As the Father, Son, and Spirit were leaving earth, they admitted that the entire creation was really good, and they departed to give Adam and his wife their privacy while promising to drop by often. Adam and his wife also had a twenty-four-hour access communication voice line at their disposal to reach the Creator.

The honeymoon

With the spirit of the Creator in man, he was empowered directly by the Creator and existed in the domain where only good existed, and that is all he and the woman knew. Though connected to the Creator, man was aware that he could detach himself and live an autonomous life which would let him decide between good and evil for himself. Having the Creator's Spirit in him eliminated the need for any laws to live by.

The only law he knew was to love and he needed no effort to keep it because it was all he knew and it was as easy as breathing, considering that it was very beautiful and fulfilling. To stay connected to the Creator as a regent, man was asked not to eat of the fruit of the tree of knowledge of good and evil, the only commandment he was given. This was to remind him of his responsibility and his role as a steward and not the creator of the domain assigned to him. He had been made to understand that every creature has a role and responsibility in the world to give them a reason to live for and fulfilment in living.

Another peculiar tree in the garden, the tree of life, bore fruit that represented a choice to live forever if eaten. Man could eat it if he so desired as well as every other of the countless fruit trees. He clearly understood the implications of what life and death meant in the context of existence.

None of the two trees were of concern to the man because he lived a very gratifying and fulfilling life between his company with his wife and the Creator. Life was ecstatic and very good and was free of any worries, pain, fatigue, sorrow, anxiety, or sickness, and there was nothing but joy, peace, and contentment. Adam and his wife enjoyed playing and swimming with the water creatures for fun, and they played and lived like children, greatly fond of each other.

A created angel, a covering cherub who had at one time served in the presence of the throne of the Creator, called Lucifer was in awe of man's commanding position and bestowed authority over an entire planet with many forms of living creatures. As he pondered about man, many thoughts crossed his mind. Today, this creature is also known by additional names which include the devil, Satan, etc.

The love the man and the woman had for each other was incredibly wholesome, and the affection they shared was as the taste of honey. Their total devotion and passion to please each other in great abandon was effortless, and the manifestation of pure inhuman selflessness in the marriage union is yet to be duplicated on earth since then. They had greatly captured the giving nature of their creator, and it was awesome and a reflection of his image especially the loving and caring way they dealt with the other creatures.

They cherished each other, loving each other as they desired to be loved, and looked forward eagerly to their times of fellowship with the Creator at the end of each day. They flooded him with questions in unobvious and very intricate aspects of science, anatomy, botany, the universe, and about everything they encountered in the day, and he enjoyed the fellowship. They grew in knowledge, and the Creator gave them their privacy and room to explore and start implementing their creative knowledge and abilities for accommodation to their taste. Nothing was imposed on them by the Creator, and they lacked absolutely nothing.

The woman had an inexhaustible bank of recipes, and each meal was different and an amazing symphony on the palate. Their life was an unending honeymoon—no stress, no headaches, no fatigue, no boredom—just unending exploration, and blissful great research projects they were given.

Chapter 3

The Epicenter of Evil

In the shadows of invisibility paced the great fallen but powerful angel, Lucifer, with self-inflicted wounds, foaming at the mouth in great rage and jealousy as he helplessly watched the created human from a distance.

When this angel was created, he used to be the seal of perfection, who was full of wisdom and was absolutely perfect in beauty. At one time he was the anointed cherub who was assigned special responsibilities in the celestial holy mountain of the Creator and with permission to walk in the midst of the stones of divine fire, which was the closest proximity to the seat of power of the Creator. He was blameless in his ways from the day he was created and performed his duties like every other angel. He was greatly admired by all, and the Creator was praised for his great and incredible wisdom in crafting such beauty, with phenomenal music built into him. He was indeed the great music leader and a real joy to listen to. The Creator received similar praise for other angels for their different attributes appropriate for performing their respective duties.

But Lucifer's heart became lifted up in pride because of his great beauty and certain special responsibilities he had been given in addition to his great splendor. As a result, his wisdom became corrupted and warped because he felt he deserved the praises and adoration for his beauty and not the Creator. At some point between the creation of the universe and Adam being in the garden of Eden (the exact time being known only by the Creator), he had become incensed with wanting to be like and ascend above his Creator.

In this state of mind, he set in his heart to ascend to some lofty location in the heavens, to raise and establish his throne above the stars of the Creator, to sit on the mount of assembly in the recesses of the north, a position only the Creator is entitled to. He had become terribly demented and, therefore, blinded by his egregious desires and aspirations to the fact that he was just another creature with very limited power despite the authority that had been delegated to him. In earthly jargon, one could say the power went to his head. In the Creator's dwelling, every created angel has free will which can be exercised within the set boundaries, and this applied to Lucifer as well.

His madness affected many in different ways, resulting in a very unpleasant outcome, for which reason he lost his position in his original habitation with the Creator. He was cast out of there along with his accomplices generally referred to as fallen angels or demons and now lives as a transient with a generous level of travel freedom. At an appointed time determined by the Creator, he and his cohorts will be carried off to a destination any creature should dread but quite fitting for his numerous crimes by his own admission.

Lucifer, looking down during one of his trips, saw something that grieved him greatly—someone the Creator also loved and who was happy and made the Creator and the other angels happy. He moaned in agony as he wondered about what could have been if he had been content with how much he was also cherished; nothing but a dreadful fate now awaited him.

Now taking his eyes off himself to seeing the immensity of the creation of the universe, it became clear that he and the angelic host that had followed him in his sedition had totally miscalculated the Creator's infinite power. They had mistaken his incomprehensible love, offer of free will, and patience for vulnerability. Sadly, because of his great pride and narcissistic inclination, he had no remorse but kept up the hope of succeeding in his delusional and futile quest of taking the place of the Creator. The acts and activities perpetrated by Lucifer sprung out of the free will the Creator had given all his creation, resulted in a sequence of events, making him the epicenter and source of evil in the created universe with pride being its main root.

Not only did this Lucifer want the adoration and worship that was only fitting for the Creator, but he also appeared to have disdain toward the created man with a determination to drag him down with some deceptive tactic if he could, seeing man also had free will. He then set out to develop a scheme to implement his diabolic plan.

This put him and his demons on a collision course with humans who will get a chance to review his file sometime in the future, with many serving as prosecution witnesses. No known living creatures in the heavens or the earth have been able to live lives unaffected by Lucifer.

Lucifer's war room conference

LUCIFER. Fellow warriors, I do not need to give you the gory details of what the Creator has done. You all have seen or heard of it by now. I cannot understand him loving that miserable new creature. He created a whole massive universe for that puny little man. I get sick just watching how he spends time with them and splurging lovingly over them. He created the earth for him to inhabit, loaded with some gems we had in heaven and an unlimited number of toys for him to create and explore with. He has just given the whole thing to him for free, and to make matters worse, we are not allowed to physically enter the earth in human forms or talk to the man directly. As if that was not bad enough, the Creator has given him procreative power and ability! He can have offspring, and he is responsible for populating the entire earth. He can create things, procreate, but we cannot—and for eternity. This is even worse than being kicked out of heaven—the little puny man created in all the glory and protected from us by the Creator.

DAG. I can't believe another creature can create music that great; that beautiful voice the woman has reminds me of the good old days in heaven. Her voice is as lovely as—

LUCIFER, *cutting in*. No one plays music better than I do! No one! I was created with music built in me, and no one is better looking and lovelier than I! No one—and do not forget it!

BELZE. Luc, we understand that, but even you can't stand your own music anymore. I have bigger concerns. In looking at the way the galaxies have been designed, unless I am missing something, I do not know if any of you share some concerns I see. Did you see the black holes in the various galaxies especially the sneaky roaming ones that can show up where needed? I wonder what they are there for. They just look like bottomless pits with forces I won't even want to test out? I remember the words of the Creator when judgment was passed on us for our crimes. It brings the scary thoughts of the dreaded lake of fire. Could it be our final abode when it is all over for us? This is dreadful, and I am beginning to feel the walls closing in.

LUCIFER. Belze, pull yourself together. I need to think. This little created man is technically replacing us, yes. Like us all, he has been given free will, and he can choose to stay in the Creator's side by accepting to knowing just good and be fully dependent on the Creator. That will ensure that he will have an eternal existence of bliss, liberty, and splendor like no other—like we once did. However, if we could deceive him into doubting the Creator and relying on himself in deciding right and wrong, the choice of knowing good and evil, he could become just like one of us, narcissistic, with insatiable desires, and vile, which will break the Creator's heart. This could be an opening for the man and his offspring to spend eternity with us in pain and anguish instead of with the Creator.

DAG. We are not allowed to take physical human forms when on the earth in the presence of humans. We are free to roam across the interstellar space and even Earth's solar system if we operate as unidentifiable flying objects (UFOs) especially in remote places, but we are ordered not to physically meddle, or we would face immediate incarceration.

LUCIFER. But we can go in through a creature willing to allow us to possess it for a season—call it a demonic possession. The serpent

is a wise and beautiful animal, and I will try to get its cooperation to use its voice to reach out to man—if the serpent allows
me. Remember, I am the silver-tongued prince charming.

BELZE. Which is why we are in this predicament today. If I were to
recommend a strategy, I would not go to the man. He will kick
your teeth in...well, that of the serpent, and technically you.
Wait till you see the woman by herself, away from the man, and
then lay on the charm—thick and sticky—and lots of luck, Luc.
You better sweet talk the serpent into allowing you to use it. I
wonder what it will charge for that service. My second choice
should the serpent turn you down would be the peacock, who
reminds me of the old you, but the serpent will do, I suppose.

The ill-fated encounter

After an intense and prolonged period of planning and waiting,
during which Lucifer (now with the operational title of Satan the
devil) had to endure the ecstatic silky voice of the woman singing so
happily through the garden. This was something she did while she
harvested fruits and vegetables to prepare food for her family, and on
this occasion, she just happened to be passing by the tree of knowledge of good and evil. His patience had paid off.

He had somehow succeeded in persuading the serpent to allow
him to use his voice with the promise of a hefty reward to be paid
later. The serpent and Satan had kept vigil around the tree, patiently
waiting for the opportunity; and this fateful day, the woman passed
by the tree. Now the serpent was more subtle than any beast of the
field which the Creator had made.

SERPENT. Hello, sweet lady. The sound of your voice is one of the best
things the Creator graced this earth with. The other creatures
and I love to listen to you, and if you listen carefully, you can
hear the singing birds trying to match your lovely silky notes.

WOMAN. How are you doing today, Serpent?

SERPENT. Never felt better. I greatly enjoy the morning walks as I
have the most spring in my steps while inhaling the smell of

the floral blooms, foliage, the fruits, and those fruit cocktails you make…such wisdom and creativity. In a few years, you and your husband will have an impacting transformation of the general view with your floral arrangement and landscaping.

WOMAN. Thanks, Serpent. My husband should be home soon for lunch, and I need to prepare some dishes with new recipes I put together. I also have a surprise dish for the Creator when he visits us this evening. Feel free to stop by sometime during your walks.

SERPENT. Yea, just out of curiosity, didn't the Creator say you should not eat of the fruit of the garden?

WOMAN. Wrong, we may eat of the fruit of all the trees of the garden except for one tree—the fruit of this tree, the one you are leaning on. The Creator has said we shall not eat of it, neither shall we touch it, lest we die.

SERPENT. Die, who are you kidding? Someone as knowledgeable as you should know better than that. You will not surely die. The Creator knows that in the day ye eat of it, then your eyes will be opened, and you will be as gods, knowing good and evil. Look at me. I am holding the fruit in my hand and I am still alive and you know no other creature here is as wise as I am in certain matters like these, as well as better looking…well, of course, except you. Imagine not having to wait for him to visit you in the evenings to discuss matters on questions you may have or go bothering him any time you have a question. With your eyes opened, you will be as the gods and won't have to bother the Creator. He has this whole universe to run, and he gave you and your husband the whole earth and its creation to manage. You could use the additional wisdom.

After extensive persuasion, the woman took another closer look and saw that the tree was good for food and that it was pleasant to the eyes and a tree to be desired to make one wise. The luscious aroma from the tree played on her senses, and in the invisible dimension of existence, the devil and his cohorts held their breath. Seeing that the serpent did not die from touching the fruit, she took of the fruit thereof, and took a bite. It was luscious and delicious, and based on her judgment, it was not as sweet as the pineapple.

Lucifer immediately sent out to his lieutenants to have the giant cigar boxes laid out for their celebration, not being sure if Adam will fall for it. Shortly thereafter, he left the serpent and headed out to join the others to await the anticipated revelry. The serpent was not entirely certain on what to make of it all, but somewhere in its mind, it was expecting a shoe to drop, and it wondered what it would be and when.

After eating the fruit, nothing happened immediately to her physically. She took some home to share with her husband. But a certain listlessness befell her, and a strange foreboding slowly started crawling over her as she walked home.

As her husband headed home from his garden-tending activities and inspections, he missed the sweet melodic voice that always served as a beacon of where his wife was. It seemed a little odd, but he pressed on home. He could see her standing with a basket of fruits, and as he drew closer, her beautiful glow and blissful aura appeared tempered ever so slightly.

As he strode toward her, she appeared at a loss for words, a rare occurrence, knowing she was a chatterbox at times, something he cherished. Standing there and looking down the path in the direction of her husband, she did not appear very surefooted as always; and as he got closer, he noticed the slight twitching around the corners of her lips. He rushed in and gently held her with his eyes questioning. She pointed at the basket, and then he saw the fruit—the forbidden fruit. He gasped in sheer terror. Pointing to her mouth, she told him what the serpent had said and indicated that she had indeed eaten it.

"My love, I touched and ate the fruit, and though I am alive, I do not feel right. You promised me your love, and you told the Lord and I that you will always love me and we would always be together. Remember all the children we are supposed to have and blissful company and life we have and our affection for each other. I really hate to be the one to ruin this for us, but it is your call whether you will eat the fruit too so our fate will be same. I believe now that I will die, and when I do, I do not want to die alone, but if we live, we shall live together. Between the two of us, we should be able to easily separate evil from good and do what is good and teach our children together to do just the good. Alone, I am not likely to succeed easily, but together we can increase our odds of success."

From the look on her face, it was becoming clearer by the minute that her glorious covering on her was slowly depleting, and she was shaking all over. Knowing the Creator was visiting them in a little while that evening, her plight had become urgent. So, with little time to waste, she extended her hand holding the fruit, and with the unmistakable dread written all over her, he had to make a choice, the only difficult choice he ever made to this point.

Trying not to delve into the hard facts, he knew about the outcome he had been clearly informed by the Creator, their Lord. Her apparent helplessness seemed to win over his heart, and he gently guided the fruit to his mouth. He knew she would die, and he did not want her to die alone because his love for her was still pure due to the divine nature still in him at this point. In this one and only rare moment, he failed to check things out with the Creator his Lord, who was available to address any questions at any time, something he always did joyously. He took a bite and, looking down into her somewhat haunted eyes, ate it, thereby deciding to die with her by his own free will.

Immediately after the man ate the fruit, the Creator's Spirit departed from them, followed by the glorious enveloping glow that overlaid their bodies. Their appearance became plain just like the other animals in the garden except without the fur, feathers, or scales. The woman shrieked in horror as both their eyes were opened, and they knew that they were embarrassingly naked as the Spirit and glory of the Creator departed their bodies.

The Spirit had been a buffer that kept out any evil desires from the heart of man. He had been created with only good in all that he did and his thoughts. Not a hard word had ever been exchanged between them nor the desire to hurt each other, the creation around them, or the Creator himself. They did not even know how to be bad or evil.

What the man had been told will happen happened. They both looked like the walking dead, and they sewed fig leaves together and made themselves aprons to cover their nakedness. They had never known fear or confusion until today, and it was terrifying and just plain embarrassing because the disobedience was uncalled for.

They were regents who had been put in charge of everything created on earth and given complete dominion, and everything was to happen as they directed; in effect, they were the lords of the earth until now. Adam knew they had also lost their dominion by disobeying the Creator in wanting to be those who determined what was right and wrong over the rest of the creation outside of the authority of the Creator. Other than man's cognitive superiority, he had reduced himself almost to the same level as other creatures and would have to compete with them for survival going forward.

And then not long after, they heard the voice of the Lord their Creator walking in the garden, which was always preceded by a gentle whirlwind to alert them of his presence in the cool of the day. Adam and his wife hid themselves from his presence among the trees of the garden. He knew hiding was futile because the Creator was invisible though he always made his presence known to them by the sound of his voice, and that had never been an issue until now—and then the call:

CREATOR. Adam, where are you?

ADAM. I heard your voice in the garden, and I was afraid because I was naked, so I hid myself.

CREATOR. Who told you that you were naked? Have you eaten of the tree which I commanded you that you should not eat?

ADAM. The woman, whom you gave to be with me—she gave me of the fruit, and I did eat.

CREATOR. Woman, what is this that you have done?

WOMAN. The serpent deceived me, and I did eat.

CREATOR. Serpent, because you have done this, in allowing yourself to be used by the devil to deceive my children, you are cursed above all cattle and above every beast of the field. Upon your belly will you crawl, and dust will you eat all the days of your life. And I will put enmity between you and the woman and between you and her offspring. Her offspring, the Redeemer, will bruise your head, and you will bruise his heel.

The serpent was not permitted to say anything, and the judgment was swift and immediate. As the verdict was uttered, the serpent's anatomy was immediately transformed. Its limbs were instantaneously eliminated, and the magnificent, graceful, and once very elegant dinosaur became a slithery beast that crawled on its belly from that day forward. Greatly humiliated below all other cattle, the serpent had been reduced in stature below every other beast and would have to raise its head to look up at any other beast of the field.

The serpent let out a heart-wrenching wail in terror as it saw its great comeliness reduced to a loathsome monster in the same rank as a worm which does not need limbs for its earth-tunneling job. The echo of the wail from the serpent reverberated across the entire planet. In listening and conspiring with the devil, he ended up with an outcome like the angelic host that had fallen for his falsehood and lost everything they had including their dignity. The other dinosaurs in its size class watched as the giant anaconda crashed down into a massive heap of embarrassing wriggling flesh in real time. There was great chaos as all species of the serpent were visibly transformed, and they did their best to slither off into hiding from the shame of their appearance.

CREATOR. Woman, I will greatly multiply your sorrow and pain when you bear and deliver children, and your desire shall be to your husband, and he will rule over you. Adam, because you listened to the voice of your wife in disobedience to me and have eaten of the tree of which I commanded you, saying, "You shall not eat of it," cursed is the earth and the ground for your sake. In sorrow shall you eat of it all the days of your life. Thorns, thistles, and a lot of undesirable elements will it bring forth because of your choice—and remember, it is your choice. You were the lord in your garden and never needed to toil. The whole earth was meant to be an extension of your garden for you and your offspring. From now henceforth, in the sweat of your face will you eat bread till you die and return unto the ground, for out of it was your body made. For dust you are, and unto dust your body shall return.

The painful exit

In the presence of the woman and the man, the Creator killed some animals, poured their blood into the soil, then took the skins and lovingly created protective and supple leather jumpsuits for the man and the woman. These were created for beauty, comfort, and functionality. Leather shoes did the Lord make as well, knowing their next place of residence was going to need these protective coverings.

They were devastated when they saw the ugliness, coldness, and pain of physical death—the first death in the created universe—in order to clothe them. Now they knew what physical death was, and what followed next was the prelude to spiritual death.

CREATOR. It is with a heavy heart I am saying this, but behold, the man has become as one of us, to know good and evil, so lead the man and the woman out of the garden, lest they reach out and eat of the tree of life and live forever. Maintain a guard at the entrance into the garden to keep them and their offspring out of it. The man has been taught and has the necessary knowledge to cultivate and sustain his own habitation outside the garden. Adam, you and your wife have made your decision, and I will respect it. I will leave a conscience in you as a guide to enable you to judge between good and evil as you have chosen. A choice to do evil has consequences as I explained to you. I created you because I love you, and with a heavy heart, I send you out of what you have rejected. Remember, evil choices will always trigger painful sequences of events that will affect you, your offspring, and the entire earth. The earth was created for you to dwell and thrive in. Living in it with all that it offered was all yours and the whole world at large as well as the dominion I had given you over all my earthly creation. You were created to live eternally with me and your offspring will make a way to redeem you and it will be entirely up to you whether you and your progeny appropriate the offer or not. Remember, the life of a human being is more valuable than all the riches of the earth put together in my sight. No human can afford the price of another human being, for you are that important, valuable, and loved by me.

The saddest song

And Adam called his wife's name Eve because she was the mother of all living. As they stepped away from the Creator and slowly trudged off, Eve broke into one of the saddest songs Adam ever heard as the impact of the devil's deception came full circle. The notes were so sad that even the other creatures felt it. Covered in tears, they walked off and away from the garden, and the goldilocks climate was no more.

As they stepped out of the threshold of the garden of Eden, the velvety walkways and extra comfortable atmosphere transitioned into a hardened earth with a very plain landscape. Gone was the beauty and immaculately self-manicured and plush habitat with its gleaming streams of water littered with chunks of gold and onyx stones among a plurality of minerals and gemstones. The only lone point of comfort was the hope of the redeemer the Creator had promised.

Life outside the garden

For the first time in their lives, Adam and Eve saw a side of life they never knew could even exist. A monster of a challenge called narcissism and self-preservation reared its head and challenged every decision they had to make. Gone were the days when they selflessly cared for each other's needs. Now things were degenerating into slights, disagreements, groans, and the promised euphoria of being just like the gods (at least to the woman) brought in by the knowledge of good and evil turned into a nightmarish life capped with incessant misery and pain.

The blissful life they once had become a distant memory, and how they missed it! Oh, how they missed it! How they longed for the now-gone evening visits of laughter and fellowship with the Creator. The food did not even taste the same as they now ate to stay alive instead of enjoying it. Their work became a loathsome drudgery and toiling to survive instead of the fun-filled days of tending and administration they had in the garden. There was nothing ultimately tangible to look forward to anymore except the dreaded physical death, whereby their carcasses will return into the dust.

Adam and his wife settled into their new environment and built a habitation to protect them from the prevailing new climatic elements. Even Earth seemed to be convulsing with shifting tectonic plates that signaled an ominous warning of a planet in trouble. Their very advanced intellect enabled them to see that their once-beautiful planet was on a course to eventually disintegrate. Without deliverance out of this state, life was worthless, and they had to find things to occupy and immerse themselves in and fill the gaping void left behind by the departure of the Creator's Spirit.

Over time, they had lots of sons and daughters and could see the onset of the deterioration of their physical bodies as they aged. They taught the children about their fall and the promised redeemer, with great emphasis on the need to maintain their relationship with the Creator. They taught them how to maintain that relationship and to use their conscience as a guide on how to live until the arrival of the Redeemer. Nothing did they hide from the children. They taught them about their own failure in disobedience to the Creator and the evil side of the devil, who now had direct access to the mind of man with the primary intent of making a man's every decision contrary to the Creator's directive known as sin. Since man now had to make a choice in every decision he made, these decisions could be for good or for bad, in which case, it could hurt them personally or each other.

They taught their children about the consequences of sin because it always resulted in decisions that hurt others or themselves, and this was why sinning was unacceptable to the Creator; he was never pleased with seeing his creatures hurt each other.

The enormity of the horror and ravaging effect of the choice of the knowledge of good and evil were beyond anything Adam and Eve could have ever imagined. The unimaginable cruelty in the murder of their son Abel, including other murders among their other grandchildren and great-grandchildren while they were still alive, was a foreboding picture of the horrors to ensue following the devastating decision of their choice of independence. Even they realized the problem was of a magnitude that only the Creator himself could fix.

Adam and his wife watched themselves age and deteriorate like old cloth exposed to harsh weathering elements. Their beautiful plump bodies slowly fell apart over the hundreds of years into unrecognizable wrinkled prunelike masses of flesh that slowly emitted the odor of physical death as their body organs slowly closed shop irreversibly. Death was not only painful, but it was also ugly. Oh, how they wished they had stayed with the Creator and had their abode back at the garden.

At 930 years of age, when Adam believed it was time for him to die, he called a solemn assembly of all his exponentially expanded family. He pleaded with the children, reminding them of his failure in bad choices in life which had resulted in their Creator removing his Spirit from them. He reminded them of restoration through the promised redeemer.

Chapter 4

The Drumroll for Recreation

One of the things that made Adam's heart sink before his death were the whispers about the Creator, the descendants questioning the existence of the Creator who was invisible, and even whether he had indeed created Earth or whether Earth and the entire cosmos was an accident. And so it was that at the age of 930 years, after having given birth to lots of sons and daughters, he died—one of the saddest men—and was buried.

Excerpts from Lucifer's demonic conference

LUCIFER. I call to order this conference of the leading elite of the luciferous kingdom. We succeeded beyond my wildest expectation. Man chose to live with the knowledge of good and evil, and his death is technically a massive victory for us.

AGAG. How is that?

LUCIFER. If man had opted to stay with the knowledge of only good, we would never have had access to his soul. All he had to do was not eat the fruit. You all know the problem was not the fruit but, rather, man's decision to take on the responsibility of deciding what is wrong or right instead of the Creator. Eating the fruit was just letting the Creator know, and we know he is true to his word, and with the decision made, he graciously and respectfully took his Spirit away from man. Man has lost dominion of the earth, and he is now fully accessible.

BELZE. Without the Creator's Spirit ruling over that of the man, the man is fair game.

LUCIFER. Well, not entirely. If he is smart enough to call on and lean on the Creator, we will not be able to exploit his situation. We must make him believe he can work his way out of the mess by himself. We need to work on his pride and keep him destabilized with excessive busyness and try to keep him blind to the fact that he dies physically, and if we succeed with that, we can make him believe there is no life after the physical death.

BELZE. Deception is the key then—lies garnished with partial truths. We must keep him unbalanced and get him to the point where he despises the good and loves evil as best as we can.

LUCIFER. He is probably no longer likely to fall for our lies and be more inclined to tread carefully. We need to keep him from fully trusting the Creator's word—that is the key. We need to try and make man hate the Creator.

AGAG. He can't be that stupid. He has no reason now not to trust the Creator's word.

LUCIFER. That is our job. He will have to make choices in every decision he makes and every decision has consequences and we need to make sure he leans on the wrong side.

BELZE. Let us study him over the course of time and strategize accordingly.

LUCIFER. As the humans spread out, I want you all to be organized into a structured hierarchy that covers every corner of the earth man moves into just as the Creator is doing with his angels. This will allow us to communicate strategies and pretend to humans like I am omnipotent and omnipresent like the Creator.

BELZE. Are you implying that we should be organized and structured like the Creator's kingdom but create counterfeits of whatever the Creator offers where possible? Brilliant!

AGAG. We do not have any creative abilities anyway, nor are we allowed to introduce anything new. We just need to continue with the lies and half-truths and introduce sorcery where possible.

LUCIFER. Bottom line, we are to do our best in causing men to create their own gods and belief systems similar but different from the

Creator. This way, there will be enough confusion when the earth is covered with all types of religions and belief systems, and most people won't care to know what is true and what is not. Just make them believe this life is all there is and throw in reincarnation.

AGAG. Brilliant. We shall establish principalities, powers, and operation centers over every nation we can and expand as populations grow. And we shall empower whichever human we can and use sorcery and pride where possible.

LUCIFER. Just do your best to make people believe I am equal to the Creator—even more powerful than him if possible. Men will believe a lie, it looks like, if you say it long and loud enough. Let's do our best to cause man to look at life in the short term and make decisions that gratify their flesh at any cost and pull them away from things pertaining to knowledge of the Creator.

AGAG. I thought we were crazy and stupid, but humans are teaching us a thing or two in those departments. Can man really be made to believe that there is no Creator, that there isn't a spiritual dimension to existence, and that life ends after the physical death? That would be like saying there is no Creator and that life sprang out of nothing, not with a living Creator who is only too ready to engage with his creation and makes himself available to those who really want to know him.

LUCIFER. Agag, like we said already, our job is to deceive him and make him believe he is extremely intelligent than he really is but make him believe the lies. We might even succeed in making man to worship us, all of you included, naturally. Now that would be something to behold! Could it really happen?

BELZE. I'll bet you anything man can't be that stupid.

The effect of man's disobedience

And it came to pass when men began to multiply on the face of the earth that most of the descendants of Adam ignored his warnings and opted to living their lives the way they wanted to and disregarded the consequences.

And the Creator saw that the wickedness of man was great in the earth and that every imagination of the thoughts of his heart was only evil continually, and it grieved him that he had created man on the earth. The earth, the animals, and all in it were so badly infected with the sin element that man lost his dominion in many areas, and he even became part of the food chain of the wild beasts on land, air, and water. Even the earth itself was not spared of man's self-destructive odyssey. In all this time, the earth never saw rain, but it was adequately watered by a nightly mist.

Of the descendants of Adam, the thorns, thistles, and hardship on work made some of them despise the Creator instead of calling on him for help as their father Adam had told them. While they liked what they could get from him, they wanted that on their own terms.

One line of descendants decided to follow the advice from Adam in seeking the Creator, and so he drew nearer to them as he had promised Adam. Their fathers had seen the garden and cherubim with flaming swords from a safe distance. There was a clear contrast between the garden environment and where they were, and that was all they needed to accept the gracious and merciful offer from the Creator.

A descendant called Enoch had decided to walk with the Creator, embracing the hope of the redemptive promise, and kept his precepts which they all knew. He taught his children and walked before the Creator as an example to them. It was refreshing to the Creator, and he drew close and walked with him. After the end of his life on earth, his grandchild, Noah, continued to walk on the precepts of the Creator as passed down from Enoch. He was a just man and perfect in his generations, and Noah and his family walked with the Creator contrary to what humanity did in his day.

Chapter 5

Sailing the Ocean without a Rudder

During Noah's time, as men multiplied and filled the earth, it continued growing corrupt before the Creator, and the earth was filled with violence. Man had turned to all forms of perversions to fill the void in him created when the Spirit of his Creator withdrew from him. Nothing could satisfy or gratify the human desires—not material wealth or food. All the divinely created pleasures for man had become perverted; getting satisfaction out of any aspect of life was like drinking saltwater to quench one's thirst.

This was the beginning of the perversion of genetic science. Man understood the principles underlying much of the scientific knowledge including the knowledge of species preservation through DNA. The Creator never took back that gift from man, and he made additional provision with knowledge for man to help preserve him from self-annihilation.

Man started dabbling in genetic mixing across species in all efforts to overcome his shortcomings and ways to improve on his ever-declining physical prowess and moral spiral. Though man lived over nine hundred earth years then, his physical deterioration was a pitiful sight to behold.

Man wanted to live forever; therefore, many in the then-science world got into a mad quest to uncover the chemical composition of the fruit of the historied tree of life which their ancestors had failed to eat of. Many alive had lived to tell of the flaming swords that guarded the entrance of the garden seen with their very own eyes.

The garden could be visually seen from a distance, and there was a visible marked contrast between its foliage environment and that of the earth outside its bounds.

Then men turned the Creator's gift of pleasure of sexual intimacy in a marriage bed into a powerful weapon of merchandise fueled by malicious and depraved lust. This exploded into a contemptible industry that even got the involvement and participation of luciferous forces. This gift from the Creator, like other gifts, shifted from the marriage bed to a perpetual source of misery and death. In great sadness, the Creator watched the exploits in sinful sexual desires and impurity as men and women degraded their bodies with one another.

Because of this, the Creator gave them over to their shameful lusts. With sex taken out of the marriage bed, it became so vile and contemptible with no holds barred to the point where it extended into pedophilia. It even got pushed over the threshold of human interaction into bestiality, resulting in illicit sex becoming a perpetual fire that was not easy by natural means to be quenched.

Human and sex trafficking became a prosperous industry because the desire was insatiable, with the poor and helpless being fair game to the rich, strong, and powerful. The perversion of sex and its insatiable desire introduced wholesale prostitution, with pimps armed with drugs culminated into horrible diseases introduced into vast human populations across humans and beasts.

The great breach

The luciferous fallen angels, looking at the sexual revelry in which man was wallowing in, could not help themselves but jump into the fray. Some of the fallen angels took human forms, dived into the sexual morays, selected wives from human women, and had children with them. This unauthorized genetic mixing resulted in Nephilim, whose remains and remnants of their fabricated artifacts are with us till this day, thanks to archeology.

At dusk on a given day, during these chaotic times swept down a powerful squadron of a heavenly angelic host unto earth while the devil was having one of his demonic conferences with his top brass.

In a flash, a select group of these powerful luciferous beings were seized, chained, and unceremoniously piled on a heap, covered in dirt. The demons shrieked in terror, and their leader, Lucifer, was seen lying on the ground on his back with the foot of a powerful angel on his neck, though not chained but shivering in fear. It was a very humiliating sight for the devil, who lay there helplessly and unable to help himself or any of his followers. The powerful angel then took his foot off the devil, giving him room to compose himself and try to regain whatever was left of his dignity. He scurried off to the side, claiming that it was not yet incarceration day for him and his followers based on the Creator's schedule.

The leader of the squadron of angels read out the verdict, which described the infraction. They were summarily warned that any luciferous angel who breached the bounds on earth set by the Creator would be swiftly taken into custody and kept there chained in solitary darkness until the day of their final judgment. They stepped over a line they had been prohibited from crossing.

Every one of these majestic beings who had participated in the sexual exploits anywhere across the earth had been seized and were then dragged off into the darkness of the bottomless pit. They cried out to Lucifer for help while the nonparticipants bowed their heads in shame, fully coming into terms with the fact that they and Lucifer were doomed and will truly end up in the lake of fire despite the false hope he gave them. Even he still stood in fear as he considered the very sudden and unexpected encounter and the unimaginable power the relatively small squadron possessed, and the last thing they saw was a humiliated, terror-stricken, and angry devil with his head bowed in helpless defeat.

As the dust settled, the devil breathed a sigh of relief as he realized that it was not yet their expected end. He then warned the rest of his demonic empire to remember not to venture outside of their allowable limits if they did not want to hasten their expected demise.

This was a day of mourning in Lucifer's kingdom as they were all acutely reminded of their helplessness and the fate that awaited them. The devil looked so frail and helpless in the presence of the mighty angelic host, and it made many of his followers wonder how they could have been so stupid to have fallen for his deception.

And the Creator, looking upon the earth, saw that all humans had corrupted their way upon the earth, thereby committing evil in his sight; and it was not bad enough that they had drifted from their Creator, but they turned even science into something that even challenged him. The beauty of scientific principles the Creator had taught their fathers himself for their use for good were suddenly applied for use in many nefarious applications.

They also turned to various forms of witchcraft to the point where they served a host of gods to the extent of offering live human sacrifices by fire, especially little children, to them. The screams of the babies in pain in death throes shot straight up to heaven and have kept the audio center continually lit and memorialized up there.

The people totally disregarded the possibility of the wrath of the Creator being revealed against all the wickedness of people, who suppressed truth by their wickedness. For since the creation of the world, his invisible qualities, eternal power, and divine nature had been clearly seen and known, being understood from what had been made so that the people were without excuse. For although they knew him, they neither glorified him as the Creator nor gave thanks to him, resulting in humanity with darkened hearts and perverted minds.

They became filled with every kind of wickedness—evil, greed, and depravity. The earth was full of envy, murder, strife, deceit, malice, Creator haters, insolence, arrogance, and boasting. People even went as far as inventing ways of doing evil to the extent where violence ruled societies among the very young to the old.

What made it even so much more hideous is that although they knew the Creator's righteous decree and that those who chose not to abide by them would face very unpleasant and even irreversible eternal consequences, they not only continued to do these very things but also approved of those who practiced them. These were really bad times for humanity.

Furthermore, because they did not think it worthwhile to retain the knowledge of the Creator, he gave them over to their depraved minds so that they continued in their madness to their own hurt. The vileness was compounded by diseases that spread through the populations, and the people received in themselves the due natural outcome of activities they participated in, and violence in the land was the end result.

In looking at this ugliness, the Creator was saddened that he had created man, for he had become as vile as the devil. In fact, man had become so vile that even the luciferous gangs followed him into sexual perversion.

Noah stood steadfast in his walk with the Creator to follow in his grandfather's footsteps and lived a righteous life. The Creator looked at Noah and was gracious to him as he saw the ridicule hurled at him from those around him at his stance at trusting him and living a life following his precepts, and this pleased the Creator greatly. To the Creator, it did not matter whether it was one person or a thousand who called on him—he answered and stood faithfully by them.

The ark and the rainbow

One day, the Creator called unto Noah and said to him, "Noah, the end of all flesh is come before me, for the earth is utterly filled with violence, and behold, I will destroy them with the earth. Build for yourself an ark with gopher wood, with many rooms, and seal it inside and outside with pitch.

"I am bringing a flood of waters upon the earth to destroy all flesh in which is the breath of life from under heaven, and everything that is in the earth shall die. But with you will I establish my covenant, and you will come into the ark—you and your sons and your wife and your sons' wives with you.

"Of birds, of cattle, of every creeping thing of the earth, all after his kinds, two of every sort will I personally send to come to you at the appointed time to keep them alive. You will not need to go search for them, and you shall stock all the food that is eaten, and you will gather it to you and for them."

And Noah believed the Creator and immediately began the construction of the ark, following the exact dimensions and details the

Creator had given him. During the construction process and time, he warned the people of the Creator's impending judgment and the need to turn from their evil ways to escape the judgment.

But the people far and near laughed Noah to scorn. Over the decades during which Noah built the ark, his work was made to look like a spectacle, as he was teased and mocked. Whole excursions from people around the known world then came to see the ark he was building for an impending flood from water falling from the sky—something no one had ever seen before. The scientists and philosophers were able to explain to everyone why this was not possible especially since the water content of the sky could not possibly flood the earth. Many asked Noah for evidence of precedence, and they decided he was just superstitious and a nutcase. While Noah saw the logic in some of their postulations and he himself could not explain how and why it would happen, he was just content to trust what the Creator had said and leave it at that.

The people laughed and could not understand why the Creator, whom none of them had seen, would care about one person and family of all the millions of people milling around. Many even believed the Creator was dead, had abandoned the world, or had no more power over man because man had become too intelligent.

Not long after the completion of the construction of the ark, Noah started stocking up all manner of foodstuffs as he had been commanded. The people thought it was the easiest form of making money by selling anything that Noah requested—grain, hay, fresh water, dried fruit, and all manner of foodstuff for humans and animals. It took 120 years to complete the construction of the ark. Even Noah's family sometimes quietly wondered how embarrassing this could turn out if nothing happened. But then, they remembered the incredibly detailed instructions and dimensions the Creator had given him.

Soon after, when all the stockrooms were filled in the ark, it happened. One of the strangest phenomena ever witnessed by man took place. Land-based animals and birds of different species flew or walked up to Noah's ark in pairs of male and females, with no one leading them on, and none were seen to threaten or attack each other. Noah, standing by the ark ramp, graciously received them into the ark while his children directed them to their respective pens. They had absolutely no fear of Noah and were in no way threatening either. No science could explain this. Noah knew he had been exonerated by the Creator in the sight of his family and the people, and he knew the end for humanity was imminent.

It was somewhat perplexing to some watching but then shrugged it off as some fluke of nature. With all the creatures safely in the ark, the Creator commanded Noah to board the ark because in seven days from that moment, he was going to send rain on the earth. The rest of the people were technically given seven more days to have a change of heart and join Noah especially after the supernatural arrival of the animals, but none did.

Upon seeing this, Noah continued a desperate final appeal to those who could hear him and called them to escape the coming destruction by joining him in the ark. The people responded by stating that he was free to make a fool of himself, but not them. There was no science or evidence that showed there was enough water in the clouds to flood the earth, and furthermore, there was no precedence, and so thanks but no thanks.

Noah and his family finally settled in, and while they gathered for dinner, to their amazement, they saw the door slowly close itself and snapped shut. They knew the Creator had locked the door of the ark, and no one could go out or come in anymore. Noah and his family knew the end of man was now days away as the Creator had warned him. One of the things Noah had found a little perplexing was that the ark had no rudder or oars, and he was not sure how he would direct the giant craft if he was asked to. But then, he remembered that the Creator had sent him the animals, and he would take care of the navigation detail; so great was his faith in the Creator.

The people in large multitudes camped around the ark to see the rain come, but nothing happened. They watched Noah and his family and the animals with mocking laughter. They could not understand where on earth the water will come from that will fall from the sky unto the earth—so much so that their homes and the entire earth with its great hills will be covered. Not even Noah knew what rain was, but he took the Creator's word for it and just followed the instructions he had been given.

The people concluded that he was just eccentric due to madness of some sort, the only human and family that abstained from the common and prevailing practices which he described as evil. They were happy to be rid of him, and his property and possessions were already occupied by the community leaders who expected a huge retrieval payment from Noah when he eventually ran out of victuals from his wooden boat—if he escaped being eaten up by the animals in it. By the sixth day, all the people were gone and went about their normal business of revelry, eating and drinking, fishing, farming, merchandising, weddings, honeymoons, and daily rituals.

The seventh day

On the seventh day after Noah boarded ark, the Creator gave the order to the angelic host to begin the flood process. In a flash, the beautiful bright afternoon was interrupted by huge and extremely bright lightning flashes across the sky from horizon to horizon so bright that they outshone the light of the sun. On the heels of these were successive and deafening thunderclaps so loud that the sonic booms shook the very foundations of everything standing on the earth's crust.

Men shrieked in terror as there was no letup between the terrifying and gigantic lightning bolts that hit the ground and set things on fire, electrocuting men and beasts alike in their path. The panic-stricken people could tell they were in trouble but had nowhere to run, for there appeared to be no place safe to hide in. They had never seen or imagined anything like this, and many of them remembered Noah's warning, but it was too late.

As if the thunder and lightning were not bad enough, enormous fissures suddenly appeared along the earth's crust that sealed the fountains of waters under the earth running around the globe, travelling at unfathomable speeds. This led to the creation and shifting of Earth's tectonic plates around the globe with the release of magma and the interaction of the intense heat of the magma under the earth encountering the waters above the magma.

The result was the generation of superheated geysers that shot jet streams of subterranean water and rocks clear across the earth's atmosphere and some possibly into space, some which are likely orbiting around the sun to this day.

The force was so violent that the shockwaves travelled across the whole earth, resulting in giant trenches and canyons around the earth, like the great oceanic ridges. Other land formations on the earth resulted with an opposite effect to the trenches as the rocky hydroplanes pushed into each other, creating some of the mountain ranges still on earth today, mostly running parallel to these trenches as the moving plates pressed against each other. So great were the forces.

The water from the super geysers fell back unto the earth as torrential rain like the earth had never known or imagined. The rain and resulting tsunamis from the cataclysmic forces created massive landslides that entombed massive herds of land animals alive, human dwellings, as well as vegetation.

Even equally terrifying were the exploding volcanoes that blasted vegetation, man, and animals, reducing giant trees into poles that sank into the prevailing deluge of mud and water.

The sea of humanity that was witnessing this great calamity cried out to the Creator for mercy as they looked up to the terrifying red-and-black sky, but there was no answer. Those who could see the ark could not reach it as it buoyed in the swelling water surrounded by death and the dying. Death was everywhere. Men had totally underestimated the Creator as they sized him through the eyes of men.

None on the earth, not even Noah, could have imagined the fierceness of the forces unleashed on the earth. As men perished, they could hear the echo of Noah's voice and his warnings. Some who were able to have a glimpse of the power of the Creator saw just how minuscule humanity was. Seeing this had happened as Noah promised, those who could did not want to look forward to meeting their

Creator at death as Noah had warned will happen. Many perished without even having a chance to give it a second thought.

Even Noah and his family, hearing the sonic booms and explosions all around them, cowered and huddled together as the craft shuddered. For forty days, the rain kept coming on the earth; and as the waters increased, they lifted the ark high above the earth. The waters rose and increased greatly on the earth, and all the high mountains under the entire heavens were covered. The waters rose and covered the mountains to a depth of more than seven meters, or about twenty-three feet.

Now the water from the springs of the deep and the floodgates of the heavens had been closed, and the rain had stopped falling from the sky. The waters flooded the earth for 150 days, and the massive craft floated with no rudder, implying that only the Creator could determine where its occupants will land.

Every living thing on the face of the earth was wiped out; people and animals and the creatures that move along the ground and the birds were wiped from the earth. Only Noah was left and those with him in the ark.

But the Creator remembered Noah and all the animals and the livestock that were with him in the ark, and he sent a wind over the earth to begin the recession of the excess water from the face of the earth. As he had done at creation, large quantities assuaged into the reopened gigantic caverns and fountains under the earth's crust, parts of it back into the moisture-laden clouds and the gigantic intercontinental troughs, and other depressions created by the shifting plates served as the reservoirs for the bulk as the rest of the receding waters.

The rapid flooding waters flowing down the inclines carved out more canyons as the powerful mud and debris blasted their paths across the rock strata, entombing any vegetation and decaying corpses in their path as well as remains trapped as fossil under thousands of feet in some areas across whole continents.

As the water continued receding steadily from the earth's surface into its bowels, the ark came to rest on the mountains of Ararat. The waters continued to recede until the tenth month, and on the first day of the tenth month, the tops of the mountains became visible.

When the earth was completely dry, the Creator asked Noah to step out with his family and bring out all the animals. Noah therefore came out, built an altar, and offered burnt offerings on it to the Creator as he had been taught by the line of men and women who had worshipped and obeyed him in the past.

When the Creator smelled the pleasing aroma of the offering, he said in his heart, "Never again will I curse the ground because of humans even though every inclination of the human heart is evil from childhood, and never again will I destroy all living creatures as I have done. As long as the earth endures, seedtime and harvest, cold and heat, summer and winter, day and night will never cease."

He then blessed Noah and his sons, saying to them, "Be fruitful and increase in number and fill the earth. The fear and dread of you will fall on all the beasts of the earth and on all the birds in the sky, on every creature that moves along the ground, and on all the fish in the sea. They are given into your hands. Everything that lives and moves about will be food for you. Just as I gave you the green plants, I now give you everything.

"Remember, whoever sheds human blood by humans shall their blood be shed, for in my image is mankind created. Any wickedness extended towards any human being will be judged accordingly. As for you, be fruitful and increase in number. Multiply on the earth and increase upon it."

Continuing, he said to Noah and to his sons with him, "I now establish my covenant with you and with your descendants after you and with every living creature that was with you. I have set my rainbow in the clouds, and it will be the sign of the covenant between me and the earth. Whenever I bring clouds over the earth and the rainbow appears in the clouds, never again will the waters become a flood to destroy all life. Whenever the rainbow appears in the clouds, I will see it and remember the everlasting covenant between me and all living creatures of every kind on the earth."

The sons of Noah who came out of the ark were Shem, who was brown, Ham, who was dark, and Japheth, who was fair complexioned. These were the three sons of Noah from the same mother, and from them came all the postflood humans and every ethnic group on the earth today.

True to form, Noah had maintained the tradition of animal sacrifice as a reminder, pointing to the Redeemer to come destined to be the sacrifice to permanently pay for the sins of humanity. Noah taught this to his sons and held them responsible for teaching their offspring to look forward to the day this promise is fulfilled by the Creator.

After the flood, Noah lived 350 years and he lived a total of 950 years and then he died and his sons became responsible for populating the earth; and according to their lines of descent, they multiplied and spread out over the earth.

Coming out of the ark and seeing the terrestrial carnage and their deliverance, Noah did not need to emphasize the point. They experienced the greatest worship service of their lives as they gazed at the totally changed landscape. The fear of the Creator settled mightily upon them as they realized that even they had been spared by an inexplicable act of mercy.

The gigantic canyons, mountains, and the physical ark itself were all in plain sight for them as a memorial to their children, grand-great-grandchildren, and for generations to come. As best as they knew how, they lived in the awe and reverence of the Creator, and they grew and multiplied in number greatly given the longevity of life they enjoyed then.

Postflood life

At this time, the whole world had one common language— one that Noah and his family were raised up with. As they moved eastward, they found a plain in Shinar and settled there. A few generations after the flood, man's steady drift away from the Creator and regression into evil and self-destructive tendencies continued to manifest themselves in all aspects of life.

The animal sacrifices that pointed to the Redeemer became perverted, and even the worship and relationship to the Creator degenerated into very contemptible practices. The combination of ancestral worship, sorcery, and other forms of mysticism exploded to the point where live babies were again being offered to idol gods to pacify their supposed wrath as well as for requests for their intervention when deadly acts of nature were experienced. Not all groups followed the same path in the spiritual and moral degeneration, and some rifts were becoming apparent among them.

In about 604 BC, a large number of the more vocal leaders of the families of the descendants of Noah's children, realizing the apparent schisms among themselves, got together. They said to each other, "Come, let's make bricks and bake them thoroughly, and let us build ourselves a city with a tower that reaches to the heavens so that we may make a name for ourselves. Otherwise, we will be scattered over the face of the whole earth."

The plan for the tower was apparently one with very dubious and diabolical intents and not one of reverence for the Creator. Here again, men were setting out to reach the Creator on their terms and not as instructed by him. The rapid spiritual regression of man into depravity was very remarkable.

They used brick instead of stone and tar for mortar due to the material available in abundance and their ability to replicate the strength of stones for the structure they had in mind. But the Creator came down to see the city and the tower the people were building. With concern for those who were intent on staying with the teachings of Noah and his sons as they looked forward to the Redeemer, the Creator decided to intervene.

He said, "If as one people speaking the same language they have begun to do this, then nothing they plan to do will be impossible for them, for I have given them the knowledge and ability, and I will not take it back. Let us go down and confuse their language so they will not understand each other—at least long enough to create enough separation among them."

So the Creator interjected multiple new languages among them such that they could not all understand the same language. Different groups of the people coalesced around a language they could understand and practices the subgroups could agree to. The result was that they stopped building the city and tower found today in present-day

Babylon in Iraq and were scattered from there to other parts of the earth, and that is why it was called Babel—because there the Creator confused the language of all of humanity, resulting in a multilingual world.

As the people scattered over the earth, the migration took some to Asia, Africa, Europe, and the Americas. They did the best they could to create governing systems that could support stable communities and create harmony among the people.

In the face of intertribal fighting over resources, city-states and whole nations were created for mutual protection and survival. Covetousness and other forms of greed led to increased violence and continuous wars. This created a new enterprise of weaponry for war and the continuous quest for weapons of mass destruction. Some of these nations became very powerful and preyed on the weak, and many built cities with impenetrable walls for protection. The world was becoming a dangerous place to live in as the people became even more adversarial.

Some of the nations totally disavowed the existence of a Creator, while others created or adopted their own gods. In the land of Canaan, like the others, the knowledge and reverence of the Creator of the heavens and the earth was almost obliterated except for a few remnant communities. As depravity set in, the Creator allowed them to reap of the rewards of their contemptuous lifestyles which was rife with self-inflicted diseases especially sexually transmitted ones, where sexual morality was no longer regarded as relevant.

Chapter 6

The Day a Man Knocked the Devil Out Cold

Despite the depths of human depravity man was rapidly spiraling into, there were still a few men who believed in and honored the Creator. One of those men was Job who lived in the land of Uz, and he had seven sons and three daughters.

The devil knew and feared Job because he was a man who understood the simplicity of faith in the Creator. Job never deviated from his personal relationship with the Creator and did his best to instruct his children to also do so. For this reason, Job never started a day without talking to the Creator in prayer, especially since the postflood artifacts and whole continental shifts around the globe served as a daily reminder to him. He was also conscious of the barrier the Creator provided between him and the forces of evil propagated by the devil, who is partly responsible for the beginning of man's problems here on earth. He knew he wholeheartedly chose to walk with and be obedient to the Creator, and Job knew the Creator was his protector and provider of everything he had with absolutely no reservation. His faith in the invisible Creator was as childlike as faith could get.

He was the wealthiest man in the East and very well respected by the community because of his integrity. He was in every way a righteous man and upright in all his ways to his fellowmen and the Creator. He believed the Creator was the ultimate authority in his life and that in living, he had to be accountable to him in every decision he made, and he did his best to shun even the very appearance of evil. That was the lot man had chosen and had to live with until the advent of the Redeemer. He believed in the promised Redeemer and stood very firmly on that belief and lived his life accordingly. He was one human who was willing to stand on the declarations and promises of the Creator unconditionally and found absolutely nothing wrong about life in being obedient to him; rather, to him, it was most fulfilling and the way life was supposed to be.

The devil hated Job because he was a true example of what the Creator believed and knew humanity could live up to. The devil had failed to make Job feel he was a self-made man who did not need the Creator or depend on his own ability. He chose to be dependent on the Creator just the way Noah did and taught.

Many times, the devil and his foul spirits had tried attacking Job with the intent to hurt him and discredit the integrity of his faith and confidence in the Creator but realized he was untouchable.

In the spiritual realm, which the devil and his followers exist and operate, the Creator put a hedge around him and his household and everything he had. It was a band of very powerful angels standing guard and keeping Job and all he had untouchable by the devil and his followers.

The devil, determined to destroy Job whenever he got a chance, decided to establish an attack base at a very safe distance away from whatever belonged to Job but with his demons staying on watch should an opportunity arise. He was never going to let Job get away with the act of a human being humiliating the most powerful spiritual adversary who dwells in the kingdom of darkness without even lifting a finger.

He considered it an unacceptable precedent which could expose his extremely limited professed power claim. However, Job's daily prayers and his absolute dependence on the Creator created a permanent impregnable base of defense that the devil and his demons could not breach.

As it is the routine, on a given schedule, all the created angels come to present themselves before the Creator, and the devil also is required to come and present himself. During these gatherings, he always goes in with a long laundry list of accusations of those who have the Creator as their Lord. He accuses them of every little infraction his followers observe while demanding access to terrorize them to verify their true loyalty. Almost every time, the answer from the Creator is no.

During one of these gatherings, the Creator said to him, "So, what have you been up to, and where you have been roaming lately?" And the devil answered, "From roaming throughout the earth and space, wandering back and forth on it and just doing my routine rounds with the record of the visited areas as submitted before you."

Then the Creator, being fully aware of Satan's wicked attempts at interfering in Job's life, said to him, "From your submitted records, I see you have been spending a lot of time around my servant Job's neighborhood. There is no one on earth like him. He is blameless and upright, a man who obeys and loves his Creator and shuns evil."

"Does Job fear the Creator for nothing?" the devil replied. "Have you not put a hedge around him and his household and everything he has so that I am unable to touch him? You have blessed the work of his hands so that his flocks and herds are spread throughout the land. I can assure you that if you will remove the hedge from around him and allow me to take away everything he has, he will surely curse you to your face."

Then the Creator said to him, "Very well, then, everything Job has is in your power, but on the man himself, do not lay a finger."

Then the devil went out from the presence of the Creator, ecstatic for the opportunity to lay hands on this foe. At the same time, the angelic host protecting Job was temporarily withdrawn from around him and all that he owned.

The devil immediately unleashed one of the most vicious attacks ever directed at the possession of a servant of the Creator. The devil, whose primary inclination toward humanity is to steal, kill, and destroy, attacked Job's thriving businesses, and they were utterly leveled to the ground in absolute destruction. In one day, all his worldly possessions completely evaporated through a combination of armed raids, unexplainable arson, and other destructive acts of nature; and to cap his day, his home collapsed on and killed all his children and servants, leaving just his wife and a few servants. It all happened in one day.

This was unprecedented in a nonwarring scenario and quite baffling to the entire community as to how such a calamity could befall someone as righteous as Job and all within a day. There was no one who could point an accusing finger at him because as far as anyone knew, this was a righteous man. Then arose the age-old question of "why do bad things happen to good people?"

By the end of the day, after the carnage had been reported to Job, he got up on wobbly knees because of the shock, tore his robe, and shaved his head in a sign of profound grief and mourning. To the bewilderment of all around him, he fell to the ground on his knees in worship to his Creator and declared, "Naked I came from my mother's womb, and naked I will depart when I die. The Creator gave, and he has taken away. May his name be praised." In all this, Job did not sin by charging the Creator with wrongdoing. As the people left, they beat their breasts in shock and awe at the incredible declaration and resolve. Never had anyone seen or heard anything like this before.

At this declaration, in one of the largest and very raucous gathering of the devil and his fallen angels since their expulsion from heaven, one could hear a pin drop. While they had all gathered with great excitement to see their enemy and humiliator squirm and the Creator cursed with giant cigars in one hand and spiritual drug cocktails in others, the ugly smoke-filled gathering became most solemn with reverberating humiliating shock waves.

Satan could not believe a mere mortal human could love and honor for the sake of love and honor under the circumstances. He knew man was specially created with an incredible brain and abilities of which he is not even aware, but he did not expect this reaction. He dreaded his return to the next meeting when the angelic host had to present itself before the Creator.

He had watched countless number of humans transformed into greedy, narcissistic, and proud monsters the moment they came into wealth. It was one of the devil's most successful tools of deception on humanity. He had learned that after humans came into wealth, the next thing they craved for was power as greed fueled insatiable desires. As far as he could remember, very few humans had ever been satisfied with what they had, and many killed and destroyed to retain what they had even when it killed them doing it. In great distress, he spent a good portion of his time conferring with his fallen demons on their best options regarding Job before the next meeting, and they finally settled on a plan shortly before the meeting.

On the given day, as the angels came to present themselves before the Creator as required, the devil had come this time with a new strategy, the last one having failed badly. This time he was armed with accusations targeting the Creator and Job directly. After the review of the presentation of his activities, the Creator said to him, "Have you considered my servant Job? There is no one on earth like him. He is blameless and upright, a man who obeys and loves his Creator and shuns evil. And he still maintains his integrity though you incited me against him to ruin him without any reason."

"Skin for skin!" the devil replied. "A man will give all he has for his own life. But now give me permission to strike his flesh and bones with sickness, and he will surely curse you to your face."

The Creator said to him, "Very well, then, he is in your hands, but you are not allowed to take his life."

With that, the devil went out from the presence of the Creator and afflicted Job with very painful sores from the soles of his feet to the crown of his head. The oozing pus from his flesh boils and the pain from the resulting sores were so grievous so much so that only the dusting of ashes could keep away the flies and stench in the makeshift shelter he had from broken timber. He was a hideous and contemptuous sight to behold, and all his acquaintances and relatives fled from him except his wife.

The devil and his fallen angelic host kept vigil, waiting; and as his grief grew, they monitored his wife and saw her extreme frustration which grew by the day. They were extremely encouraged especially after they saw that all his acquaintances had scattered away from him like rats fleeing a sinking ship on fire. From a human standpoint, it was impossible to explain Job's predicament.

They had the largest pile of cigars and spiritual narcotics for celebration, for this time they were confident that Job would be broken and will recant his position and curse the Creator. The devil knew Job was just a man like any other human because he knew his parents and friends, and the problem, according to the devil, was his childlike faith in the Creator like Noah, Enoch, and a few others in the past.

There were things Job held onto for dear life. He remembered what had been passed down from Adam to Noah. He knew there was life after death, and he had a Redeemer who would restore the faithful to the position Adam had lost. He remembered how the Creator had saved one family, Noah, who dared trust in him. The earth was littered with scars from the flood. He knew his Redeemer and Creator was trustworthy, faithful, and all-knowing; and since he was all-knowing, Job knew he had not broken his Creator's law nor was living in disobedience intentionally and was, therefore, willing to die with his integrity intact even though he did not know why he was being afflicted. He trusted the fact that the Creator knew why though he himself did not.

Job agonized through months of futility and nights of misery. When he lay down, he wondered how long before he would get up. The night dragged on as he tossed and turned until dawn. His body was clothed with worms and scabs. His skin was broken and marred with the festering sores.

His wife, overwhelmed by the situation, said to him, "Are you still maintaining your integrity? I find this too hard to handle and can't take it anymore. Watching you slowly decompose to death with no way for me to even comfort you in my arms breaks my heart, so do me a favor—curse the Creator so he should just kill you off quickly to stop the pain!" she screamed.

Fully understanding her sentiments, he replied, "You are talking like a foolish woman in great distress and grief. Shall we accept good from the Creator and not trouble? These are aspects of life we cannot explain or understand at this time, and so let's trust him." In all this, Job did not sin in what he said nor charge the Creator with any wrongdoing.

When Job's three friends heard about all the troubles that had come upon him, they set out from their homes and met together by agreement to go and sympathize with as well as comfort him.

Upon arriving, when they saw him, they could hardly recognize him; his state was so bad beyond anything they had even imagined— so much so that they began to weep aloud, tore their robes, and sprinkled dust on their heads in profound grief. Overwhelmed by his grief, they sat on the ground with him for seven days and seven nights, unable to even utter a word to him because they saw how great his suffering was.

After a while, they tried to speculate on the possible cause of the calamity as they struggled with the question of why the Creator would cause such painful suffering on Job without cause and, therefore, questioned his innocence. Seeing that this was very uncharacteristic of the Creator, they wondered openly whether he was living a sinful life in secret, to which Job declared that his suffering was not due to sin or any injustice in his hands and that his prayers and relationship with the Creator was pure. To remind them of his innocence amid his distress that appeared to be getting the best of him, he made the following declaration to them:

> I made a covenant with my eyes not to look lust-
> fully at a young woman, a prevalent area of sin to
> men. For what is our lot from the Creator above,
> our heritage from him? Is it not ruin for the
> wicked, disaster for those who do wrong? Does
> he not see my ways and count my every step? If I
> have walked with falsehood or my foot has hur-
> ried after deceit, let the Creator weigh me in his
> honest scales and he will know that I am blame-
> less, if my steps have turned from the path, if my
> heart has been led by my eyes, or if my hands
> have been defiled, then may others eat what I
> have sown, and may my crops be uprooted.
>
> If my heart has been enticed by a woman,
> or if I have lurked at my neighbor's door, then

may my wife grind another man's grain, and may other men sleep with her. For that would have been wicked, a sin to be judged. It is a fire that burns to destruction; it would have uprooted my harvest. If I have denied justice to any of my workers, whether male or female, when they had a grievance against me, what will I do when the Creator confronts me? What will I answer when called to account? Did not he who made me in the womb make them? Did not the same one form us both within our mothers?

If I have denied the desires of the poor or let the eyes of the widow grow weary, if I have kept my bread to myself, not sharing it with the fatherless, but from my youth I reared them as a father would, and from my birth I guided the widow, if I have seen anyone perishing for lack of clothing, or the needy without garments, and their hearts did not bless me for warming them with the fleece from my sheep, if I have raised my hand against the fatherless, knowing that I had influence in court, then let my arm fall from the shoulder, let it be broken off at the joint. For I dreaded destruction from the Creator, and for fear of his splendor I could not do such things.

If I have put my trust in gold or said to pure gold, 'You are my security,' if I have rejoiced over my great wealth, the fortune my hands had gained, if I have regarded the sun in its radiance or the moon moving in splendor, so that my heart was secretly enticed and my hand offered them a kiss of homage, then these also would be sins to be judged, for I would have been unfaithful to the Creator on high.

If I have rejoiced at my enemy's misfortune or gloated over the trouble that came to him, I have not allowed my mouth to sin by invoking a curse against their life, if those of my household have never said, 'Who has not been filled with Job's meat?', but no stranger had to spend the night in the street, for my door was always open to the traveler, if I have concealed my sin as people do, by hiding my guilt in my heart because I so feared the crowd and so dreaded the contempt of the people that I kept silent and would not go outside, (Oh, that I had someone to hear me! I sign now my defense, let the Creator answer me; let anyone who accuses me put his indictment in writing. Surely, I would wear it on my shoulder, I would put it on like a crown. I would give him an account of my every step I would present it to him as to a ruler.)

If my land cries out against me and all its furrows are wet with tears, if I have devoured its yield without payment or broken the spirit of its tenants, then let briers come up instead of wheat and stinkweed instead of barley. This is my testimony and defense, and the words of Job are ended.

His friends and the whole community knew him and knew this was the truth—as far as overt things they could see—and no one challenged him for any secret violation of his claims, and this only furthered deepened the mystery of his calamity.

Though in great pain and grief, he further declared that he knew that his Redeemer lives and that in the end he was confident he will come down from heaven to the earth. And after his body had been destroyed in death, yet in his resurrected flesh he will see him; he himself will see him with his own eyes.

The devil and his host were a little nervous listening to Job but were still waiting with bated breath for him to break as they watched him moan and groan. After having been pushed to the point where he finally wished he had not been born, they sensed the declaration was imminent, and then it came. As Job looked at his friends, knowing that his fate was in the hands of his Creator, he declared, "Though the Creator slays me, I will always trust him however this ordeal plays out."

Life stopped in the assembly of the devil and his followers. Never had they seen or heard anything like this since the creation of man. The devil's humiliation was complete—a man stood up to him by staying faithful and trusting in the Creator. This was an incident he hoped the rest of humanity will never find out about. It was the dreaded knockout sucker punch that flattened the devil's world on its back in complete defeat and taking out his front teeth permanently. He had not seen it coming, and he was knocked out cold.

His great assembly was confounded, and his powerful followers quietly picked themselves off the floor and took one final look in the direction of Job and his habitation. They knew it was over, and as they looked, the protective hedge around Job, his security detail from out of this world started moving back into position and looking even more lethal than ever before.

The devil was flabbergasted and he stood with his head bowed in shame and his attendees quietly and slowly stole away from the assembly, dumping their unlit giant cigars, and returned to their assigned duties on different parts of the earth, completely despondent. As they slowly left the gathering, it was clear that their greatest job of the future was to have men not trust their Creator because trust in him automatically resulted in the immediate deployment of this formidable protective hedge—invisible to man but dreaded by the devil and his demons to whom it was quite visible.

The devil and his fallen angels and demons know that they cannot touch a servant or child of the Creator or touch anything that belongs to him without the Creator's permission, and when he allows it, there is a reason.

The Creator, impressed by Job's resilience, showed up, but staying invisible, spoke to Job audibly in the presence of his friends from a whirlwind in an exchange in which he recounted certain life mysteries only the Creator had answers for but never explained to Job why he had suffered the ordeal.

Job was so overwhelmed and awed by the presence and power of the Creator that he declared to him, saying, "Surely I spoke of things I did not understand—things too wonderful for me to know. You said, 'Listen now, and I will speak; I will question you, and you shall answer me.' My ears had heard of you, but now my eyes have seen you. Therefore, I despise myself and repent in dust and ashes."

The Creator proceeded to fully restore Job's health and his wealth but never explained to Job why he went through the ordeal, and he didn't care to know but was gratified that the Creator had remained true to his word and had exonerated him and validated Job's faith and innocence.

All his brothers and sisters and everyone who had known him before came and ate with him in his house. They comforted and consoled him over all the trouble that he had suffered over this period of months.

The Creator blessed the second part of Job's life more than the first part. He restored to him twice the wealth he had before, and he also had seven sons and three daughters, and nowhere in all the land were there found women as beautiful as Job's daughters.

After this, Job lived a 140 years; he saw his children and their children to the fourth generation. And so, Job died an old man and full of years, someone Satan never wanted to lock horns with ever again. He is also a reminder and shining beacon to humanity that the devil is no match to a man who trusts in the Creator's guaranteed protective covering and his redemptive plan, and this promise is perpetual even into eternity as promised on his honor and name.

Chapter 7

An Offer Too Good to Refuse (1921 BC)

Excerpts of a postflood conference

FATHER. Seeing how things have developed, we have arrived at the point where we need to initiate the next phase of the redemption plan we promised Adam. It is now many hundreds of years since the end of the flood, and man has had the opportunity to see life in the path Adam and Eve took.

SON. It is very painful to watch. Noah had 120 years to build the ark and warn the people to change from their wicked ways and save themselves from the impending destruction. They just laughed him to scorn, and only his family was saved. Man just keeps crawling in life's mire, oblivious to his actual destiny.

FATHER. With the greater part of humanity now corrupt again and in a moral freefall, we need to seek someone who will accept our call through whom we can build a nation taught in righteousness and use that nation as a model to lead the world back to its Creator. We need man to recognize the ugliness of sin, have a taste of the kingdom he was created for, and experience his Creator's love for humanity. These generations trudge through life not knowing the beauty and purpose for which they were created. This way, the man who accepts the call will be a blessing to the entire earth, and through him will the Redeemer reach the world.

SPIRIT. It is not yet clear how you would like this executed, though I see that you would like us to intervene more in the activities of men to lift off the self-inflicted blinders.

FATHER. Quite right. Seeing the heart of man is desperately wicked continually with a propensity for violence and self-destruction, we need to increase your presence on earth to contain the spread of evil. Otherwise, man's conduct will fall further beneath that of deranged wild beasts.

Spirit, we shall increase your influence on earth. Secondly, we shall sporadically send angels from here to the earth with specific messages to individuals to speak to them on our behalf. They would be manifestations of the Creator in human forms, fire, wind, or however we deem appropriate for each specific job. Thirdly, we shall select certain men and women on whom you would temporarily rest on, and they would be able to declare messages from the Creator to the people.

The messages of these prophets or seers would mostly be prophecies to warn, guide, and direct the people to reveal the heart of the Creator to man. These would be recordable and verifiable prophecies with very clear timelines spanning the start of human time into the end of human time and eternity. This will give man time to process the information accurately, starting with the patriarch of the nation we are set to establish, and thread the timeline back to the creation of the universe, which is the start of human time. Humanity was created with an unlimited mental capacity, and we should, therefore, provide him with verifiable evidence to support our promises to help guide his decisions.

As man transitions into this new phase of divine revelation and your push against the expanded deceitful influence of the devil, we need to increase all the scholastic and life preservation tools he needs to stay alive. Apparently, the global scars and continental shifts resulting from the flood are not enough in reminding him of the consequences of sin. The additional pieces of written information will endure time and stand as a witness to humanity when it exercises its free will. We shall increase knowledge significantly in the future so that man will have no excuse to reject the authenticity of the lineage of the Redeemer based on the historical record of who accepts the call to be the patriarch of this nation.

We know that the redemption of man is the most important event on earth, second only to his creation, and we should provide him with every available tool and support.

Son, talk to Abram, who is currently an idol worshiper and one of the offspring of Shem. Propose to him and see if he will be willing to accept the call. If he does, we shall work with him and set the plan in motion.

SON. Abram and Sarai, who is barren, are perfect as they shall have a firsthand experience of the power of the Creator over nature when it comes to being the father of nations.

FATHER. It will be a long teaching experience. We must teach him that there is a living someone who created the heavens and the earth and not the idols he currently worships. He will experience the power of life and death as executed by us, and he will teach his children. He needs to know the difference between a creature and the Creator. A barren wife conceiving will be a personal miracle and in what is naturally impossible.

He will need to teach his children the way of truth because as we can see, truth now in man's eyes is relative. Abram is seventy-five years old, and all he knows is the lifeless gods of created things and its associated practices. He will need some years of patient teaching to merge his heart and head knowledge.

We shall also make room for the Canaanites to come to a better knowledge of the Creator, and those of them who do and change their ways will be kept in the land, but those who reject us will be driven out, and that piece of real estate will be given to Abraham and his descendants for the model nation.

SPIRIT. Directions totally understood, and we shall proceed as directed.

FATHER. It would be important to upgrade the protective security detail around Abram. The devil will increase his deceptive tactics to try and intimidate his family. Speak and empower them in such a way that their enemies will recognize the presence of the living Creator in their lives. Stay in frequent communication with them that they may know and remember that the Creator speaks, hears, and answers prayers.

SON. How do we bridge the knowledge gap between the created and the eternal? This seems to be a limitation I see in the newer generation of man's understanding as they sink further into depravity.

FATHER. You are correct. Though we shall have some angelic intervention and messaging, man will be primarily responsible for reaching others. For those who are so far out that we need to extend the revelation through divine manifestation of the Creator, those would serve as catalysts and trigger points in ways that fit the circumstances. This way man can be reached no matter his proximity to another human with knowledge of the eternal and true Creator of the universe.

Two years after the flood, one of the sons of Noah, Shem, turned one hundred years old, and he became the father of Arphaxad. And after he became the father of Arphaxad, Shem lived five hundred years and had other sons and daughters.

At this time, the people still lived for very long, but the longevity started a gradual decline. Terah, a descendant of Shem, became the father of a man called Abram. The name of Abram's wife was Sarai, and she was barren and was, therefore, not able to conceive children. Abram's family were staunch idol worshippers.

During this time, the debilitating effect of man's evil ways had resulted in an explosion of idolatry, with the resurgence of human sacrifices. The symbol of an animal sacrifice, meant as a reminder of the promise the Creator made to Adam, passed through to Noah and his sons—Japheth, Shem, and Ham—had become perverted. The time to initiate the execution of the promise he had made to Adam had come.

The Creator had decided to choose someone through whom he would build a people and a nation, establish a covenant with them, and use them to teach the rest of the world how the Creator intended to relate to humanity. This was to be the lineage through whom the redeemer promised to Adam would come into the world so that the Creator could deal with the sin problem of humanity.

On a given day around *1921 BC*, Abram was sitting alone in the quiet of his home, reflecting on his life's accomplishments and considering the bleakness of his life. He was now seventy-five years old and childless. His family was quite prosperous from their family businesses and he had huge herds of livestock and a lot of servants and so was everyone else in his family. The only difference was that they all had children except him. The implication was that his wealth was going to be inherited by his lead servant, and the thought of this outcome was depressing, seeing that he had labored all his life in vain.

His wife was very supportive, loyal, gracious, loving, and incredibly physically attractive. He could not even entertain the thought of getting a second wife who could bear him children because he loved her dearly. He and the rest of his family had offered all kinds of gifts to the idol gods especially Ashtoreth, the fertility goddess, and prayed for years to no avail. This afternoon, as he sat there reflecting, he decided he would accept his fate and just comfort his wife till either one of them died. He made sure not to make her feel she was less than a woman or in any way blame her.

In the quiet, he heard someone call his name very audibly and very distinctively. Abram, knowing there was no one near or within voice distance, looked around him carefully. This was a voice like he had never heard before but one with authority yet not intimidating or demanding.

The Creator introduced himself to Abram and then said, "I want you to leave your country, your people, your father's household, and the idolatrous worship of false gods in the form of graven images and devilish practices that are as worthless as the lifelessness in the images, and I want you to go to the land I will show you.

"If you will trust me and go, I will make you into a great nation, and I will bless you. I will make your name great, and you will be a blessing. I will bless those who bless you, and whoever curses you I will curse, and all peoples on earth will be blessed through you. I am the Creator of the heavens and the earth, and through you, I will let the whole earth find their way back to me, and one of your direct descendants will be the Redeemer I promised Adam to reconcile man back to his Creator."

Abram needed no convincing, for he had heard things like these regarding creation of man, the garden of Eden, the great flood, and had assumed they were just legends but now knew this was real. Abram, hearing the mention of the possibility of children of his own—an offer too good to refuse—emphatically accepted, seeing he had nothing to lose. He then told his wife what the Creator had said and that they were leaving Ur to a land the Creator had promised him. When she asked him where the land was, he told her he really did not know but believed he would receive further instructions on where to go. She found this quite peculiar, but she knew Abram was a very logical and rational man of reliable character and with very good judgment for as long as they had been married. While this was very unusual, he had never given her reason to question his judgment, so she cast in her lot with him to head out to the unknown.

Abram was seventy-five years old when he set out from Harran. He took his wife, Sarai, his nephew Lot, all the possessions they had accumulated, and the people they had acquired in Harran, and they set out for the land of Canaan, to where he was now directed to go. Abram traveled through the land as far as the site of the great tree of Moreh at a place called Shechem. At that time, the Canaanites were in the land.

When the Creator saw that he had indeed travelled out of Ur and finally in the land of Canaan, he then appeared to Abram and said, "To your offspring I will give this land." He then encouraged him to travel through the land and promised to be always with him. Seeing that the Creator had indeed visited him as promised, this was a mighty boost of encouragement which further strengthened his faith and resolve. In the place where the Creator had appeared to him this time, he built an altar in reverence and worship to him for appearing again to him. This was more like the stories about the Creator he had heard about, and there were no confusing things with the idols they had been worshipping all his life.

From there, he went on toward the hills east of Bethel and pitched his tent, with Bethel on the west and the city of Ai on the east. There he built an altar to worship and called on the name of the Creator and referred to him as the Lord and then set out and continued toward the Negev.

Abram meets Pharaoh

Abram's euphoria was punctuated by an unexpected problem which he assumed the Creator may have missed. An unexpected famine happened in the land, and Abram headed down to Egypt to live there for a while because the famine was severe. He was still trying to understand and familiarize himself with the ways of the Creator whom he called Lord before whom he now walked. One thing he understood was that he acted just like his ancestors had described before and after the flood. He wondered how man could have drifted so far away from the living Creator into worshipping lifeless manmade idols of stone, gold, silver, trees, the sun, moon, and other celestial bodies.

Not being sure how protective his Lord would be over him and his possessions, as he was about to enter Egypt, he said to his wife Sarai, "I know what an attractive woman you are. When the Egyptians see you, they will say, 'This is his wife.' Then they will kill me but will let you live. Say you are my sister so that I will be treated well for your sake, and my life will be spared because of you." In his mind, he felt he needed to give his Lord a helping hand in staying alive to fulfill the promise the Creator had made to him.

Upon arriving in Egypt, when Pharaoh's officials saw her, they praised her to Pharaoh, and she was taken into his palace. He treated Abram well for her sake just as he had predicted, and Abram acquired sheep and cattle, male and female donkeys, male and female servants, and camels.

But the Creator, wanting to let Abram understand he was the Creator and his protector, inflicted serious diseases on Pharaoh and his household because of Abram's wife, Sarai. Pharaoh, seeing that this was beyond a mere coincidence because the assault was too obvious even to his wise men, he summoned Abram.

"What have you done to me?" he said. "Why didn't you tell me Sarai was your wife? Why did you say, 'She is my sister,' so that I took her to be my wife? Now then, here is your wife. Take her and leave!" Then Pharaoh gave orders about Abram to his men, and they sent him on his way with his wife and everything he had. The Creator saw to it that not even the gifts given to Abram for Sarai were taken back, and it was obvious to Abram that this intervention was supernatural.

The greatness and might of the Creator was beginning to dawn on Abram, and it made him happy that his faith had not been misplaced. The protective covering and the apparent invincibility began settling even more so on him. This was the Creator in the folklore and legends he had heard of, one who could see, speak, hear, one who was just, frighteningly powerful yet incomprehensibly gracious and gentle—yes, a Creator of justice.

Now he was becoming more confident and certain about the promise of the Redeemer promised for the deliverance of humanity from the bondage of sin. How the Creator planned to do this was still a mystery to Abram, but one of the things that was becoming obvious to him was that the Creator had a plan and timing that only he knew and Abram was very respectfully afraid to dare inquire about. For one thing, he had a lot to learn from and about the Creator, and he was enjoying the relationship so far.

So Abram went up from Egypt to the Negev with his wife and everything he had, and Lot, his nephew, went with him everywhere he did. Abram had become very wealthy in livestock and in silver and gold.

From the Negev, he went from place to place until he came to Bethel, to the place between Bethel and Ai where his tent had been earlier and where he had first built an altar to the Creator. There Abram called on the name of the Lord, and he was no longer looking at the Creator just as the Creator but his sovereign Lord who really cared for him.

The enhanced walk of faith

Now Lot, who was travelling about with Abram, also had flocks and herds and tents; but the land could not support them, for their possessions were so great that they were not able to stay together, and quarreling arose between Abram's herders and Lot's. Therefore, Abram said to Lot, "Let's not have any quarreling between you and me or between your herders and mine, for we are close relatives. Is not the whole land before you? Let's part company. Please choose which way you prefer. If you go to the left, I'll go to the right. If you go to the right, I'll go to the left." Abraham was becoming very gracious because he was beginning to understand that the sovereign Lord would prosper him regardless if he stayed anywhere in the land of Canaan, and he did not need to strive to choose first, and his faith pleased his Lord greatly.

Lot looked around and saw that the whole plain of the Jordan toward the city of Zoar was well watered, like the garden of the Lord, like the land of Egypt along the Nile River, and this was before the Lord destroyed Sodom and Gomorrah. Lot, therefore, chose for himself the whole plain of the Jordan and set out toward the east, and the two men then parted company on the greatest of terms and mutual respect. Abram lived in the land of Canaan while Lot lived among the cities of the plain and pitched his tents near Sodom. Now the people of Sodom were quite prosperous but wicked and were sinning greatly against the Creator, and they even prided themselves in their sinful ways.

The Creator said to Abram after Lot had parted from him, "Look around from where you are, to the north and south, to the east and west. All the land that you see I will give to you and your offspring forever. I will make your offspring very populous. Go, walk through the length and breadth of the land, for I am giving it to you." So Abram went to live near the great trees of Mamre at Hebron, where he pitched his tents. There he built an altar to worship the Lord, and he was enjoying the privilege of being able to speak to and be spoken to by the living Creator and his sovereign Lord of the universe.

As was the practice at that time, nations fought each other for resources, and the strong just seized what they desired and subjected the weak to taxes and other forms of levy, and so it was with the cities of Sodom and its neighbors.

And so it was that for twelve years, the Kings of Sodom, Gomorrah, Admah, and Zoar, all neighboring cities, had been subject to a king called Kedorlaomer, but in the thirteenth year they rebelled.

Therefore, in the fourteenth year, as a lesson to the rebellious kings, Kedorlaomer and three other kings allied with him, went out to fight, and conquered the whole territory of the Amalekites as well as the Amorites who were living in the area, seized all the goods of Sodom and Gomorrah, the people and all their food, and then they went away.

They also carried off Abram's nephew Lot and his possessions since he was living in Sodom. A man who had escaped came and reported this to Abram. Now Abram was living near the great trees of Mamre the Amorite, a brother of Eshkol and Aner, all of whom were allied with Abram.

When Abram heard that his relative had been taken captive, buoyed by the promise his Lord had made to protect him, he called out the 318 trained men born in his household and his three allies and went in pursuit. After he located them, they waited till nightfall, during which Abram divided his men to launch a surprise attack. With the Creator's backing, he routed them, and successfully recovered all the goods and brought back his relative Lot and his possessions together with the women and the other people.

Returning from the victorious battle, an unusual person called Melchizedek, king of Salem, brought out bread and wine to meet and welcome Abram from the remarkable victory. He was described as the priest of God Most High, and he blessed Abram, saying, "Blessed be Abram by God Most High, Creator of heaven and earth. And praise be to God Most High, who delivered your enemies into your hand." Seeing and knowing this was a true servant and priest of the

Most High God, Abram gave him a tenth of everything as an offering directed at his Lord, whom he believed was sending a direct message to him to help strengthen his faith and further enhance his status in a very positive and unthreatening way among the Canaanites.

After Abram returned from defeating Kedorlaomer and the kings allied with him, the king of Sodom and his allies also came out to meet him. The king of Sodom said to Abram, "Give me the people, and keep the goods for yourself." But Abram said to the king of Sodom, "With raised hand I have sworn an oath to the Creator of heaven and earth that I will accept nothing belonging to you, not even a thread or the strap of a sandal, so that you will never be able to say, 'I made Abram rich.' I will accept nothing but what my men have eaten and the share that belongs to the men who went with me to Aner, Eshkol, and Mamre. Let them have their share." This pleased the Creator greatly because Abram's faith was growing, and he was beginning to be a light bearer of the Creator in the idolatrous land of Canaan. The kings were also very impressed with Abram's graciousness.

Chapter 8

An Eternal and Irreversible Real Estate Grant

Blunt honesty

After this, the Creator came to Abram in a vision and said to him, "Do not be afraid, Abram. I am your shield, your very great reward." In a remarkable act of truthfulness and sincerity in interacting with the Creator, Abram said, "Sovereign Lord, what can you give me since I remain childless and the one who will inherit my estate is my servant Eliezer of Damascus?" Continuing, he said, "You have given me no children. At this point and time, a servant in my household will be my heir, and to compound the problem, my wife and I are old and past childbearing age, and how does a man become a nation with no children."

The ever-interacting Creator replied to him, saying, "This man will not be your heir, but a son who is your own flesh and blood will be your heir." He took Abram outside and said, "Look up at the sky and count the stars—if indeed you can count them." Then he said to him, "So shall your offspring be."

Abram believed the Creator, and in so doing, it pleased him so much that he credited his belief as an act of righteousness. Then he also said to him, "I am the Lord, who brought you out of Ur of the Chaldeans to give you this land to take possession of it."

But Abram, knowing he was old and outmatched in numbers by the Canaanites, said, "Sovereign Lord, how can I know that I will gain possession of this land?" So the Lord said to him, "This evening, I want you to bring me a heifer, a goat, and a ram, each three years old, along with a dove and a young pigeon."

Abram brought all these to him, and he was instructed to cut them in two, and he arranged the halves opposite each other; the birds, however, he did not cut in half. Then he sat there with the slaughtered animals, waiting for further instructions. While he waited, birds of prey came down on the carcasses, but he drove them away and kept waiting.

The one-sided irrevocable covenant

As the sun was setting, Abram fell into a deep sleep, and a thick and dreadful darkness came over him. Then the Creator said to him, "Know for certain that for four hundred years, your descendants will be strangers in a country not their own and that they will be enslaved and mistreated there. But I will punish the nation they serve as slaves, and afterward, they will come out with great possessions. You, however, will die in peace and be buried at a good old age. In the fourth generation, your descendants will come back here, for the sin of the Amorites has not yet reached its full measure. I am a God of justice, but I am determined to extend their probation for over four hundred more years to give them the opportunity to turn to me—if they want to—as they learn more about me."

When the sun had set and darkness had fallen, a smoking firepot with a blazing torch appeared and passed between the pieces. On that day, the Creator made a covenant with Abram and said, "To your descendants I give this land from the Wadi of Egypt to the great river, the Euphrates, the land of the Kenites, Kenizzites, Kadmonites, Hittites, Perizzites, Rephaites, Amorites, Canaanites, Girgashites and Jebusites." In this, he made an irrevocable covenant with Abram.

Typically, in a covenant like this, both parties declared the covenant and passed between the cut pieces; but in this case, the Creator assumed the responsibility and made it irrevocable and not dependent on Abram and, therefore, passed between the pieces alone, thereby making Abram a witness to a covenant that could be verified all the way to the end of time by any man.

Abram also came to understand that the Creator was very righteous and merciful and was in no hurry to punish or destroy people but to give them even hundreds of years to change their ways if they were willing. He was not getting the land of Canaan at this time because the Canaanites were being given a chance to change from their evil and detestable ways.

A boy called Ishmael

Abram, still buoyant from the covenant the Creator just made with him, recounted the experience and promise to his wife Sarai. Having seen all that had transpired in their lives to this point, she believed him.

However, Sarai knew that her barren condition had not changed and the throes of menopause were already in the rear view and so she felt that she could not bear him children herself. But she had an Egyptian maid named Hagar. So she said to Abram, "The Creator has kept me from having children. I give you permission to go sleep with my maid. Perhaps I can build a family through her."

Since this was a common practice in their culture, she felt she could give the Creator a hand with his effort in trying to raise descendants for Abram. Abram, on his part, willing to please his wife, also assumed that this might be the avenue the Creator was pursuing, and without asking his Lord, Abram agreed to what Sarai said.

So after Abram had been living in Canaan ten years, at the age of eighty-five years, Sarai his wife took her Egyptian maid Hagar and gave her to him to be his wife. He slept with Hagar, and she conceived. When she knew she was pregnant and was now the natural mother to the heir to Abram, she began to despise her barren mistress.

Sarai felt betrayed and sidelined by the Creator and Abram. She felt Abram should have asked him to intervene on her behalf, to let her be a direct part of the action for such an important undertaking. She then lashed out in frustration and said to Abram, "You are responsible for the wrong I am suffering. I put my maid in your arms, and now that she knows she is pregnant, she despises me. May the Creator judge between you and I."

"Your maid is in your hands," Abram pleaded. "Do with her whatever you think best." He felt a measure of guilt in what his wife had said. Then Sarai mistreated Hagar so much so that she fled from her into the desert.

However, the Angel of the Lord found Hagar near a spring in the desert, and he said, "Hagar, maid of Sarai, go back to your mistress and submit to her. I will increase your descendants so much that they will be too numerous to count. You will give birth to a son, and you shall name him Ishmael, for the Creator has heard of your misery. Your son will be a wild donkey of a man. His hand will be against everyone and everyone's hand against him, and he will live in hostility toward all his brothers."

Now knowing the Creator cared that much about her too to the extent of revealing himself to her and promising to take care of her, she returned home, submitted herself to her mistress, and bore Abram a son. Abram was eighty-six years old when Hagar gave birth to the boy, and he gave the name Ishmael to the son she had given birth to, as instructed by the angel of the Lord through Hagar.

The advent of circumcision

Thirteen years after the birth of Ishmael, when Abram was ninety-nine years old, the Lord again appeared to him and said, "I am the Creator. Continue to walk before me faithfully and blamelessly in keeping with the covenant between me and you, and I will greatly increase your numbers." Abram bowed with his face to the ground in worship and reverence before the sovereign Lord. Continuing, he said, "As for me, this is my covenant with you: You will be the father of many nations. No longer will you be called Abram. Your name will be Abraham, for I have made you a father of many nations. I will make you very fruitful. I will make nations of you, and kings will come from you. I will establish my covenant as an everlasting covenant between me and you and your descendants after you for the generations to come to be your Lord and the Lord of your descendants after you.

"The whole land of Canaan, where you now reside as a foreigner, I will give as an everlasting possession to you and your descendants after you, and I will be their Lord." Continuing, he said, "As for you and your descendants after you, the covenant you are to keep is as follows: every male among you shall be circumcised. You are to undergo circumcision, and it will be the sign of the covenant between me and you.

"For the generations to come, every male among you must be circumcised when he is eight days old, including those born in your household or acquired foreigners. Those who are not your offspring must be circumcised. My covenant in your flesh is to be an everlasting covenant. Any uncircumcised male who has not been circumcised in the flesh will be cut off from his people because he will not be under this covenant.

"As for Sarai, your wife, you are no longer to call her Sarai. Her name will be Sarah. I will bless her and will surely give you a son by her. I will bless her so that she will be the mother of nations. Kings of peoples will come from her."

Abraham fell facedown. He laughed internally in amusement and said to himself, "Will a son be born to a man a hundred years old? Will Sarah bear a child at the age of ninety?" And Abraham, attempting to be gracious and helpful in not allowing the Creator to put himself in an exceedingly difficult and challenging position, said to him, "If only Ishmael might live under your blessing!" Then the Creator, knowing what Abraham was trying to insinuate, said, "Yes, but your wife Sarah will bear you a son, and you will call him Isaac. I will establish my covenant with him as an everlasting covenant for his descendants after him.

"And as for Ishmael, I have heard you. I will surely bless him. I will make him fruitful and will greatly increase his numbers. He will be the father of twelve rulers, and I will make him into a great nation. But my covenant I will establish with Isaac, whom Sarah will bear to you by this time next year." When he had finished speaking with Abraham, the Creator went up from him.

As soon as he was done talking to Abraham, on that very day Abraham took his son Ishmael and every male in his household and circumcised them as he had been instructed. He did not wait till the next day but did as he was commanded, and it pleased the Lord greatly. Abraham was ninety-nine years old and his son Ishmael was thirteen and both were circumcised on that very day.

A special visit

Shortly after his household had fully healed from the circumcision procedure, an unusual visitor called on Abraham near the great trees of Mamre while he was sitting at the entrance to his tent in the heat of the day.

As he looked up, he saw three men nearby who looked as though they were on their way on a journey past where he was staying. When he saw them, he hurried from the entrance of his tent to meet them and bowed low to the ground. As was the custom for great hospitality, he said, "If I have found favor in your eyes, my lord, do not pass your servant by. Let a little water be brought, and then you may all wash your feet and rest under this tree. Let me get you something to eat, so you can be refreshed and then go on your way now that you have come to your servant."

"Very well," they answered. "Do as you say."

So Abraham hurried into the tent to Sarah. "Quick," he said. "Get plenty of the finest flour, and knead it and bake some bread." Then he ran to the herd and personally selected a choice tender calf and gave it to a servant, who hurried to prepare it. He then brought some curds and milk and the calf that had been prepared and set these before them. While they ate, he stood near them under a tree as he personally and respectfully waited on them.

"Where is your wife, Sarah?" they asked him.

"Inside the tent," he said, pointing to his tent.

Then one of them said, "I will surely return to you about this time next year, and Sarah, your wife, will have a son."

Now Sarah was listening at the entrance to the tent, which was behind him and out of their sight. Somehow, to her, and even more so to Abraham, the men had an air of mystery about them though they looked very much like any other travelers with dusty sandals and feet.

Abraham and Sarah were already very old, and Sarah was well past the age of childbearing, therefore being out of their sight, she laughed quietly to herself as she thought, *After I am worn out, the factory shutdown and my lord is old will I now have this pleasure?* Then one of the visitors said to Abraham, "Why did Sarah laugh and say, 'Will I really have a child now that I am old?' Is anything too hard for the Lord? I will return to you at the appointed time next year, and Sarah will have a son."

Sarah was very terrified because her laughter was silent, and there was no way they could have seen her, let alone hear her, and that confirmed her suspicion that these were no ordinary men. Being afraid, she lied and said, "I did not laugh." But he said, "Yes, you did laugh," and he left it at that with an amused shadow of an ever so slight a smile.

Abraham shadows the Creator

After their meal, which they seemed to have enjoyed, when the men got up to leave, they looked down toward the city of Sodom, and Abraham walked along with them to see them on their way. Then one of the visitors said, "Shall I hide from Abraham what I am about to do? Abraham will surely become a great and powerful nation, and all nations on earth will be blessed through him. For I have chosen him so that he will direct his children and his household after him to keep the way of the Creator by doing what is right and just so that he will bring about for Abraham what he has promised him."

Continuing, he said, "The outcry against Sodom and Gomorrah is so great and their evil so grievous that I will go down and see if what they have done is as bad as the outcry that has reached me. If not, I will know."

The men turned away and went toward Sodom, but Abraham remained standing before him. He knew there was a familiarity in that voice. Abraham knew of the wickedness of the people of Sodom and Gomorrah, and he knew his nephew and his whole family and servants lived there. Then Abraham, having ascertained what was about to happen to those cities, approached him and said, "Far be it from you to do such a thing—to kill the righteous with the wicked, treating the righteous and the wicked alike. Far be it from you! Will not the righteous Judge of all the earth do what is right? Will you sweep away the righteous with the wicked? Will you really sweep them away and not spare the place if you found fifty righteous people in it?"

Then he replied and said, "If I find fifty righteous people in those cities, I will spare the whole place for their sake."

Then Abraham spoke up again, "Now that I have been so bold as to speak to the Lord, though I am nothing but dust and ashes, what if the number of the righteous is five less than fifty? Will you destroy the whole city for lack of five people?"

"If I find forty-five there," he said, "I will not destroy it."

Once again, he spoke to him, "What if only forty are found there?" He said, "For the sake of forty, I will not do it." Then he said, "May the Lord not be angry, but let me speak. What if only thirty can be found there?"

He answered, "I will not do it if I find thirty there."

Abraham said, "Now that I have been so bold as to speak to the Lord, what if only twenty can be found there?"

He said, "For the sake of twenty, I will not destroy it."

Then doing a quick computation in his mind about the number of the household population of Lot, he said, "May the Lord not be angry, but let me speak just once more. What if only ten can be found there?"

He answered, "For the sake of ten, I will not destroy it."

When the Lord had finished speaking with Abraham, he left, and Abraham returned home. Abraham had done a quick calculation about the odds of finding ten righteous people in that whole region, and he felt good because his nephew's family was likely to have at least that many between his wife, children, and herdsmen.

After the departure of the Lord, Abraham sat down for a moment to meditate on what had just transpired. He was just recovering from the fact that he had just been in the presence of a manifestation of the Creator or one of his angels who had come down in the form of humans. It was not easy for him to make a proper evaluation because each time an angel visited with a message, he spoke in the first person as if it was the Lord himself speaking since they spoke for him. There was something about that voice that sounded so familiar. But why would the Lord visit him in a human manifestation, enduring a trek in the heat with dusty feet?

Upon reflecting on it, it made sense. If he were visiting a horse, a calf, an ant, or any other creature, it would make sense to manifest himself in their corresponding form for them to understand him. He had now seen a side of his Lord that showed a very deep human concern and friendship he would never have believed possible for the one who created everything that is, seen and unseen. What a Creator! What love.

It rained brimstone

The two messengers arrived at Sodom in the evening, and Lot was sitting in the gateway of the city, a seat of great administrative authority. When he saw them, he got up to meet them and bowed down with his face to the ground in humility to offer his hospitality as he had been raised.

"My lords," he said. "Please turn aside to your servant's house. You can wash your feet and spend the night safely and comfortably there and then go on your way early in the morning."

"No," they answered. "We will spend the night in the city square." But knowing the place, he insisted so strongly that they were embarrassed in the presence of the other administrators and did go with him to his house. After dinner, before the men went to bed, all the men from every part of the city of Sodom, both young and old, surrounded the house.

They called out to Lot, "Where are the men who came to you tonight? Bring them out to us so that we can have sex with them." Lot went outside to meet them and shut the door behind him and said, "No, my friends. Don't do this wicked thing. Please don't do anything to these men, for they have come under the protection of my roof."

"Get out of our way," they replied. Speaking among themselves they said, "This fellow came here as a foreigner, and now he wants to play the judge! We'll treat you worse than them." Some of them were already stripped down to their undergarments and some others even beyond any semblance of pretentious decency. They mounted pressure on Lot and lunged forward to seize Lot and break down the door.

But the two men inside reached out and pulled Lot back into the house and shut the door. Then they struck the men who were at the door of the house, young and old, with blindness so that they could not find the door; and the men, incensed with lustful cravings like wild beasts in heat, wore themselves out trying to find the door. Lot's suspicion was confirmed that these were no ordinary men but rather angels who had taken human forms.

The two men asked Lot if he had anyone else here—sons-in-law, sons or daughters, or anyone else in the city who belongs to him. They then instructed him to get them out because they were going to destroy this place. They explained that the outcry to the Creator against its people was so great that he had sent them to destroy it, and destroy it they will.

Lot, therefore, went out and spoke to his sons-in-law, who were pledged to marry his daughters. He told them to hurry and get out of this place because the Creator was about to destroy the city. But his sons-in-law thought he was joking and laughed him to scorn. They had no regard for the Creator and were content and confident that no such thing unheard of before could happen, and they brushed him off. As he stared at the young men and their families, whom he had become very familiar with and cared for, it broke his heart to know a terrible thing was about to happen, and it was not going to end well for them.

With the coming of dawn, the angels urged Lot to hurry and take his wife and two daughters who were there and leave or be swept away when the city was punished. When he hesitated, the men grasped his hand and the hands of his wife and of his two daughters and led them safely out of the city, for the Creator was merciful to them.

As soon as they had brought them out, they were told to flee for their lives, not to turn and look back and not to stop anywhere in the plain. The men recommended that they flee to the mountains. But Lot pleaded with them, indicating he was afraid of the mountains for fear of what could happen to him there and asked rather to be allowed to flee into the small town which was nearby.

One of the angels then said to him, "Very well, I will grant this request. I will not overthrow the town you speak of. But flee there quickly because I cannot do anything until you reach it." (That is why the town was called Zoar.) By the time Lot reached Zoar, the sun had risen over the land.

Then it happened: burning sulfur rained down on Sodom and Gomorrah and the associated cities out of the heavens but spared Zoar for Lot's sake. It was a very frightening sight as the whole place was engulfed in a fiery storm, destroying all those living in the cities and the vegetation in the land. During the fiery avalanche, thunderous hail of flying sulfur, and the loud shrieks and screams, Lot's wife looked back, against the warning of the angel, and she froze and became a pillar of salt.

Early the next morning, Abraham got up and returned to the place where he had stood before the Lord. He looked down toward Sodom and Gomorrah, toward all the land of the plain, and he saw dense smoke rising from the land like smoke from a furnace, and he knew the Lord had not found up to ten righteous people, but he did not know at the time that the Lord had remembered him and had brought Lot out of the catastrophe.

From a sprawling mansion to a cave

As Lot stood and looked at the utter destruction across the plains, a lot crossed his mind. For fame and fortune and revered as a leading member of society with great prominence, he had tolerated all the filth of Sodom even though he knew better. It all came crashing down in a moment, and were it not for the mercy of the Creator, he would be a goner like the rest of the populace. With all his wealth, he had been tolerated and was easily among the society elite, and life from the top looking down at the murk of the place was morally revolting. It was the life he had chosen, and he learned that day that a whole nation and its wealth can be wiped out in one hour especially if that nation shows disdain to the righteous ways of the Creator.

Lot quickly found out that the people of Zoar were as wicked as those of Sodom, and he now understood why it was to have been destroyed as well. As images of Noah's flood and the fiery winds sweeping the plains of Sodom flashed through his mind, he and his two daughters fled from evil Zoar to go live in a cave in the mountains just in case there was a repeat order. He was through with that life, and he was never going to let riches own him again. He just now worried about his daughters, hoping they had not embraced any of the evil practices of the people of Sodom and that they were not too late for redemption.

King Abimelek encounters the Creator

The Creator, whom Abraham now acknowledge as the sovereign Lord God, was not through manifesting himself to Abraham and the Philistines as a way of revealing himself to them.

The Creator had supernaturally maintained Sarah's physical attractiveness which was garnished by an untamable allure of gentleness, grace, and meekness which was irresistible. She never allowed her physical beauty to be a distraction in her life and rather reverenced her husband with sincere endearment. With that attitude, Abraham was willing to do whatever she requested, and they both knew it. This made the affection they had for each other so enduring especially when he came to a full understanding that his wife, Sarah, was an equal partner in his mission and covenants in the sight of the Creator.

For a while, he stayed in Gerar, a region of the very formidable Philistines, and there Abraham again informed the people that his wife, Sarah, was his sister. Then Abimelek, king of Gerar, sent for Sarah and took her. But the Creator came to Abimelek in a dream at night and said to him, "You are as good as dead because of the woman you have taken. She is a married woman." It took an awful lot to intimidate the powerful Philistine king, and this time, he was not just intimidated; he was frightened to death, for he knew this was no ordinary voice, and he was not only the one in danger but his very whole nation.

Now Abimelek had not gone near her yet, so he said, "Lord, will you destroy an innocent nation? Did the man not say to me, 'She is my sister,' and didn't she also say, 'He is my brother'? I have done this with a clear conscience and clean hands."

Then the Creator said to him in the dream, "Yes, I know you did this with a clear conscience, and so I have kept you from sinning against me. That is why I did not let you touch her. Now return the man's wife, for he is a prophet and he will pray for you and you will live. But if you do not return her, you may be sure that you and all who belong to you will die."

The wise old king could not wait for sunrise as he was unable to fall back to sleep. He had finally laid hands on something that was sure to cause major indigestion for him, and he could not wait to get rid of it.

Early the next morning, Abimelek summoned all his officials; and when he told them all that had happened, they were very much afraid. Then Abimelek called Abraham in and said, "What have you done to us? How have I wronged you that you have brought such great guilt upon me and my kingdom? You have done things to me that should never be done." And Abimelek asked Abraham, "What was your reason for doing this?"

Abraham's reply was that he felt the people there had no fear of the Creator and that he was likely to get killed for his wife; therefore, he had asked her to say she was his sister if they ran into that situation.

Then Abimelek brought sheep and cattle and male and female servants and gave them to Abraham, and he returned Sarah, his wife, to him. And Abimelek said, "My land is before you. Live wherever you like." To Sarah, he said, "I am giving your brother a thousand shekels of silver. This is to cover the offense against you before all who are with you. You are completely vindicated."

Then Abraham prayed to the Creator, and he healed Abimelek, his wife, and his female servants so they could have children again, for he had kept all the women in Abimelek's household from conceiving because of Abraham's wife, Sarah.

As Abraham walked away humbled, for the first time in his life, it finally dawned on him that the Creator had power over conception, life and death, and that he was really a delegate and an ambassador for him. He could be delegated to speak on the Creator's behalf.

This pleased the Lord because he could now finish off Abraham's preparation and establish him as the patriarch of the nation through whom he would be sending the Redeemer, and he would be teaching his descendants as one who truly knew the creator of the heavens and the earth.

Then came Isaac

Now the Creator was gracious to Sarah as he had said, and he did for Sarah what he had promised. Very shortly after the interaction with Abimelek, while staying in the time frame he had given Abraham, Sarah became pregnant and bore a son to him in his old age, and he named him Isaac. He was a hundred years old when his son Isaac was born, and he was circumcised when he was eight days old.

Sarah's whole demeanor changed and laughter filled the home and it was a very joyful home as she came to grips with the fact that a special miracle had to be performed to give her her greatest desire, and it was done in style. As they sat relaxing after dinner one evening, her eyes glistening with profound joy and gratitude, she leaned over to Abraham, tickling him fondly, and said, "The Creator has brought me laughter, and everyone who hears about this will laugh with me." And she added, "Who would have said to Abraham that Sarah would nurse children? Yet I have borne him a son in his old age. The Creator most certainly has a divine sense of humor."

Sarah was remarkably reinvigorated to handle the demands of childbearing and rearing, and no one could argue that the youth of these two had not been supernaturally renewed like the eagle.

Isaac grew, and on the day that he was weaned, Abraham held a great feast. All was going well, and there was great joy in the immense Abrahamic community until the day when Sarah saw Ishmael mocking Isaac.

Sensing a very serious potential for deadly family strife, Sarah told Abraham to get rid of the woman and her son, for that woman's son was never going to share in the inheritance with her son, Isaac. The matter distressed Abraham greatly because it concerned his son and this time he turned to the Creator for counsel and the Creator was pleased. Reassuring Abraham, he said, "Do not be so distressed about the boy and his mother. Listen to whatever Sarah tells you because it is through Isaac that your offspring will be reckoned. I will make Ishmael into a nation also because he is your offspring, and I will see to that."

As had become Abraham's custom, he did whatever the Creator asked him to do without delay. Early the next morning, Abraham took some food and water and gave them to Hagar. He set them on her shoulders and then sent her off with the boy, knowing the Creator will do to him as he had promised.

To comfort and reassure her, he reminded her of the promise the angel had told her the first time she ran away from home. She went on her way and wandered in the desert of Beersheba. When the water in the skin was gone, she put the boy under one of the bushes. Then she went off and sat down about a bowshot away, certain that he would die from dehydration, and she did not want to watch him die. And as she sat there, she began to sob.

The Creator decided to reassure and comfort her in reminding her that he keeps his promises and intervenes when he sees it necessary. So when the Creator heard the boy start to cry, he called to Hagar from heaven and said to her, "What is the matter, Hagar? Do not be afraid. I have heard the boy crying as he lies there. Lift the boy up, and take him by the hand, for I will make him into a great nation as I had promised."

Then he opened her eyes, and she saw a well of water, so she went and filled the skin with water and gave the boy a drink. The Creator was with the boy as he grew up, and he lived in the desert and became an excellent archer. While he was living in the desert of Paran, his mother got a wife for him from Egypt. As the Creator had promised, he prospered the boy, and he grew into a great nation.

The humble ambassador of peace

As the Philistines observed Abraham, it was clear that he was extremely wealthy and a potential threat. However, unlike those in the surrounding nations, Abraham was a man of peace and never threatened others or used his wealth to bargain with. They observed that his moral code of conduct was dictated by the one he claimed to be the creator of the heavens and the earth.

The amazing thing about this great prince was that they could not find any fault against him, and it was a thing of beauty. The scariest of all was that they knew if they touched him, the Creator would destroy the Philistine nation without Abraham lifting a finger. This pleased the Lord greatly because the Philistines had an opportunity to see the true and living Creator in action and a chance for them to have him as their Lord.

So, at that time Abimelek and Phicol, the commander of his forces, said to Abraham, "The Creator is with you in everything you do. Now swear to me here before him that you will not deal falsely with me or my children or my descendants. Show to me and the country where you now reside as a foreigner the same kindness I have shown to you."

Abraham said, "I swear it." Then the two men made a treaty. So that place was called Beersheba because the two men swore an oath there. After the treaty had been made at Beersheba, Abimelek and Phicol, the commander of his forces returned to the land of the Philistines. Abraham planted a tamarisk tree in Beersheba, and there he called on the name of the Lord, the eternal creator. And Abraham stayed in the land of the Philistines for a long time.

Abraham's final test and legacy

Job had left an incredible legacy for mankind showing how Satan, the evil one, could be tamed. The Creator decided it was time to put Abraham to the final test so he could establish his own legacy. Abraham's legacy would not be just for himself but for all the nations and his descendants.

So after some time had elapsed and Isaac was fairly grown, the Creator tested Abraham. He said to him, "Abraham!"

"Here I am," he replied.

Then he said, "Take your son, your only son, whom you love, Isaac, and go to the region of Moriah. Sacrifice him there as a burnt offering on a mountain I will show you."

True to form, as was Abraham's custom, early the next morning he got up and loaded his donkey. He took with him two of his servants and his son Isaac. When he had cut enough wood for the burnt offering, he set out for the place that the Creator had told him about, which he was familiar with. After three days of travel, Abraham looked up and saw the place in the distance. He then told his servants to stay behind with the donkey while he and the boy went over to worship and to rejoin them upon completion.

Abraham took the wood for the burnt offering and placed it on his son Isaac, and he himself carried the fire and the knife. As the two of them went on together and got close to the place, Isaac spoke up and said to his father Abraham, "Father?"

"Yes, my son?" Abraham replied.

"The fire and wood are here," Isaac said. "But where is the lamb for the burnt offering?"

Abraham answered, "The Creator himself will provide the lamb for the burnt offering, my son."

And the two of them went on together. Abraham knew the Lord well enough now to be confident that his son will somehow be restored by the Creator because he had established an irreversible, one-sided covenant with him, and he knew the Creator never went back on his word. According to his promise to Sarah and Abraham, Isaac was the son of promise, and he was willing to do what the Lord had asked him and let the Creator sort out the details because he believed that was his Lord's problem and not his.

When they reached the place, Abraham built an altar there and arranged the wood on it. Here, Abraham explained to Isaac that he would be the sacrifice as requested by the Creator. It was very puzzling to Isaac because the sovereign Lord his father served despised these horrible practices which were part of the Canaanitic culture and had warned them never to do them. However, he knew his father had always been prompt in obeying and following through with whatever thing the Creator had asked him. He also knew and believed that he was the son of promise, and the Creator always kept his promise, so he was likely to do something miraculous though he did not know what.

Isaac, now about thirty-five years of age, put his hands together in a sign of free-will submission to his father and to the Creator. He extended them to him to be bound. He was too physically strong for his father to offer him against his will, and they both knew it. Gratefully, Abraham bound his son Isaac and laid him on the altar, on top of the wood.

Then Abraham reached out his hand and took the knife, lifting it to slay his son. At that point, the angel of the Lord called out to him from heaven, "Abraham! Abraham!"

"Here I am," he replied.

"Do not lay a hand on the boy," he said. "Do not do anything to him. Now I know that you have reverential fear and honor for the Creator because you have not withheld from me your son—your only son with Sarah."

Taking a mighty deep breath, he heard a rustling sound to the side of him; and as Abraham looked up, there in a thicket he saw a ram caught by its horns. He went over and with the help of his son, took the ram, and sacrificed it as a burnt offering instead of his son. So Abraham called that place "The Lord Will Provide."

The angel of the Lord called to Abraham from heaven a second time and said, "I swear by myself that because you have done this and have not withheld your son, your only son, I will surely bless you and make your descendants as numerous as the stars in the sky and as the sand on the seashore. Your descendants will take possession of the cities of their enemies, and through your offspring, all nations on earth will be blessed because you have obeyed me."

The Creator noted that Isaac had indeed abided by the teaching received from his parents and that he had come to trust the Creator too, and it pleased him greatly.

Then Abraham returned to his servants with a double spring in his steps, and they set off together for Beersheba in the best spirit they had ever seen him in. The servants were quite joyful that his worship session with his son had been special.

And Abraham stayed in Beersheba. He had now seen multiple facets of the Creator he never knew, and he cherished the blissful life when walking with him. He knew he could never trade his relationship with his Lord for anything in the world; life had never been so good and secure.

Unknown to Abraham, his experiences were what the Creator has in mind for every human who chose to walk with him as his Lord. He desired this to the point where he pulled all stops to show humanity his heart using Abraham as the model.

Sarah lived to be a 127 old and enjoyed her son's company for decades as she taught and watched him grow into a God-loving young man, and she was very content when she died. Though the birth was late in her life, the Creator gave her decades to enjoy and nurture him in full strength; and at her good old age, she died in Hebron, in the land of Canaan. Abraham mourned and wept over her and appealed to the Hittites to sell him a piece of land with the cave of Machpelah to bury his wife. They graciously did, and the piece of land became the purchased property of Abraham in the land of Canaan.

Isaac gets married

With time, Abraham became very old, and the Creator had blessed him in every way as he had promised. Seeing that the end was coming, he was determined to get a wife for his son, but not from the Canaanites; they were almost incorrigible without divine intervention as far as the ways of righteousness were concerned. Therefore, under oath, he sent his lead servant to go and get a wife for his son in his own country where he had come from from among his relatives. He was very confident the Creator will provide the wife of his choice for Isaac his son.

Then the servant left, taking with him ten of his master's camels loaded with all kinds of good things from his master. He set out for Aram Naharaim and made his way to the town of Nahor, where Abraham's relatives lived.

The Creator did indeed prosper his journey remarkably, and he succeeded in finding a very beautiful and gracious young woman among Abraham's relatives who was willing to come to the land of Canaan and be the wife of Isaac. Her name was Rebekah and the two loved each other dearly and Isaac was greatly comforted after the death of his mother. With his wife, they lived and walked in reverence of the Creator, and Abraham was very happy knowing she complemented Isaac's faith in many ways.

Abraham's exit

Abraham had been so physically revived that he took another wife, whose name was Keturah, after the death of his wife Sarah. She bore him Zimran, Jokshan, Medan, Midian, Ishbak, and Shuah.

Abraham left everything he owned to Isaac, the son of promise; but while he was still living, he gave gifts to the sons of his concubines and sent them away from his son Isaac to the land of the east. Then Abraham breathed his last and died at a good old age, an old man full of years at 175 years. His sons Isaac and Ishmael buried him in the cave of Machpelah near Mamre where his wife, Sarah, was buried.

After Abraham's death, the Creator blessed his son Isaac, who then lived near Beer Lahai Roi in the land of Canaan, and Ishmael returned to the eastern boarder of Egypt where he lived among his people.

Ishmael's Sons

As the Creator promised, he blessed Ishmael, the son of Hagar the Egyptian, whom she bore to Abraham. The Creator had prospered him greatly while Abraham was still alive and, therefore, had no reason to contend with Isaac for any inheritance. They therefore buried their father and parted in peace and the best of terms of peace.

These are the names of the sons of Ishmael listed in the order of their birth: Nebaioth the firstborn of Ishmael, Kedar, Adbeel, Mibsam, Mishma, Dumah, Massa, Hadad, Tema, Jetur, Naphish, and Kedemah. These were the sons of Ishmael, and these are the names of the twelve tribal rulers according to their settlements and camps. Ishmael lived a hundred and thirty-seven years. He breathed his last and died, and he was gathered to his people. His descendants settled in the area from Havilah to Shur, near the eastern border of Egypt, as you go toward Ashur. And they lived in hostility toward all the tribes related to them.

Chapter 9

A Nation Born in Turbulence

Sometime after Abraham's death, there was a famine in the land of Canaan besides the previous famine in Abraham's time, and Isaac went to Abimelek, king of the Philistines, in Gerar.

With Abraham dead, Isaac now bore the covenant, and the Creator decided to direct him more closely and strengthen him. This time the Creator appeared to Isaac and told him not to go down to Egypt but rather to live in the land where he directed him with the promise to watch over him and prosper him. He reaffirmed the promise he had made with Abraham regarding the land and his descendants, with Isaac thereby letting him know that the promise and the blessings were transferred to him.

Like his father, despite his great wealth and might, he continued the legacy of peaceful coexistence and maintained the high level of righteousness he had established. This allowed the Creator to present him as a witness to the Canaanites and the opportunity to see what a life with the Creator entailed. Isaac's wealth had continued to grow exceedingly in flocks, herds, and servants that the Philistines envied him while he stayed in Gerar. When Abimelek sensed the envy, he gave strict orders to all his people prohibiting anyone from harming Isaac or his wife, and the punishment for doing so would be death.

Later, Abimelek told Isaac to move away from them because he had become too powerful for them, and though he was a man of peace, his might made them very uneasy. Isaac graciously accepted and kept moving and eventually reached Beersheba. That night, the

Creator appeared to him and continued to earnestly encourage him and remind him of the covenant.

Meanwhile, Abimelek, the commander of his forces, and advisers decided to pay him a visit. Isaac asked them why they had come to see him since they had been hostile to him and sent him away. Their response was that it was obvious now to everyone in the land that the Creator was with him, and they meant him no harm; they just wanted a sworn agreement between Isaac and them to not harm each other. Isaac, therefore, made a big feast for them when they signed the sworn treaty of peace between them, after which they parted ways peacefully.

They made their Choices

Isaac was forty years old when he married his wife, Rebekah, brought from Abraham's relatives. She conceived and gave birth to twins when he was sixty years old. Isaac, being the only child of Sarah, established him easily as the heir. Only one person could be in direct line of succession, and as always, it typically fell on the eldest son, based on the birthright. However, the Creator left it entirely up to the twins to decide who wanted to be the one—a privilege that came with significant responsibilities.

Isaac was sixty years old when Rebekah gave birth, and Esau, the older boy, became a skillful hunter, a man of the open country, while Jacob was content to stay at home among the tents.

Isaac taught the boys the promise of the Creator for humanity and how important it was for them to be the light bearers of the Abrahamic covenant and serve as his ambassadors.

Isaac, who had a taste for wild game, loved Esau, but Rebekah loved Jacob, and the boys developed their individual personalities. Once when Jacob was cooking some stew, Esau came in from the open country, famished. He had not had time to cook, so he asked Jacob for some of that red stew he had just made. Jacob promised to give him in exchange for Esau's birthright. After some exchanges, Esau swore an oath to give Jacob his birthright in exchange for the food.

Then Jacob gave Esau some bread and some of the lentil stew. He ate and drank and then got up and left. So Esau despised his birthright, essentially giving up the privilege of being in the direct ancestral line of the promised Redeemer of humanity. Part of the benefits of having the birthright is that it entitles one to a greater portion of the family inheritance besides being the family priest. With this transaction, the boys determined their personal priorities and chose their preferred paths in life.

When Esau was forty years old, he married Judith, daughter of Beeri the Hittite, and Basemath, daughter of Elon the Hittite. They were hardcore Canaanites, and their abominable practices were a source of grief to Isaac and Rebekah. This was not what they had hoped for especially after all that they had taught the boys. It was up to them to make their choices though, and Isaac was fully aware that the Creator never forced anyone to obey him, but he and his wife did their best to instruct the boys on the consequences of choices, whether good or bad.

The family blessings and covenant passed down

Isaac's faith and confidence in the Creator helped him maintain a very peaceful life. He was now old, and his eyes were so weak that he could no longer see; and believing that his days were now numbered, he called for Esau, his older son, and told him he believed he could soon die from old age. He then asked him to go out to the open country to hunt some wild game for him. He wanted it prepared the way he was fond of so that he could eat and formally pass on the Abrahamic blessings to him in the presence of the Creator before he died.

Now Rebekah was listening unnoticed as Isaac spoke to his son Esau. As soon as Esau left for the open country to hunt game, Rebekah told her son Jacob what their father had said to Esau. Together with her son, they concocted a dangerous scheme which involved preparing some tasty food just the way Isaac liked it, and Jacob pretending to be Esau. If Isaac found out Jacob was lying, he would end up with a curse, and he was deadly afraid; but the mother was very persuasive, and the desire for the blessings provided the additional motivation for Jacob.

The mother then cooked the food, and Jacob took it to his father, disguised as Esau and wearing his clothes that bore his field odor. With his near blindness, Isaac was unable to tell that this was indeed Jacob, so he ate the food and prayed for the transfer of the blessings to him.

A cry of regret

After Isaac finished blessing him, and Jacob had scarcely left his father's presence, his brother, Esau, came in from hunting. He too prepared some tasty food and brought it to his father. Then he said to him, "My father, please sit up and eat some of my game, so that you may give me your blessing."

His father asked him, "Who are you?"

"I am your son," he answered. "Your firstborn, Esau."

Isaac trembled violently and said, "Who was it, then, that hunted game and brought it to me? I ate it just before you came and I blessed him and indeed, he will be blessed!"

When Esau heard his father's words, he burst out with a loud and bitter cry and said to his father, "Bless me—me too, my father!"

But he said, "Your brother came deceitfully and took your blessing."

Esau said, "Isn't he rightly named Jacob? This is the second time he has taken advantage of me. He took my birthright, and now he's taken my blessing!" Then he asked, "Haven't you reserved any blessing for me?"

Isaac answered Esau, "I have made him Lord over you by the authority the Creator has bestowed upon me and have made all his relatives his servants and I have sustained him with grain and new wine. So what can I possibly do for you, my son?"

Esau said to his father, "Do you have only one blessing, my father? Bless me too, my father!" Then Esau wept aloud.

His father Isaac answered him, "Your dwelling will be away from the earth's richness, away from the dew of heaven above. You will live by the sword, and you will serve your brother. But when you grow restless, you will throw his yoke from off your neck."

Upon hearing that Esau had earlier passed over his birthright to Jacob, it dawned on Isaac that this might have been divinely ordained especially if Esau had intentionally and voluntarily given away his birthright with little regard for it.

Esau held a grudge against Jacob because of the blessing his father had given him. He was heard to say that after the death of their father, he will kill Jacob and the inheritance will be his then and this way, he comforted himself.

When Rebekah was told what her older son, Esau, had said, she asked Jacob to flee to her brother Laban in her home country in Harran and stay there with him for a while until Esau's fury subsided. She solemnly promised to send word for him to come back from there as soon as she thought it was safe.

Then Rebekah said to Isaac, "I'm disgusted with living because of these Hittite women Esau is married to. If Jacob takes a wife from among the Canaanite women, like these Hittite women, my life will not be worth living."

Rebekah had been a dream wife for Isaac in character and beauty, the best woman a man could wish for as a partner, in many ways like his own mother. Doing a quick mental algebra, he computed how awesome it would be for his son to get a wife from the same stock of character like his wife. So Isaac called for Jacob, and he commanded him not marry an idol-worshipping Canaanite woman but to go at once to Paddan Aram, to the house of his mother's father, Bethuel, and take a wife for himself there. He was reminded to return to Canaan as soon as he was able. He prayed and handed Jacob over to the care of the Creator and then sent him away.

Word got to Esau that Isaac had blessed Jacob and had sent him to Paddan Aram to take a wife from there and that when he blessed him, he commanded him to not marry a Canaanite woman and that Jacob had obeyed his father and mother and had gone.

Esau then realized how displeasing the Canaanite women were to his parents, so he went to Ishmael and married Mahalath, the daughter of Ishmael son of Abraham, in addition to the wives he already had. His deliberate act of marriage to the wicked Canaanites was in disobedience to his father and of great potential danger to his posterity because of the vile Canaanite practices.

Jacob's encounter with the Creator

Jacob fled Beersheba and set out for Harran, going as fast as he could for fear of his brother Esau, only stopping when the sun had set. Taking one of the stones there, he put it under his head and lay down to sleep. Up to this point, his personal relationship with the Creator was not quite existent. Being one for very personal relationships, the Creator had decided to confirm to Jacob that he had indeed inherited the blessings of Abraham and that he was now the heir and therefore, he needed to introduce himself.

As he slept, he had a dream in which he saw a stairway resting on the earth, with its top reaching to heaven, and the angels of the Creator were ascending and descending on it.

There above it stood the Lord, and he said, "I am the Creator, the Lord God of your father Abraham and of Isaac. I will give you and your descendants the land on which you are lying. Your descendants will be like the dust of the earth, and you will spread out to the west and to the east, to the north and to the south. All peoples on earth will be blessed through you and your offspring. I am with you and will watch over you wherever you go, and I will bring you back to this land. I will not leave you until I have done what I have promised you."

When Jacob awoke from his sleep in the early morning, he thought, *Surely the Lord is in this place, and I was not aware of it.* He was afraid and said, "How awesome is this place! This is none other than the house of the Creator. This is the gate of heaven." This was the first time Jacob had a direct encounter with the Creator, and the reality of him outside the teachings of his parents was driven home.

He took the stone he had placed under his head and set it up as a pillar and poured oil on top of it as an act of worship like his fathers did when they built altars to worship the Creator. He called that place Bethel though the city used to be called Luz. Then Jacob made a vow, saying, "If you will be with me and will watch over me on this journey I am taking and will give me food to eat and clothes to wear so that I return safely to my father's household, then you will be my Lord and this stone that I have set up as a pillar will be your house and of all that you give me I will give you a tenth."

True to his promise, this vision which he gave Jacob was his initiation into the world of the personal relationship he wants with everyone who chooses to trust and walk with him.

Jacob builds a family and wealth in Paddan Aram

Then Jacob continued his journey and eventually found his uncle Laban and in the course of time served him in raising and tending his flocks. In exchange for his service, he ended up being married to two of Laban's daughters, Rachel and Leah, and their respective maids, Zilpah and Bilhah, for a total of four wives over a span of fourteen years. During this time, he had eleven sons and one daughter between the four wives.

His family was very dysfunctional, in fact, as dysfunctional as can be expected when a man is married to multiple wives, including two sisters, with contentions among the wives that naturally brew rivalry and animosity between the children. Blatant favoritism from the father toward some of his children garnished the dysfunctionality.

The Creator had to work with what he had and helped tame Jacob to the point where he would stop relying on his worthless menial efforts of trickery and face the job of raising a family that reflected the values of righteous living and knowing the Creator. Like the rest of humanity, he was a true prince of the Almighty and did not know it.

After twenty years of living with Laban, his father-in-law, the Creator appeared to him in a dream and asked him to pack up and return to the land of Canaan. Jacob then told his family, and they packed up and fled with the cattle and herds that he had earned in serving Laban all these years. It was not a pleasant separation, but the Creator appeared to Laban in a dream and warned him against interfering with the return of Jacob to Canaan, which he obeyed and let Jacob return with his whole family and his acquired possessions.

The dreaded encounter

As much as Jacob wanted to return home, he dreaded having to face his brother, Esau, especially since he had not received word from his mother that it was okay to return home. The threat of dying at the hands of his brother was still as vivid as the day he fled from home. He knew he had to face his brother whether he liked it or not, and so he concocted a plan, Jacob's style, to try and make possible amends with him.

Jacob then sent messengers ahead of him to his brother, Esau, in the land of Seir, with a gift that comprised of two hundred female goats, twenty male goats, two hundred ewes, twenty rams, thirty female camels with their young, forty cows, ten bulls, twenty female donkeys, and ten male donkeys. He instructed them to communicate to Esau as follows: "Your servant Jacob says, 'I have been staying with Laban and have remained there till now. I have cattle and donkeys, sheep and goats, male and female servants. Now I am sending this message to my lord that I may find favor in your eyes.'"

When the messengers returned to Jacob, they told him that his brother Esau was coming to meet him with four hundred men. The thought of four hundred armed men led by his brother who had in the past planned to kill him resulted in very great consternation and distress for Jacob.

In desperation, after having kept the Creator at arm's length, Jacob remembered to pray and cried out to him saying, "O Lord of my father Abraham, God of my father Isaac, Lord, you who said to me, 'Go back to your country and your relatives, and I will make you prosper,' I am unworthy of all the kindness and faithfulness you have shown me. I had only my staff when I crossed this Jordan, but now I have become two camps. Save me, I pray, from the hand of my brother Esau, for I am afraid he will come and attack me and the mothers with their children. But you have said, 'I will surely make you prosper and will make your descendants like the sand of the sea, which cannot be counted.'"

It had been a while since Jacob prayed to ask for help from the Lord. This was hard for him because he had the mind of a self-made man who depended on his own abilities to accomplish anything he set his mind to, but this time, this was too great a challenge for him.

Jacob Meets Esau

Somewhat spiritually strengthened by heartfelt prayers of desperation through the night, Jacob pushed forward, and as he looked up, he saw Esau coming with his four hundred men. Fearing the potential carnage that could ensue, he divided the children among Leah, Rachel, and the other two wives. He put the two wives and their children in front, Leah and her children next, and Rachel and Joseph in the rear.

He went alone ahead and bowed down to the ground seven times as he approached his brother, but Esau ran to meet Jacob and embraced him; he threw his arms around his neck and kissed him. And they wept. Then Esau looked up and saw the women and children. "Who are these with you?" he asked.

Jacob answered, "They are the children the Creator has graciously given me, your servant." Sensing no evil intent from Esau, the wives and their children approached and bowed down.

Esau asked, "What's the meaning of all these flocks and herds I met?"

"To find favor in your eyes, my lord," he said.

But Esau said, "I already have plenty, my brother. Keep what you have for yourself."

"No, please!" said Jacob. "If I have found favor in your eyes, accept this gift from me. For to see your face is like seeing the face of the Creator now that you have received me favorably. Please accept the present that was brought to you, for the Creator has been gracious to me, and I have all I need."

And because Jacob insisted, Esau accepted it.

Then Esau said, "Let us be on our way. I'll accompany you."

But Jacob said to him, "My lord knows that the children are tender and that I must care for the ewes and cows that are nursing their young. If they are driven hard just one day, all the animals will die. So, let my lord go on ahead of his servant while I move along slowly at the pace of the flocks and herds before me and the pace of the children until I come to my lord in Seir."

Esau said, "Then let me leave some of my men with you."

"But why do that?" Jacob asked. "Just let me find favor in the eyes of my lord."

So that day, Esau started on his way back to Seir. Jacob, however, went to Sukkoth, where he built a place for himself and made shelters for his livestock. After Jacob came from Paddan Aram, he arrived safely at the city of Shechem in Canaan and camped within sight of the city. For a hundred pieces of silver, he bought from the sons of Hamor, the father of Shechem, the plot of ground where he pitched his tent. There he set up an altar and called it El Elohe Israel.

As Jacob sat and reflected on all that had happened in the last week, it started to occur to him that he had been negligent on teaching his family more about the Creator and to seek his help. He also realized for the first time that all the wealth he had sought for really was not all he thought it will be, for it could have been lost in the hands of Laban or Esau had there not been a divine intervention in both cases.

His brother had grown into a formidable nation with more wealth and stature in twenty years than he could ever have imagined even though he had decided to adopt the ways of the Canaanites. Secretly, he started believing that he had been able to avert a disaster by bribing his way out of annihilation, and it was now time to figure out what his next move was to be in acquisition of the land of Canaan as promised him by the Creator.

Excerpts from luciferin emergency meeting

LUCIFER. Our anticipated slaughter of the Jacob family by Esau failed miserably. As you all know, we have a very serious problem because Jacob's family has successfully made it back to Canaan.

AGAG. We did all we could to sabotage his return, but the hedge around him is impenetrable like the ones around Job, Abraham, Isaac and all those who choose to walk truthfully with the Creator. We never have problems with those who are the Creator's children by name only—you know the drill.

LUCIFER. As the Creator has stated to Jacob, his family will be the line in which the nation will be built and, therefore, the lineage of the Redeemer. We need to encourage Jacob to rely on his personal efforts to try and help the Creator fulfill his mission. There is no better way to foul up the Creator's purpose than humans offering to help him their way.

BELZE. If only humans knew that they become untouchable by us unless with express permission from the Creator, imagine how that will embolden them and improve on their quality of life!

AGAG. The Creator's Spirit over them is like a neon sign which makes it quite easy to determine who belongs to him and who does not, and that helps us. I wish all we had were members of all these myriads of religions we have helped to create. They are as dumb and blind as the things and people they worship. The true covenant-keeping followers of the Creator are our problem.

LUCIFER. We must protect that truth from man with all the lies you can drum up. For every male, make them feel they must be self-made men with no need to trust or call on the Creator so that they do not have to appear weak or look foolish in front of their peers.

AGAG. So what is our plan of action with Jacob?

LUCIFER. He knows that some members of his family still possess idols, his family is quite dysfunctional, and so he is likely to spend very little time with the Creator, and that is good—very good for us. Let's do our best to maintain that dysfunctionality through division and encourage him to mix with the Canaanites in marriage and worship. Encourage his daughter however is possible to start mixing with the Canaanite women. She appears to find their women sort of interesting, and then see what comes of it—anything to trip Jacob or his crazy sons off.

BELZE. Brilliant! Those Canaanites might be a great help for us if she does. We should dangle some additional alluring elements regarding their good beauty customs as bait and trap them later when the barb sets after it is swallowed.

AGAG. Don't forget about the power of sensuality. We know that we are succeeding in destroying the value of women by making them feel that all that matters and gives them values in life is their physical beauty. We must help make them forget that it wanes with time and it seems to be a great primer for covetousness. Though it is short-term, most humans live with only short-term expectations anyway and overlook eternity.

LUCIFER. As for Jacob, he is a great prince and heir to Abraham and Isaac, but he does not fully understand the privileges that come with that. Therefore, keep him very busy so that he spends very little time praying to the Creator, and let's see what happens.

The heir at wit's end

While Jacob thought the worst was over for him and he could now settle down and strategize his way forward, the unexpected happened. One day, not long after arriving at Shechem, Dinah, his daughter, had this fancy urge to go and visit the women of the land to see if there was anything interesting she could learn from them. She did not disclose her plans to her father but went out with a few other maids. When the son of the ruler of that area saw her, he took her and raped her. This was typical of the ways of the Canaanites.

The rest of the accompanying maids went home and relayed what had happened and that Dinah was not coming back home. Unknown to Jacob, when his sons found out, they crafted an evil and possible self-destructive plan that resulted in the slaughter of the unsuspecting people. As if that was not bad enough, the boys then looted the city where their sister had been defiled in the process of her retrieval from the palace.

Upon discovering the carnage, Jacob, in total exasperation, said to his sons, "You have brought trouble on me by making me obnoxious to the Canaanites and Perizzites, the people living in this land.

We are few, and if they join forces against me and attack me, I and my household will be destroyed."

Jacob could see that he was doomed, and after having survived Esau, he now faced an enemy far deadlier with a justification to exterminate him. He had never felt more helpless in his life except when he had to face Esau, his brother. The dread of seeing his wives and children hacked up to bits while he stood by helplessly was too much for him. He could not come up with a scheme to save him, and so he resigned and looked up to the Creator for help and mercy.

Jacob returns to Bethel

Seeing Jacob was at wits' end, out of compassion, the Creator then answered his call for help and asked him to pack up, go up to Bethel, and settle there. He was encouraged by the Creator to build an altar there, something his fathers did out of reverence without having to be asked. So Jacob, who had been very spiritually laxed with his household, decided it was time to do things the Creator's way and give him full access and control of his life moving forward.

For starters, he ordered his household to get rid of the foreign gods he knew they had with them and to purify themselves and change their clothes. He then declared to them that they were going up to Bethel so he could build an altar to the Creator, who answered him in the day of his distress and who had been with him wherever he had gone.

So they gave Jacob all the foreign gods they had and the rings in their ears associated with idol worship, and Jacob buried them under the oak at Shechem. He did this as an act of submission to the Creator and request for his leadership and guidance and fully accepting him as his Lord.

As they set out, the terror of the Creator was unleashed on the towns all around them so that no one pursued Jacob's family. He and all the people with him successfully made it to Bethel, and there he built an altar in the place where the Creator revealed himself to him when he was fleeing from his brother.

The Creator appeared to him again and blessed him, saying to him, "Your name is Jacob, but you will no longer be called Jacob. Your name will be Israel." So he named him Israel and confirmed on him the covenant he had made with Abraham and Isaac and restated it as a reminder to him.

The deaths of Rachel and Isaac

After a while, they moved on from Bethel; and while they were still some distance from Bethlehem, Rachel, the wife Jacob loved the most, went into labor to give birth and had great difficulty. As the child was being birthed, the midwife said to her, "Don't despair, for you have another son." As she breathed her last, for she was dying, she named her son Ben-Oni, but his father named him Benjamin. So Rachel died and was buried on the way to Bethlehem. Over her tomb, Jacob set up a pillar; and to this day, that pillar marks Rachel's tomb.

Jacob then made it home to his father, Isaac, in Mamre, near Hebron, where Abraham and Isaac had stayed. Isaac had lived 180 years, living much longer than either he or his family had thought he would. Then he breathed his last and died and was gathered to his people, old and full of years and having witnessed the peaceful reunion between his sons, who jointly buried him.

The formation and separation of two nations

After they buried their father, seeing that they both had too much livestock between them, Esau took his household as well as his livestock and all the goods he had acquired in Canaan and moved to a land some distance from his brother Jacob because their possessions were too great for the land to support them both. So Esau (that is Edom), the father of the Edomites, settled in the hill country of Seir.

Jacob, on the other hand, lived in the land where his father had stayed, the land of Canaan. Trying to dig himself and his family from the great dysfunctionality that had prevailed over them to this point, he spent as much time as he could teaching his young son, then Joseph, about the ways of the Creator and the promises he had made to them.

Jacob was greatly motivated to teach Joseph as much as he could when he saw the level of interest he showed in the ways of the Creator. Jacob was extremely joyful when Joseph started sharing visions the Creator gave him. This made his brothers hate him because not only was their father showing very overt favoritism toward him but the revelations and dreams the Creator showed him seemed to indicate that they were all going to be subservient to Joseph, including his parents.

He became the conscience of the family and brought reports of misconduct of his brothers to his parents, and they despised him even more, but the Creator was with him especially when he resolved in his mind that he would live blamelessly before the Creator like his grandfather and great-grandfather.

Jacob had twelve sons

The sons of Leah, his first wife, were Reuben, the firstborn of Jacob; Simeon; Levi; Judah; Issachar; and Zebulun.

The sons of Rachel, the wife he loved the most; were Joseph and Benjamin.

The sons of Rachel's maid, Bilhah, given to him as a wife by Rachel were Dan and Naphtali.

The sons of Leah's maid, Zilpah, given to him as a wife by Leah were Gad and Asher. These were the sons of Jacob, who were born to him in Paddan Aram.

And so it was that the Creator had to build a nation from the dysfunctional family of Jacob, now called Israel, a nation whose patriarchs were his twelve sons from his four wives.

Chapter 10

Then Came Mighty Egypt

Joseph and Egypt

In the course of time, having settled in the land of Hebron, Joseph's brothers had gone to graze their father's flocks near Shechem and had been gone for quite a while, and his father was concerned.

He then sent Joseph to go and see if all was well with them and with the flocks and bring word back to him. So Joseph went after his brothers and eventually found them near Dothan.

But when they saw him in the distance, the animosity they had for him came welling up; and before he reached them, they had plotted to kill him to put an end to those dreams of dominance he had been having.

They decided to kill him and throw him into one of the many cisterns in the area and then lie to his father that a ferocious animal devoured him. When Reuben, the oldest son, heard this, he realized he was going to need tact if he had to rescue the boy because he could see they were really determined to kill him. He therefore recommended to them to throw him into a cistern here in the wilderness instead of outright killing him, with the intent to rescue him from them and take him back to his father. He knew he was outnumbered, and force would not work because they could turn on him too just as they did in Shechem when Dinah was raped.

Their disdain for their brother was so deep that when Joseph came to them, they stripped him of the special ornate robe he was wearing and threw him into the empty cistern as there was no water in it. Pleased with themselves, they then sat down to eat their meal as if they were celebrating a great accomplishment. Not long after the meal, they looked up and saw a caravan of Ishmaelites coming from Gilead. Their camels were loaded with spices, balm, and myrrh, and they were on their way to take them down to sell in Egypt.

Judah, now having an internal conflict with his conscience, said to his brothers, "What will we gain if we kill our brother and cover up his blood? Come, let us sell him to the Ishmaelites and not lay our hands on him. After all, he is our brother, our own flesh and blood." His brothers agreed. So when the Midianite merchants came by, his brothers pulled him up out of the cistern and sold him for twenty shekels of silver to the Ishmaelites, who took him to Egypt.

After some time had elapsed and Reuben felt it was safe to sneak back to the cistern by himself to rescue his brother, he was beside himself in anguish when he saw that Joseph was not there, and he tore his clothes in grief. He then went back to his brothers and said, "The boy isn't there! Where can I turn now?" In desperation, he agreed to a plan in which they got Joseph's ornate robe, slaughtered a goat, and dipped his robe in the blood which they then took back to their father. They then told him they found it in the field and asked him to examine it to see whether it was his son's robe.

Upon examination, he recognized it and let out a gut-wrenching and agonized wail, "It is my son's robe! Some ferocious animal has devoured him. Joseph has surely been torn to pieces!" Then Jacob tore his clothes, put on sackcloth, and mourned for his son for a long time. All his sons and daughters came to comfort him, but he refused to be comforted. "No," he said. "I will continue to mourn until I join my son in the grave." So his father wept for him, and almost nothing seemed to matter to him anymore.

He was now utterly confused because the one son whom he was counting on to carry the spiritual legacy was now dead. He could not explain why the Creator would allow that to happen. He could not help wondering whether the dysfunctionality in his family may have resulted in rejection. He recalled that the Creator, who never goes back on his word, had just recently confirmed the Abrahamic covenant with him. Nothing made any sense, and he spent his time mourning for his beloved son. He finally realized that age and not spending as much time teaching all his children had caught up with him, and he resigned himself to just live out the last of his days until death came.

Joseph's life in Egypt

Meanwhile, Joseph had been taken down to Egypt. Potiphar, an Egyptian who was one of Pharaoh's officials, in fact, the captain of the guard, bought him from the Ishmaelites at the slave market.

Despite his apparent fate, Joseph had sworn not to walk back from the Creator, whom he had come to cherish and was more than ever determined to live by the statutes of the covenant he had established with his family. As a result of this resolve, the Creator had seen to it that he was bought by Potiphar where his literacy allowed him to easily learn the Egyptian language and customs at the highest level of Egyptian society. Also being hardworking, Joseph lived in the house of his Egyptian master and prospered.

His master, having watched him for some time very closely, noticed that Joseph believed fervently in his invisible or imaginary Creator, exhibited an exceedingly high moral standard, and was therefore trustworthy. Even more so, as a huge economic benefit to Potiphar, he seemed to succeed in everything he did which brought his master great wealth. Joseph therefore found favor in his eyes, and Potiphar put him in charge of his household.

From the time he put him in charge of his household and of all that he owned, the Creator blessed the household of the Egyptian both in the house and in the field. Potiphar, instinctively recognizing this, therefore left all his investments and everything he had in Joseph's care; and with Joseph in charge, he did not concern himself with anything except the food he ate.

Now Joseph was well-built and handsome, and after a while his master's wife took notice of him and tried repeatedly to have sex with him, but each time he found a way to escape without embarrassing her.

She then set a trap for him in a way he could not easily escape, and so in this occasion, he was blunt with her. "With me in charge," he told her. "My master does not concern himself with anything in the house. Everything he owns he has entrusted to my care. No one is greater in this house than I am. My master has withheld nothing from me except you because you are his wife. How then could I do such a wicked thing and sin against the Creator?"

He was determined to be obedient to the Creator even though he knew not yielding to her could result in very undesirable outcomes especially his job security and his life. His grandfather, great-grandfather, and Job had stuck with the Creator and he never let them down and Joseph was going to walk the moral high ground regardless of the cost.

The woman did not give up especially since she did not care for his so-called Creator God. They had numerous gods in Egypt, and she had never heard of them being moral in any way. And though she spoke to Joseph day after day, he refused to have sex with her or even be with her. So one day, she skillfully kept all the servants fully occupied out of the house at the time when Joseph was to attend to his duties inside. She was ready for him in the inner room, and knowing they were alone, she pounced on him.

She caught him by his cloak and said, "Come to bed with me!" But he left his cloak in her hand and fled out of the house. When she saw that he had left his cloak in her hand and ran out of the house, she felt scorned. Seething with anger and hate, she called her household servants and told them that the Hebrew boy had tried raping her, seeing she was alone in the house. She said her loud screams for help sent him on the run, leaving his cloak behind.

She kept his cloak beside her until her husband, his master, came home. Then she told him this story: "That Hebrew slave you brought us came to me to make sport of me. But as soon as I screamed for help, he left his cloak beside me and ran out of the house." When his master heard the story his wife told him, he burned with anger and disappointment.

For a crime like that, things could have been very bad for Joseph; but Joseph's master took him and put him in prison, the place where the king's prisoners were confined.

But while Joseph was there in the prison, the Creator was with him; he showed him kindness and granted him favor in the eyes of the prison warden. The warden, seeing that he was very good administratively, decided to put Joseph in charge of all those held in the prison, and he was made responsible for all that was done there. The warden paid no attention to anything under Joseph's care because the Creator was with Joseph and gave him success in whatever he did just as he had done with Potiphar. While it was a very challenging time for Joseph, how he was treated helped him somewhat tolerate the situation; and he still believed that if he stood faithful, the Creator he served would bring him through, as he had done his forefathers, and find a way to send him home to his father.

A bridge built with grapevines and clusters

It just so happened that during this time of his imprisonment, Pharaoh, the king of Egypt, was angry with two of his officials—the chief cupbearer and the chief baker—and put them in custody in the house of the captain of the guard, in the same prison where Joseph was confined.

The captain of the guard assigned them to Joseph, and he attended them. After they had been in custody for some time, each of the two men had a dream the same night. When Joseph came to them the next morning, he saw that they were dejected, and he asked them why they looked so sad that day. They then informed him that they both had dreams, but there was no one to interpret them.

Then Joseph said to them, "Do not interpretations belong to the Creator? Tell me your dreams."

The chief cupbearer told Joseph his dream. He said to him, "In my dream, I saw a vine in front of me, and on the vine were three branches. As soon as it budded, it blossomed, and its clusters ripened into grapes. Pharaoh's cup was in my hand, and I took the grapes, squeezed them into Pharaoh's cup, and put the cup in his hand."

"This is what it means," Joseph said to him. "The three branches are three days. Within three days, Pharaoh will restore you to your position, and you will put his cup in his hand just as you used to do when you were his cupbearer. But when all goes well with you, remember me and show me kindness by mentioning me to Pharaoh to get me out of this prison. I was forcibly carried off from the land of the Hebrews, and even here I have done nothing to deserve being put in a dungeon."

The confidence with which he interpreted the dream and the noticeably short time of its fulfillment was stunning. They all understood that if the interpretation was wrong, Joseph would be in trouble, and it would be an embarrassment to the Creator he talked about a lot. This provided the officer with a massive wave of hope, and even he knew he was innocent, but at a word from Pharaoh, innocent or not, he could die.

When the chief baker saw that Joseph had given a favorable interpretation, he said to Joseph, "I too had a dream. On my head were three baskets of bread. In the top basket were all kinds of baked goods for Pharaoh, but the birds were eating them out of the basket on my head."

"This is what it means," Joseph said with great sadness in his voice. "The three baskets are three days. Within three days, Pharaoh will lift off your head and impale your body, and the birds will eat away your flesh." Somehow, the officer believed him, and those were the shortest days of his entire life because he knew he had only three days to live if Joseph's interpretation was right.

Though the officer believed Joseph was likely right, he could only wish that the interpretation was incorrect. He looked at Joseph with eyes begging for a more favorable interpretation which he knew would not be forthcoming. With a wry smile, he waived off the interpretation of an invisible Creator who was not known by any great nation especially the great Egypt with the most powerful gods known to those alive at the time. *No nation was greater than Egypt,* he thought.

Now the third day was Pharaoh's birthday, and he gave a feast for all his officials. He lifted up the heads of the chief cupbearer and the chief baker in the presence of his officials: He restored the chief cupbearer to his position so that he once again put the cup into Pharaoh's hand, but he impaled the chief baker just as Joseph had said to them in his interpretation.

Joseph had hoped to be vindicated by the Creator, but as time went by, his hope of release was fading. This was the first time he had vocalized his innocence in his imprisonment, seeing that the likelihood of him dying in the dungeon was high unless Pharaoh intervened. His master was out of the question because it would implicate his wife, and he had no intention of ruining their lives and would let the Creator himself deal with that. The hope of someday being able to go back home to his father as a free man would be an awesome treat like no other. Well, he could only dream.

Joseph felt somewhat vindicated though he knew the interpretations of the dreams were accurate. Again he wondered why the Creator had him in a dungeon but was still so gracious to him. His logical conclusion was that his ticket out of the dungeon and his return back to Canaan to his family was in the hands of the cupbearer. Sadly, for Joseph, as he waited day after day for deliverance; it never came as he had expected. The chief cup bearer did not remember Joseph; he had forgotten him as he reveled in his newfound freedom and vindication.

Joseph shatters an impregnable barrier

During the two years after the chief cupbearer's restoration to his job, he did not remember Joseph. During this time, Joseph had learned a lot about the working of Pharaoh's government and the intricacies of Egyptian governance and life from the prisoners in the dungeon whom he oversaw. However, at the end of those two years, as if on cue, Pharaoh had a very unusual dream that was in two parts.

In the morning his mind was troubled, so he sent for all the magicians and wise men of Egypt. Pharaoh told them his dreams, but no one could interpret them for him. He knew there was a significant meaning to these dreams, and his officials knew that there won't be any rest or special privileges or worse if an accurate interpretation was not provided to him.

Then the chief cupbearer said to Pharaoh, "Today I am reminded of my shortcomings. Pharaoh was once angry with his servants, and he imprisoned me and the chief baker in the house of the captain of the guard. Each of us had a dream the same night, and each dream had a meaning of its own. Now a young Hebrew was there with us, a servant of the captain of the guard. We told him our dreams, and he interpreted them for us, giving each man the interpretation of his dream. And things turned out exactly as he interpreted them to us. I was restored to my position, and the other man was impaled."

Pharaoh then sent for Joseph immediately. He was pulled out of the dungeon, bathed, shaved, given a change of presentable clothes, and then brought before Pharaoh.

Pharaoh then said to Joseph, "I had a dream, and no one can interpret it. But I have heard it said of you that when you hear a dream, you can interpret it."

"I cannot do it," Joseph replied to Pharaoh. "But the Creator of heaven and the earth will give Pharaoh the true answer he is seeking."

Then Pharaoh said to Joseph, "In my dream, I was standing on the bank of the Nile when out of the river there came up seven cows, fat and sleek, and they grazed among the reeds. After them, seven other cows came up, scrawny and very ugly and lean. I had never seen such ugly cows in all the land of Egypt. The lean, ugly cows ate up the seven fat cows that came up first. But even after they ate them, no one could tell that they had done so. They looked just as ugly as before. Then I woke up.

"In my dream I saw seven heads of grain, full and good, growing on a single stalk. After them, seven other heads sprouted, withered and thin and scorched by the east wind. The thin heads of grain swallowed up the seven good heads. I told this to the magicians, but none of them could explain it to me."

Then Joseph said to Pharaoh, "The dreams of Pharaoh are one and the same. The Creator of the heavens and the earth has revealed to Pharaoh what he is about to do. The seven good cows are seven years, and the seven good heads of grain are seven years—it is one and the same dream. The seven lean, ugly cows that came up afterward are seven years, and so are the seven worthless heads of grain scorched by the east wind: They are seven years of famine.

"It is just as I said to Pharaoh—he has shown Pharaoh what he is about to do. Seven years of great abundance are coming throughout the land of Egypt, but seven years of famine will follow them. Then all the abundance in Egypt will be forgotten, and the famine will ravage the land. The abundance in the land will not be remembered because the famine that follows it will be so severe. The reason the dream was given to Pharaoh in two forms is that the matter has been firmly decided by the Creator, and he will do it soon.

"And now let Pharaoh look for a discerning and wise man and put him in charge of the land of Egypt. Let Pharaoh appoint commissioners over the land to take a fifth of the harvest of Egypt during the seven years of abundance. They should collect all the food of these good years that are coming and store up the grain under the authority of Pharaoh to be kept in the cities for food. This food should be held in reserve for the country to be used during the seven years of famine that will come upon Egypt so that the country may not be ruined by the famine."

Pharaoh and his officials were stunned, and they could not but believe that this was the correct interpretation. The plan seemed very good to Pharaoh and to all his officials especially since this was an easy enough interpretation to verify if it happened according to his dream. So Pharaoh, looking at his officials, asked them, "Can we find anyone like this man, one in whom is the Spirit of the Creator?"

Then Pharaoh said to Joseph, "Since he has made all this known to you, there is no one so discerning and wise as you. You shall oversee my palace, and all my people are to submit to your orders. Only with respect to the throne will I be greater than you. I hereby put you in charge of the whole land of Egypt."

Then Pharaoh took his signet ring from his finger and put it on Joseph's finger. He dressed him in robes of fine linen and put a gold chain around his neck. He had him ride in a chariot as his second-in-command, and people shouted before him, "Make way!" Thus, he put him in charge of the whole land of Egypt. Then Pharaoh said to Joseph, "I am Pharaoh, but without your word, no one will lift hand or foot in all Egypt." Joseph bowed before Pharaoh in reverence and acceptance.

Pharaoh gave Joseph the name Zaphenath-Paneah and gave him Asenath, daughter of Potiphera, priest of On, to be his wife. She was a bombshell of a woman in character and physical beauty—the dream of many men in Egypt and here, handpicked specially by the Creator himself for his faithful servant. He could not have asked for a better wife, and in her eyes, she could not have asked for a better husband, and they loved each other, including Joseph's Creator. Talk about a marriage made in heaven. Joseph was thirty years old when he entered the service of Pharaoh, king of Egypt.

And Joseph went out from Pharaoh's presence, and it took him some time to fully grasp the enormity of what had just happened and the responsibility Pharaoh had just given him. He now understood that all the years spent with Potiphar and the dungeon, as much as he despised those years, they were preparing him for this assignment the faithful Creator had reserved for him, and he could never have seen it coming in a trillion years! It was just plain stunning, something only the Almighty could pull off. He now had a chance to see what the old faithful ancestors who trusted the Creator had experienced.

Under normal circumstances, the Egyptians looked at the Hebrews as very inferior and an abomination, and there was no way this could have happened naturally. The Creator had seen to it that he lacked no social graces, and he did his best to make the Potiphar family very comfortable with no plans for retribution. That made them fear him even more and raised a lot of questions in the society as to which gods were the most powerful. This pleased the Creator because Joseph was a faithful witness, and he could comfortably begin to reveal himself to the Egyptians even more.

Just as Joseph had said, the years of plenty came up; and during the seven years of abundance, the land produced in unprecedented quantities, leaving no doubt about the fulfillment of the first half of Pharaoh's dream. Joseph collected all the food produced in those seven years of abundance in Egypt and stored it in the cities. In each city he put the food grown in the fields surrounding it.

He stored up huge quantities of grain, like the sand of the sea; it was so much that he stopped keeping records because it was beyond measure. The people had never seen that much food produced in all their lifetimes.

Before the years of famine came, two sons were born to Joseph by Asenath, daughter of Potiphera, priest of On. The firstborn he called Manasseh and the second Ephraim.

Once again, the Creator of the heavens and the earth gave the Egyptians an opportunity to heed his warning of an impending calamity and at the same time made provision for deliverance for the Egyptians and surrounding nations. This shows his heart and the relentless efforts in getting humanity to wake up and heed all the warnings he has directed at man to keep him from self-destruction when they continue pursuing lifestyles that breed evil and violence.

The seven years of abundance in Egypt came to an end, and the seven years of famine began, just as Joseph had said. There was famine in all the other lands, but in the whole land of Egypt, there was food in great abundance.

When all Egypt began to feel the famine, the people cried to Pharaoh for food. Then Pharaoh told all the Egyptians to go to Joseph and do what he tells them. Joseph opened all the storehouses and sold grain to the Egyptians, for the famine was severe throughout Egypt. And all the world came to Egypt to buy grain from Joseph because the famine was severe everywhere.

High-wire drama in color

As the famine ravaged the lands, not even Joseph's family in Canaan was spared. The apparent death of his son Joseph had broken Jacob, and he did not know how the Creator was going to salvage the family that was in a wreck. When Jacob learned that there was grain in Egypt, he sent his ten sons to go down and buy food for their large family before they starved to death. But Jacob did not send Benjamin, Joseph's brother, with the others because he was afraid that harm might come to him.

Now Joseph was the governor of the land, the person who sold grain to all its people. So when Joseph's brothers arrived, they bowed down to him with their faces to the ground. As soon as Joseph saw them, he recognized them; and as they bowed low, he remembered the dreams he had told them about, and now it was happening. He pretended to be a stranger and spoke harshly to them, demanding where they came from and accusing them of being spies.

"No, my lord," they answered. "Your servants have come to buy food. We are all the sons of one man. Your servants are honest men, not spies."

"No!" he said to them. "You have come to see where our land is unprotected."

But they replied, "Your servants were twelve brothers, the sons of one man, who lives in the land of Canaan. The youngest is now with our father, and one is no more."

Joseph said to them, "It is just as I told you—you are spies! Now this is how you will be tested: As surely as Pharaoh lives, you will not leave this place unless your youngest brother comes here for me to corroborate your story. Send one of your number to get your brother. The rest of you will be kept in prison so that your words may be tested to see if you are telling the truth. If you are not, then as surely as Pharaoh lives, you are spies!" And he put them all in custody for three days.

On the third day, Joseph said to them, "Do this, and you will live, for I have reverence for the Creator of all things. If you are honest men, let one of your brothers stay here in prison while the rest of you go and take grain back for your starving households. But you must bring your youngest brother to me so that your words may be verified and that you may not die." This they proceeded to do.

The ordeal was so great they started to crack psychologically as the shadows of their sin against their brother started bearing down on their conscience. They said to one another in Hebrew, "Surely we are being punished because of our brother. We saw how distressed he was when he pleaded with us for his life, but we would not listen. That's why this distress has come on us."

Reuben replied, "Didn't I tell you not to sin against the boy? But you wouldn't listen! Now we must give an accounting for his blood." They did not realize that Joseph could understand them since he had been using an interpreter when he had communicated with them.

He turned away from them and began to weep but then came back and spoke to them again. He had Simeon taken from them and bound before their eyes. He gave orders to fill their bags with grain, to put each man's silver back in his sack, and to give them provisions for their journey. After this was done for them, they loaded their grain on their donkeys and left, trembling and exasperated.

At the place where they stopped for the night, one of them opened his sack to get feed for his donkey, and he saw his silver in the mouth of his sack. "My silver has been returned," he said to his brothers. "Here it is in my sack." Their hearts sank, and they turned to each other, trembling, and said, "What is this that the Creator has done to us?"

When they came to their father Jacob in the land of Canaan, they told him all that had happened to them. They said, "The man who is Lord over the land spoke harshly to us and treated us as though we were spying on the land. But we said to him, 'We are honest men. We are not spies. We were twelve brothers, sons of one father. One is no more, and the youngest is now with our father in Canaan.' Then the man who is lord over the land said to us, 'This is how I will know whether you are honest men—leave one of your brothers here with me and take food for your starving households and go. But bring your youngest brother to me so I will know that you are not spies but honest men. Then I will give your brother back to you, and you can trade in the land.'"

As they were emptying their sacks, there in each man's sack was his pouch of silver! When they and their father saw the money pouches, their hearts sank, and they were never so terribly frightened. Their father Jacob said to them, "You have deprived me of my children. Joseph is no more and Simeon is no more, and now you want to take Benjamin. Everything is against me!"

Then Reuben said to his father, "You may put both of my sons to death if I do not bring him back to you. Entrust him to my care, and I will bring him back."

But Jacob said, "My son will not go down there with you. His brother is dead, and he is the only one left. If harm comes to him on the journey you are taking, you will bring my gray head down to the grave in sorrow, and the answer is no."

Imprisonment of fear

Now the famine was still very severe in the land with years more to go based on Pharaoh's dream. After they had eaten all the grain they had brought from Egypt, their father said to them, "Go back and buy us a little more food."

But Judah said to him, "The man warned us solemnly, 'You will not see my face again unless your brother is with you.' If you will send our brother along with us, we will go down and buy food for you. But if you do not send him, we will not go down because the man said to us, 'You will not see my face again unless your brother is with you.'"

Jacob, finding himself in distress, asked, "Why did you bring this trouble on me by telling the man you had another brother?" They replied, "The man questioned us closely about ourselves and our family. 'Is your father still living?' he asked us. 'Do you have another brother?' We simply answered his questions. How were we to know he would say, 'Bring your brother down here'?"

Then Judah said to his father, "Send the boy along with me, and we will go at once so that we and you and our children may live and not die. I will guarantee his safety. You can hold me personally responsible for him. If I do not bring him back to you and set him here before you, I will bear the blame before you all my life. As it is, if we had not delayed, we could have gone and returned twice."

Then their father, reaching back for a usable scheme, said to them, "If it must be, then do this—put some of the best products of the land available in your bags and take them down to the man as a gift—a little balm and a little honey, some spices and myrrh, some pistachio nuts and almonds. Take double the amount of silver with you, for you must return the silver that was put back into the mouths of your sacks. Perhaps it was a mistake. Take your brother also, and go back to the man at once. And may the Creator himself grant you mercy before the man so that he will let your other brother and Benjamin come back with you. As for me, if I am bereaved, I am bereaved."

With that, the men took the gifts and double the amount of silver along with Benjamin also. They hurried down to Egypt and presented themselves to Joseph. When he saw Benjamin with them, he told the steward of his house to take the men to his house for lunch. The man did as Joseph told him and took the men to Joseph's house. Now the men were frightened when they were taken to his house. They thought it had to do with the silver that was put back into their sacks, and he likely intended to seize them as slaves.

When Joseph came home, they presented to him the gifts they had brought into the house, and they bowed down before him to the ground. As he looked about and saw his brother Benjamin, his own mother's son, he was deeply moved emotionally at the sight of him, and Joseph hurried out into his private room and wept there. After he had washed his face, he came out and, controlling himself, asked for the food to be served after a lot of cordial pleasantries.

They served him by himself, the brothers by themselves, and the Egyptians who ate with him by themselves because Egyptians could not eat with Hebrews, for that is an abomination to Egyptians.

The men had been seated before him in the order of their ages—from the firstborn to the youngest—and the Egyptians looked at each other in astonishment. They all felt fully relaxed enough to enjoy the feast, and they drank freely with him after he had reassured them that their story had been verified and they were not spies after all.

The camel's back broken

The night before the men left to head back home, Joseph gave instructions to the steward of his house to fill the men's sacks with as much food as they could carry with some additional details, and he did as Joseph directed. As morning dawned, the men were sent on their way with their donkeys. The brothers had never felt better, and they could not wait to recount the adventure and turn of events to their father. They were beginning to feel that the Creator may have forgiven them of the evil against their brother after all.

They had not gone far from the city when Joseph sent his steward after them, and when he caught up with them, he asked them, "Why have you repaid good with evil by stealing the cup my master drinks from and also uses for divination? This is a wicked thing you have done."

In replying, they asked him, "Why does my lord say such things? Far be it from your servants to do anything like that! We even brought back to you from the land of Canaan the silver we found inside the mouths of our sacks. So why would we steal silver or gold from your master's house?"

So sure and confident were they that they passed sentence on themselves, saying, "If any of your servants is found to have it, he will die, and the rest of us will become my lord's slaves."

"Very well then," he said. "Let it be as you say. Whoever is found to have it will become my slave. The rest of you will be free from blame."

Each of them quickly lowered his sack to the ground and opened it. Then the steward proceeded to search, beginning with the oldest, Rueben, and ending with the youngest, Benjamin. They were beginning to breathe a monster sigh of relief as the search finally came to Benjamin. They were certain that they were in the clear. Upon opening his sack, out tumbled the silver cup.

At this turn of events and outcome, they tore their clothes in indescribable anguish and dejection. The atmosphere was just plain melancholic and garnished with despair and indeed painful to watch. How quickly the festive mood turned to profound mourning. They all slowly loaded their donkeys and returned to the city, speechlessly and powerlessly especially after having passed their own sentence for the crime.

Joseph was still in the house when Judah and his brothers came in, and they threw themselves to the ground, fully prostrate before him. Joseph said to them, "What is this you have done? Don't you know that a man like me can find things out by divination?"

"What can we say to my lord?" Judah replied, sobbing. "What can we say? How can we prove our innocence? The Creator has uncovered our guilt from the past. We are now my lord's slaves. We ourselves and the one who was found to have the cup."

But Joseph said, "Far be it from me to do such a thing! Only the man who was found to have the cup will become my slave. The rest of you, go back to your father in peace."

Then Judah, with his head bowed very low, went up to him and said, "Pardon your servant, my lord. Let me speak a word to my lord, and please do not be angry with your servant though you are equal to Pharaoh himself. My Lord asked his servants, 'Do you have a father or a brother?' And we answered, 'We have an aged father, and there is a young son born to him in his old age. His brother is dead, and he is the only one of his mother's sons left, and his father loves him.' Then you said to your servants, 'Bring him down to me so I can see him for myself.' And we said to my lord, 'The boy cannot leave his father. If he leaves him, his father will die.' But you told your servants, 'Unless your youngest brother comes down with you, you will not see my face again.'

"When we went back to your servant, my father, we told him what my lord had said. Then our father said, 'Go back and buy a little more food.' But we said, 'We cannot go down. Only if our youngest brother is with us will we go. We cannot see the man's face unless our youngest brother is with us.'

"Your servant, my father, said to us, 'You know that my wife bore me two sons. One of them went away from me, having been torn to pieces by a wild beast, and I have not seen him since. If you take this one from me too and harm comes to him, you will bring my gray head down to the grave in misery.' So now, if the boy is not with us when I go back to your servant, my father, and if my father, whose life is tightly bound up with the boy's life, sees that the boy isn't there, he will die. Your servants will bring the gray head of our father down to the grave in sorrow.

"I, your servant, guaranteed the boy's safety to my father. I said, 'If I do not bring him back to you, I will bear the blame before you, my father, all my life!' Now then, please let your servant remain here as my lord's slave in place of the boy, and let the boy return with his brothers. How can I go back to my father if the boy is not with me? No! Please, I plead with you, do not let me see the misery that would come on my father."

The red carpet invite into Egypt

The speech was too much for Joseph as he could no longer control himself before all his attendants, and he cried out to have everyone leave his presence except the Hebrews. And he wept so loudly that the Egyptians heard him, and Pharaoh's household heard about it. Then Joseph said to his brothers, "I am Joseph! Is my father still living?" But his brothers were not able to answer him because they were now even more terrified at his presence than before, considering what they had done to him and, wishing this was just a bad dream, wailed quietly in great despair, wishing it would end and stop the psychological and mental carnage. But it was not a dream.

Seeing their consternation, Joseph said to his brothers, "Come close to me." When they had done so, trembling and very unsure-footed, he said, "I am your brother Joseph, the one you sold into Egypt! And now, do not be distressed and do not be angry with yourselves for selling me here because it was to save lives that the Creator sent me ahead of you. For two years now there has been famine in the land, and for the next five years there will be no plowing and reaping. But the Creator sent me ahead of you to preserve for you a remnant on earth and to save your lives by a great deliverance. So then, it was not you who sent me here but the Creator. He made me father to Pharaoh, Lord of his entire household and ruler of all Egypt.

"Now hurry back to my father and say to him, 'This is what your son Joseph says, "The Creator has made me Lord of all Egypt. Come down to me—do not delay. You shall live in the region of

Goshen and be near me—you, your children and grandchildren, your flocks and herds, and all you have. I will provide for you there because five years of famine are still to come. Otherwise, you and your household and all who belong to you will become destitute.'"

"You can see for yourselves, and so can my brother Benjamin, that it is really I who am speaking to you. Tell my father about all the honor accorded me in Egypt and about everything you have seen. And bring my father down here quickly." Then he threw his arms around his brother Benjamin and wept, and Benjamin embraced him, weeping. And he kissed all his brothers and wept over them. Afterward, his brothers talked with him.

When the news reached Pharaoh's palace that Joseph's brothers had come, Pharaoh and all his officials were pleased, and Pharaoh said to Joseph, "Tell your brothers to load their animals and return to the land of Canaan and bring their father and families back to me. I will give them the best of the land of Egypt, and they can enjoy the fat of the land. Also, take some wagons from Egypt for their children and not to worry about their belongings because the best of all Egypt will be theirs."

Joseph gave them wagons, as Pharaoh had commanded, and he also sent to his father ten donkeys loaded with the best things of Egypt, ten female donkeys loaded with grain and bread, and other provisions for his journey. Then he sent his brothers away, and as they were leaving, he said to them, "Don't quarrel on the way!"

So they went up out of Egypt and came to their father Jacob in the land of Canaan. They told him, "Joseph is still alive! In fact, he is ruler of all Egypt." Jacob scolded them for making an evil joke and he did not believe them, but when they told him everything Joseph had said to them and when he saw the wagons Joseph had sent to carry him back, he went into shock and almost lost consciousness. But when he recovered, the spirit of old Jacob revived. And he said, "I'm convinced! My son Joseph is still alive. I will go and see him before I die."

The memorable reunion in Egypt

After packing up, Jacob set out with all that was his, and when he reached Beersheba, he offered sacrifices to the Creator and inquired of him about the trip, considering how old he now was, and remembering that he had been ordered by the Creator himself to return to Canaan.

That night after offering the sacrifices, the Creator spoke to Jacob in a vision and said, "Jacob! Jacob!"

"Here I am," he replied.

"Do not be afraid to go down to Egypt, for I will make you into a great nation there. I will go down to Egypt with you, and I will surely bring you back again. And Joseph's own hand will close your eyes."

Then Jacob left Beersheba and headed for Egypt, transported in Pharaoh's wagons. All those who went to Egypt with Jacob, those who were his direct descendants, not counting his sons' wives, numbered sixty-six persons. With the two sons who had been born to Joseph in Egypt, the members of Jacob's family, which went to Egypt, were seventy in all.

Jacob could not remember the last time he had been so buoyed physically and spiritually. With confirmation from the Creator himself for the trip and Joseph being alive, he was now certain of the fulfilment of the covenant and his place. Having been preinstructed by Joseph, they headed off to meet him in the land of Goshen in Egypt.

When they arrived, Joseph was waiting; and as soon as he appeared before his father, he threw his arms around him and wept for a long time. When he finally caught his breath, Jacob said to Joseph, "Now I am ready to die since I have seen for myself that you are still alive."

Joseph went and told Pharaoh that his father and brothers, with their flocks and herds and everything they owned, had come from the land of Canaan. He chose five of his brothers and presented them before Pharaoh. Pharaoh asked the brothers, "What is your occupation?"

"Your servants are shepherds," they replied to Pharaoh. "Just as our fathers were." They also said to him, "We have come to live here for a while because the famine is severe in Canaan and your servants' flocks have no pasture. So now, please let your servants settle in in your land for a little while."

Pharaoh said to Joseph, "Your father and your brothers have come to you, and the land of Egypt is before you. Settle your father and your brothers in the best part of the land. Let them live in Goshen. And if you know of any among them with special ability, put them in charge of my own livestock."

Then Joseph brought his father Jacob in and presented him before Pharaoh. After Jacob met Pharaoh, intrigued by how old he looked, seeing the Egyptians on the most part did not live that long, Pharaoh asked him, "How old are you?"

And Jacob said to Pharaoh, "The years of my pilgrimage are 130. My years have been few and difficult, and they do not equal the years of the pilgrimage of my fathers." Then Jacob blessed Pharaoh and went out from his presence.

So Joseph settled his father and his brothers in Egypt and gave them property in the best part of the land, the district of Rameses, as Pharaoh had directed. Joseph also provided his father and his brothers and all his father's household with food according to the number of their children.

And so, as the Creator had promised Abraham, his descendants numbering seventy were invited by Pharaoh himself and asked to settle in the best part of the land because the Creator had delivered Egypt from annihilation through Joseph and had made Egypt an extremely wealthy nation and the breadbasket of all the surrounding nations. As promised, they were to be there for four generations before returning to Canaan.

Joseph manages the famine

During the next five years, the famine was so severe that the nations of Canaan wasted away. Pharaoh and his officials trembled at the thought of what might have happened had Joseph not been there with food for the people. Egypt got extremely wealthy from the sale of food to the other nations, and Pharaoh ended up owning almost all the land in Egypt in exchange for food to all the people as directed by Joseph. Without a shadow of a doubt, all Egypt knew their place in the world could be attributed to Joseph, and Pharaoh and his officers got a chance to experience the power and care of the Creator.

Even after the famine came to an end after the seven years, Pharaoh was in no hurry to send the family of Joseph back to Canaan or Joseph, for that matter. He and his people had become a national treasure and an insurance policy for Pharaoh just in case some other calamity came up that required divine intervention.

Besides, Joseph had made Egypt into a cash machine that was bursting at the seams in wealth, and Pharaoh's cattle had greatly multiplied to the point where the cost to the nation of having the Hebrews in the land was minuscule compared to the revenue they generated, and so the Hebrews were cherished for generations.

Now the Israelites settled in Egypt in the region of Goshen. They acquired property there and were fruitful and increased greatly in number. Jacob lived in Egypt seventeen years after meeting Pharaoh, and the years of his life were 147.

Jacob strides off the stage

When the time drew near for Jacob to die, he called for his son Joseph and made him swear in the name of the Creator to bury him in the land of Canaan in the area where his fathers were buried. Then Joseph swore to him, and Jacob worshiped as he leaned on the top of his staff.

He then called the rest of his sons together, and to them he said, "The Creator appeared to me at Luz in the land of Canaan, and there he blessed me and said to me, 'I am going to make you fruitful and increase your numbers. I will make you a community of peoples, and I will give this land, the land of Canaan, as an everlasting possession to your descendants after you.'

"May the Creator before whom my fathers, Abraham and Isaac, walked faithfully, the one who has been my shepherd all my life to this day, who has delivered me from all harm, may he bless you. I am about to die, but he will be with you and take you back to Canaan, the land of your fathers. Bury me with my fathers in the cave in the field of Ephron the Hittite, the cave in the field of Machpelah, near Mamre in Canaan, which Abraham bought along with the field as a burial place from Ephron the Hittite. There Abraham and his wife Sarah were buried, there Isaac and his wife Rebekah were buried, and there I buried Leah." When Jacob had finished giving instructions to his sons, he drew his feet up into the bed, breathed his last, and died.

Joseph wept much for his father and directed the physicians in his service to embalm him, taking the full forty days that was the time required for embalming. And the Egyptians mourned for him seventy days in a show of respect and appreciation to Joseph. When the days of mourning had passed, Joseph said to Pharaoh's court, "If I have found favor in your eyes, speak to Pharaoh for me. Tell him, 'My father made me swear an oath and said, "I am about to die. Bury me in the tomb I dug for myself in the land of Canaan." Now let me go up and bury my father. Then I will return.'"

Pharaoh said, "Go up and bury your father as he made you swear to do."

So Joseph went up to bury his father. All Pharaoh's officials accompanied him, the dignitaries of his court, and all the dignitaries of Egypt besides all the members of Joseph's household and his brothers and those belonging to his father's household. Only their children and their flocks and herds were left in Goshen.

Chariots and horsemen also went up with him. It was a very large company. Joseph observed a seven-day period of mourning for his father and then carried him to the land of Canaan and buried him in the cave in the field of Machpelah, near Mamre. After burying his father, Joseph returned to Egypt together with his brothers and all the others who had gone with him to bury his father.

When Joseph's brothers saw that their father was dead and thought retribution from Joseph would follow, they came and threw themselves down before him. "We are your slaves," they said. But Joseph said to them, "Don't be afraid. Am I in the place of the Creator? You intended to harm me, but he intended it for good to accomplish what is now being done, the saving of many lives. So then, don't be afraid. I will provide for you and your children." And he reassured them and spoke kindly to them and there settled the matter for good.

The death of Joseph

Joseph stayed in Egypt along with all his father's family, and he lived there a long time and saw the third generation of his son, Ephraim's children. Then Joseph said to his brothers, "I am about to die. But the Creator will surely come to your aid and take you up out of this land to the land he promised on oath to Abraham, Isaac, and Jacob." And Joseph made them swear an oath and said, "The Creator will surely come to your aid, and then you must carry my bones up from this place and take it with you back to the land of Canaan." So Joseph died at the age of 110. And after they embalmed him, he was placed in a coffin in Egypt.

Chapter 11

When Gods Were Asked to Prove Themselves

Oppressed

The Hebrews, being exceedingly fruitful, had multiplied greatly, increased in number, and became so numerous that the land was filled with them. After Joseph, all his brothers, and all that generation that included the Egyptians died, a new king to whom Joseph meant nothing came to power in Egypt.

The king then told his people that the Hebrews had become far too numerous for the nation and therefore needed to be handled shrewdly. He brought their loyalty to Egypt into question and suggested that they could align with Egypt's enemies and fight with them in order to leave Egypt. They had become a major workforce for Egypt, and he was determined to keep them but under very tight control.

After official consultations in the house of Pharaoh, they decided to put slave masters over them to oppress them with forced labor, and they built Pithom and Rameses as store cities for Pharaoh. They made their lives bitter with harsh labor in brick and mortar and with all kinds of work in the fields; in all their harsh labor, the Egyptians worked them ruthlessly.

It seemed like the more they were oppressed, the only place of consolation was in the arms of their wives in bed, leading to increased conceptions, causing them to spread out more. The Egyptians tried secretly killing the children especially the boys at childbirth, and when the midwives wiggled out of direct compliance, Pharaoh then gave this order to all his people. Every Hebrew boy that was born had to be thrown into the Nile, but every girl was to be allowed to live. This nationalist mandate was given to every Egyptian, and it was a mandate of infanticide of a magnitude never heard of before. Pharaoh swimming in a sea of wealth believed he could do anything he deemed good in his sight and dismissed any regard for the Creator, Joseph, and the Hebrews.

Then came generation 4

During this period of apparent hopelessness and darkness, a couple of the tribe of Levi gave birth to a son and successfully hid him for three months from the Egyptian death squad. But when his parents could hide him no longer, his mother, with the approval of his father, got a papyrus basket for him and coated it with tar and pitch. Then she placed the child in it and put it among the reeds along the bank of the Nile near the spot and time when Pharaoh's daughter went down to bathe. The little child's sister, Miriam, stood at a distance to see what would happen to him.

As Pharaoh's daughter went down to the Nile to bathe and her security detail and attendants were walking along the riverbank, they discovered the basket. When it was opened, Pharaoh's daughter saw the crying baby, and she felt sorry for him. She knew it was one of the Hebrew babies.

Upon seeing her reaction from her hiding position, the baby's sister showed up and asked Pharaoh's daughter if she could go get one of the Hebrew women to nurse the baby for her, to which she consented. So the girl went and got the baby's real mother, and Pharaoh's daughter asked her take and nurse the baby for her for a fee. The woman then took the baby and nursed him with the love only a loving mother could give. When the child grew to the appointed age determined by Pharaoh's daughter, she took him to her, and he became her son and she named him Moses.

Presumptuous deliverer

Moses received the best education Egypt had to offer. As a son of the daughter of Pharaoh, that placed him too in the line of succession for the throne, and so he was taught in all skills a Pharaoh needed to rule the nation.

One day, after Moses had grown up, he went out to where the Hebrew people were and watched them at their hard labor. He saw an Egyptian savagely beating a Hebrew, and revolted by the inhumane punishment, looking this way and that and seeing no one, he quite easily killed the Egyptian and hid him in the sand.

The next day, he went out and saw two Hebrews fighting. Trying to score more points with the Hebrew community, he intervened and reprimanded the one in the wrong for hitting his fellow Hebrew. The man, looking at Moses and seeing him as just another of the Egyptian oppressors, asked him who made him ruler and judge over them. Then he asked him if he was thinking of killing him as he did the Egyptian the other day. Saying this in the hearing of other Egyptians created a nightmarish problem for Moses.

Word spread around quickly, and when Pharaoh heard of this, he tried to kill Moses, but he fled from Pharaoh and went away from the land of Egypt to Midian. There, while defending some women at a well from a group of teasing and abusive herdsmen, he ended up meeting and living with their father, a priest of Midian called Jethro, who had seven daughters. Moses eventually married one of them called Zipporah and tended his father-in-law's sheep. He was forty years old when he fled from Egypt and Zipporah gave birth to a son and Moses named him Gershom, saying, "I have become a foreigner in a foreign land." During that long period, the king of Egypt died.

After about forty years of Moses living in Midian, the Israelites, now in the fourth generation of existence in Egypt, groaned under the weight of their slave burdens and cried out to the Creator for help, and he heard their groaning as he remembered his covenant with Abraham, with Isaac, and with Jacob.

Things in Canaan had not changed for the better but continued to deteriorate morally and spiritually, profoundly entrenched in idolatry and the resultant detestable practices and violence. The Canaanites had sealed their fate as a whole region, and the Creator decided deliverance for the Canaanites would come down to small communities, groups, or just individuals. It was time to return the descendants of Abraham to the land of Canaan just as he had promised.

Moses's first personal encounter with the Creator

One day, while Moses was tending the flock of Jethro, he led it to the far side of the wilderness and came to Horeb, commonly known as the mountain of the Creator. As he looked around to ensure there were no predators, he thought he saw what looked like fire. Fire and grazing sheep were not a good combination.

As he went over to take a closer look, he saw that the bush was indeed on fire, but the bush did not burn up. Intrigued, he decided to go over and see the strange sight, why the bush did not burn up. As he went closer, he heard a call from the flame within the bush, "Moses! Moses!" And Moses answered, "Here I am." "Do not come any closer," the voice said. "Take off your sandals, for the place where you are standing is holy ground." It turned out this was an angel of the Creator sent with a message to Moses.

Continuing, he said, "I am the Creator, the Lord of Abraham, Isaac, and Jacob." At this, Moses hid his face because he was afraid to look at a manifestation of the Creator, for he had heard about this invisible being who could speak. He did not think he will be interested in him, a hopeless sheep herder wanted for murder by Pharaoh.

Continuing, he said, "I have indeed seen the misery of my people in Egypt. I have heard them crying out because of their slave drivers, and I am concerned about their suffering. So I have come down to rescue them from the hand of the Egyptians and to bring them up out of that Egypt into a good and spacious land, a land flowing with milk and honey, currently the home of the Canaanites, Hittites, Amorites, Perizzites, Hivites, and Jebusites. And now the cry of the Hebrews has reached me, and I have indeed seen the way the Egyptians are oppressing them. So now, I am sending you to Pharaoh to bring my people out of Egypt."

But Moses answered back, "Who am I that I should go to Pharaoh and bring the Israelites out of Egypt?" And the Creator said, "I will be with you. And this will be the sign to you that it is I who have sent you—when you have brought the people out of Egypt, you will worship me on this mountain."

Moses then replied, "Suppose I go to the Israelites and say to them, 'The Creator of your fathers has sent me to you,' and they ask me, 'What is his name?' Then what shall I tell them?" He said to Moses, "I Am Who I Am. This is what you are to say to the Israelites—'I Am has sent me to you.'"

Saying further to Moses, "Go, assemble the elders of Israel, and say to them, 'The Lord of your fathers appeared to me and said, 'I have watched over you and have seen what has been done to you in Egypt. And I have promised to bring you up out of your misery in Egypt into the land of the Canaanites, Hittites, Amorites, Perizzites, Hivites, and Jebusites, a land flowing with milk and honey.'

"The elders of Israel will listen to you. Then you and the elders are to go to the king of Egypt and say to him, 'The Creator, the Lord of the Hebrews, has met with us. Let us take a three-day journey into the wilderness to offer sacrifices to him.' However, I know that the king of Egypt will not let you go unless a mighty hand compels him. Therefore, I will stretch out my hand and strike the Egyptians with all the wonders that I will perform among them. After that, he will let you go.

"And I will make the Egyptians favorably disposed toward this people so that when you leave, you will not go empty-handed. Every woman is to ask her Egyptian neighbor and any woman living in her house for articles of silver and gold and for clothing, which you will put on your sons and daughters, and you will plunder the Egyptians."

Moses, remembering his brief session as a deliverer that resulted in his flight from Egypt, answered, "What if they do not believe me or listen to me and say, 'The Creator did not appear to you'?"

Then the Lord said to him, "What is that in your hand?"

"A staff," he replied.

The Lord said, "Throw it on the ground."

Moses threw it on the ground and it became a snake and he fled from it.

Then the Lord said to him, "Reach out your hand, and take it by the tail."

So, trembling, he gently reached out and took hold of the snake by the tail as instructed, and it turned back into a staff in his hand.

"This," said the Creator, "is so that they may believe that the Creator, the Lord of their fathers, has appeared to you."

Continuing further, he said, "Put your hand inside your cloak and then take it out."

So Moses put his hand into his cloak, and when he took it out, the skin was leprous; it had become as white as snow.

"Now put it back into your cloak, and then take it out again," he said.

He put his hand back into his cloak, and when he took it out, it was restored like the rest of his flesh.

Then he said to Moses, "If they do not believe you or pay attention to the first sign, they may believe the second. Just to make certain, if they do not believe these two signs or listen to you, take some water from the Nile and pour it on the dry ground and it will become blood on the ground."

Moses, having been almost overwhelmed by the enormity of this responsibility and feeling pretty inadequate for the job, said to the Creator, "Pardon your servant, Lord, but I have never been eloquent neither in the past nor since you have spoken to me even now. I am slow of speech and tongue."

The Lord said to him, "Who gave human beings their mouths? Who makes them deaf or mute? Who has power over these? Is it not I? Now go. I will help you speak and will instruct you on what to say."

But Moses said, "Pardon your servant, Lord. Please could you send someone else?"

The Creator was not particularly pleased with Moses's response but realized that it was more from a standpoint of feeling inadequate for the job. He also realized that Moses had not had enough exposure to his way of doing things and that the outcome did not depend on his eloquence or ability to articulate in any way but entirely up to the Creator.

In consideration of the circumstances, he said to Moses, "What about your brother, Aaron the Levite? I know he can speak well. I have already sent him on his way to meet you, and he will be glad to see you. You shall speak to him and put words in his mouth. I will help both of you speak and will teach you what to do. He will speak to the people for you, and it will be as if he were your mouth and as if you were God to him. But take this staff in your hand so you can perform the signs with it. Also, just so you know, all those who were seeking your life in Egypt are now dead." Moses could not have asked for a better companion and morale support than his brother, and this pleased him and comforted him greatly as he accepted the job and set out for home.

Return to Egypt

Then Moses went back to Jethro, his father-in-law, and asked leave of him so he could return to his own people in Egypt to see if any of them were still alive and for the assignment the Creator had given him. He had been a devoted father, a hard worker, and valuable to Jethro's household, and he had known he was never likely going to keep him forever. With gratitude he reluctantly, granted him leave and wished him well. And he took the commission staff in his hand.

Aaron had had a rough day though he was over eighty years old now and was of no use to the Egyptian slave labor force, for which he had just attended to one who had been severely brutalized. After tending to the man's injuries, he went back to his home and in tears asked the Creator in a most honest prayer whether he still planned on taking the Hebrews out of this terrible bondage.

In a vision, through the tear-filled eyes, he was instructed by the Creator to go into the wilderness to where he will find Moses, his brother, who will instruct him on what to do regarding the situation. As he hesitated, wondering if this was a dream or his imagination, not having had an encounter with the Creator before, he was then instructed very clearly to leave immediately, and the location was disclosed to him as well as what Moses looked like after forty years in the desert. He took off in a hurry and met Moses at the mountain where he had been directed to, and when he met Moses, they hugged and kissed each other ecstatically.

Then Moses told Aaron everything the Creator had sent him to say and about all the signs he had commanded him to perform. Aaron also told him how the Creator had appeared to him and asked him to go down to the desert to mount Horeb, where he was to meet Moses. Now they knew without a doubt that all this was ordained by the Creator, and the dread in the trip back was neutralized and replaced with stratospheric hope of deliverance to a respecter and keeper of covenants.

As soon as they returned to Egypt and brought together all the elders of the Israelites, Aaron then told them everything the Creator had said to Moses. He also performed the signs before the people, and they believed. And when they heard that the Lord was concerned about them and had seen their misery, they bowed down and worshiped.

Moses meets Pharaoh

After the meeting with the elders, Moses and Aaron went to Pharaoh and told him that the Creator of the universe, the Lord of Israel, had sent Pharaoh a message to let his people go so that they may hold a festival to him in the wilderness. But Pharaoh retorted by asking them who the Lord was and why he should obey him and let Israel go. He declared very emphatically that he did not know the Lord and he was not letting Israel go. Moses indicated that the Hebrews were required by the Creator to take a three-day journey into the wilderness to offer sacrifices to him.

But the king of Egypt laughed and indicated that the Lord of the Hebrews was no match to his Egyptian gods as well as Pharaoh himself, considering that they were slaves—his slaves—and had been that way for over a long time. He figured that he had no reason to be afraid of a God like that whose people were his slaves and he was the master over them. He then decided that the children of Israel were slacking off on their work and were looking for an excuse to skip work, and he warned them to work harder and pay no attention to lies.

As a warning and to drive his point home, he commanded the slave drivers and the overseers to tell the Hebrews that they were now responsible for gathering their own straw needed for brick making wherever they could find it but were required to deliver the same quota of bricks as when they were provided with straw. The Israelite supervisors were severely beaten by the taskmasters when the quotas were not fully met since they now had to spend additional time looking for straw.

Amid the peril they now found themselves in, negative emotions ran high among the Hebrews; and when they found Moses and Aaron waiting to meet them, they vented to them, "May the Lord look on you and judge you! You have made us obnoxious to Pharaoh and his officials and have put a sword in their hand to kill us."

None of them remembered what the Creator had said to them earlier when he forewarned them that Pharaoh will not acquiesce to his request of letting them go. While it might have crossed their minds, they had not expected his resultant reaction and the increase of their burdens in the magnitude they were experiencing.

Moses, somewhat frustrated by the outcome of his initial interaction with Pharaoh, therefore returned to the Lord and, praying to him, said, "Why, Lord? Why have you brought trouble on this people? Is this why you sent me? Ever since I went to Pharaoh to speak in your name, he has brought trouble on this people, and you have not rescued your people at all."

The Creator, seeing the emotional conflict, decided to firmly reassure Moses and the Israelites, particularly because none of them living had ever seen or understood what he intended to do and how he was going to do it. This generation of the Egyptians and of the children of Israel had not experienced the power of the Creator of the heavens and the earth and he had a plan on how to do just that and it was not known even by Moses.

Then the Creator reassured Moses, telling him they were going to see what he had in store for Pharaoh. Not only was Pharaoh going to let them go, but he was also going to drive them out of his country. He then gave Moses a history lesson on how he appeared to Abraham, to Isaac, and to Jacob and the irrevocable covenant he had established with them to give them the land of Canaan, where they resided as foreigners. Moreover, he had heard the groaning of the Israelites, whom the Egyptians were enslaving, and he was about to bring them out from under the yoke of the Egyptians. Moses then reported this to the Israelites, but they did not listen to him because of their discouragement and harsh labor.

Then the Lord said to Moses, "Go back to Pharaoh and tell him to let the Hebrews go out of his country."

But Moses asked the Lord, "If the Israelites will not listen to me, why would Pharaoh listen to me since I speak with faltering lips?"

Then the Creator said to Moses, "You are to say everything I command you, and your brother Aaron is to tell Pharaoh to let the Israelites go out of his country. But since he is not inclined to let them go, I will at some point after his continued refusal help harden his heart even beyond reason to the point where even when I multiply my signs and wonders in Egypt, he will not listen to you. Then I will lay my hand on Egypt because of their inhumane treatment and cruelty to the Hebrews, and with mighty acts of judgment I will bring out the Hebrews. And the Egyptians will know that I am the Creator of all things when I stretch out my hand against Egypt and bring the Hebrews out of it."

Moses and Aaron did just as they were commanded. Moses was slowly beginning to understand the direction the Creator was going, and while he did not understand the magnitude, the ominous ring to his words used was somewhat foreboding on what might befall Pharaoh. Moses was eighty years old, and Aaron eighty-three when they spoke to Pharaoh.

In the mind of Moses, he would have preferred carrying out the deliverance differently, but this was the Creator's operation, and it was becoming clear that it was his and Aaron's job to follow his instructions accurately.

In the Creator's mind, he wanted the Egyptians to be reintro-duced to him as in the days of Joseph as well as to the rest of the world. The famine had been a prelude to show the world the power, military might, splendor, riches, the gods and pride of Egypt, and how that stacked against a little of what the Creator of the heavens and the earth was going to reveal of himself.

Pharaoh, his wise men, and his sorcerers were slated to meet the Creator first in the showdown he had planned. The people needed to understand that sorcery and witchcraft were real, and though mysti-fying to the common, it was powerless against the Creator's follow-ers. Though the devil had been kicked out of heaven, his powers were not taken away from him. Its use over humanity is greatly restricted and severely limited.

It is one of the tools the devil has used to mesmerize humanity in the supernatural realm like Ouija boards, palm reading, fortune-tell-ing, séances and other forms of talking to the dead, and many other forms of witchcraft. It was widely practiced in Egypt and Canaan and even the Hebrews had grown up with these practices and many quietly served and worshiped them and they too needed rehabilita-tion just like the Egyptians. So started the slow and painful process of spiritual schooling in the ways of the Creator of the heavens and the earth for both the Egyptians, the Hebrews, and the rest of the world.

Aaron's staff becomes a snake

To begin, the Lord said to Moses and Aaron, "When Pharaoh says to you, 'Perform a miracle as a way of validating the authority of your Creator,' then say to Aaron, 'Take your staff and throw it down before Pharaoh,' and it will become a snake." So Moses and Aaron went to Pharaoh and did just as the Lord had commanded when Pharaoh asked for the sign. Aaron threw his staff down in front of Pharaoh and his officials, and it became a snake. Pharaoh then sum-moned his wise men and sorcerers, and the Egyptian magicians also did the same things by their secret arts of black magic or witchcraft: Each one threw down his staff, and each became a snake. But Aaron's staff swallowed up their staffs. Pharaoh, in looking at it, declared it to be a simple magic trick even his junior magicians could perform. His heart became hard, and he would not listen to them just as Moses had been warned.

The plague of blood

Then the Lord said to Moses, "Pharaoh's heart is unyielding. He refuses to let the people go. Go to him in the morning as he goes out to the river. Confront him on the bank of the Nile, and take in your hand the staff that was changed into a snake. Then tell him that the Creator, the Lord of the Hebrews, has sent you to tell him to let his people go so that they may worship him in the wilderness. But until now he had not listened.

"By this he will know that I am the Lord: With the staff that is in your hand, you will strike the water of the Nile, and it will be changed into blood. The fish in the Nile will die, and the river will stink. The Egyptians will not be able to drink its water."

Moses and Aaron did just as the Lord had commanded in the presence of Pharaoh and his officials as he struck the water of the Nile, and all the water was changed into blood. The fish in the Nile died, and the river smelled so badly that the Egyptians could not drink its water. Blood was everywhere in Egypt.

But the Egyptian magicians did the same things by their secret arts with water dug from the ground along the river, and Pharaoh's heart became hard; he would not listen to Moses and Aaron just as the Lord had said. Instead, he turned and went into his palace and did not take even this to heart. To him, this was just a magic trick which his sorcerers could also do.

To sustain life, the Egyptians could dig along the Nile to get drinking water because they could not drink the water of the river or the reservoirs. Seven days passed after the Creator struck the Nile.

The plague of frogs

Then the Lord sent Moses to warn Pharaoh that if he refused to let the people go, he will send a plague of frogs on the whole country. The Nile will teem with frogs and will come up into his palace, bedrooms, onto beds, the houses of the officials, on the people, into their ovens and kneading troughs.

With Pharaoh not yielding, Moses told Aaron to stretch out his hand and staff over the streams and canals and ponds and make frogs come up on the land of Egypt. When Aaron did, frogs came up and covered the land; but the magicians did the same things by their secret arts—they also made frogs come up on the land of Egypt. However, now, the insurmountable challenge was getting rid of the frogs using their sorcery; they could not. Pharaoh, recognizing the problem, summoned Moses and Aaron and said, "Pray to the Lord to take the frogs away from me and my people, and I will let your people go to offer sacrifices to him."

Moses said to Pharaoh, "I leave to you the honor of setting the time for me to pray for you and your officials and your people that you and your houses may be rid of the frogs except for those that remain in the Nile." This Moses had asked for so there will be no confusion on whether it was a matter of chance or coincidence, and as anticipated by Moses, Pharaoh chose a very short time.

"Tomorrow," Pharaoh said.

Moses replied, "It will be as you say so that you may know there is no one like the Lord. Tomorrow the frogs will leave you and your houses, your officials and your people. They will remain only in the Nile."

Feeling that Pharaoh was beginning to crack under the pressure, after leaving Pharaoh, Moses and Aaron cried out to the Lord about the frogs he had brought on Pharaoh, and the Lord did what Moses asked. The frogs died in the houses, in the courtyards, and in the fields. They were piled into heaps, and the land reeked of them. But when Pharaoh saw that there was relief, he hardened his heart and would not listen to Moses and Aaron just as the Lord had said he would.

The plague of gnats, the sorcerers' turning point

Then the Lord said to Moses, "Tell Aaron, 'Stretch out your staff and strike the dust of the ground,' and throughout the land of Egypt the dust will become gnats." They did this, and when Aaron stretched out his hand with the staff and struck the dust of the ground, gnats came on people and animals. All the dust throughout the land of Egypt became gnats. But when the magicians tried to produce gnats by their secret arts, they could not. Since the gnats were on people and animals everywhere, the magicians, seeing this was no longer just a performance in the human realm and beyond their powers in sorcery, said to Pharaoh, "This is the finger of God, and it is simply beyond our mental, physical, or spiritual ability." But Pharaoh's heart was hard, and he would not listen.

The plague of flies

Then the Lord said to Moses, "Get up early in the morning and confront Pharaoh as he goes to the river and say to him, 'This is what the Lord says: If you do not let my people go, I will send swarms of flies on you and your officials, on your people, and into your houses. The houses of the Egyptians will be full of flies. Even the ground will be covered with them. But on that day, I will deal differently with the land of Goshen, where my people live. No swarms of flies will be there so that you will know that I, the Lord, am in this land. I will make a distinction between my people and your people. This sign will occur tomorrow.'"

And the Lord did this. Dense swarms of flies poured into Pharaoh's palace and into the houses of his officials. Throughout Egypt the land was ruined by the flies. Then Pharaoh summoned Moses and Aaron and said, "Go sacrifice to your God here in the land."

But Moses said, "That would not be right. The sacrifices we offer our Lord would likely be strange to the Egyptians. And if we offer sacrifices that are strange in their eyes, will they not stone us? We must take a three-day journey into the wilderness to offer the sacrifices as he commands us." Pharaoh said, "I will let you go to offer sacrifices in the wilderness, but you must not go very far. Now pray for me."

Moses answered, "As soon as I leave you, I will pray to the Lord, and tomorrow the flies will leave Pharaoh and his officials and his people. Only let Pharaoh be sure that he does not act deceitfully again by not letting the people go."

Then Moses left Pharaoh and prayed to the Lord, and he did what Moses asked. The flies left Pharaoh and his officials and his people—not a fly remained. But this time also, Pharaoh hardened his heart and would not let the people go.

The plague on livestock

Then the Lord said to Moses, "Go to Pharaoh and say to him, 'This is what the Lord of the Hebrews says: If you refuse to let them go and continue to hold them back, the hand of the Lord will bring a terrible plague on your livestock in the field, on your horses, donkeys and camels, and on your cattle, sheep, and goats. But the Lord will make a distinction between the livestock of the Hebrews and that of Egypt so that no animal belonging to the Israelites will die.'"

The Lord set a time and said, "Tomorrow the Lord will do this in the land." And the next day he did it: All the livestock of the Egyptians died, but not one animal belonging to the Israelites died. Pharaoh, in trying to ensure that this was not just a fluke of nature and to verify Moses's claim that the cattle of the Hebrews were spared, investigated and found that not even one of the animals of theirs had died. Yet his heart was unyielding, and he would not let the people go.

The plague of boils

Then the Lord said to Moses and Aaron, "Take handfuls of soot from a furnace and have Moses toss it into the air in the presence of Pharaoh. It will become fine dust over the whole land of Egypt, and festering boils will break out on people and animals throughout the land." So they took soot from a furnace and stood before Pharaoh. Moses tossed it into the air, and festering boils broke out on people and animals.

The supposedly powerful but very embarrassed magicians, by this time totally despondent and helpless, could not stand before Moses because of the boils that were on them and on all the Egyptians. But this time, the Lord hardened Pharaoh's heart, and he would not listen to Moses and Aaron.

The plague of hail

Then the Lord said to Moses, "Get up early in the morning, confront Pharaoh, and say to him, 'This is what the Lord of the Hebrews says: Let my people go, or this time I will send the full force of my plagues against you and against your officials and your people, so you may know that there is no one like me in all the earth.

"'For by now I could have stretched out my hand and struck you and your people with a plague that would have wiped you off the earth. But I have raised you up for this very purpose that I might show you my power and that my name might be proclaimed in all the earth as a reminder. You still set yourself against my people and will not let them go. Therefore, at this time tomorrow I will send the worst hailstorm that has ever fallen on Egypt, from the day it was founded till now.'"

Solemnly warning as only the Creator would, he said, "Give an order now to bring whatever livestock you have left and everything you have in the field to a place of shelter because the hail will fall on every person and animal that has not been brought in and is still out in the field, and they will die."

For this plague, the Lord gave them enough time to allow them to bring their livestock and servants to safety. Those officials of Pharaoh who feared the word of the Lord hurried to bring their slaves and what was left of their livestock inside. But those who ignored the word of the Lord left their slaves and livestock in the field. Then the Lord said to Moses, "Stretch out your hand toward the sky for the hail to fall all over Egypt, on people and animals, and on everything growing in the fields of Egypt."

When Moses stretched out his staff toward the sky, the Lord sent thunder and hail, and lightning flashed down to the ground. So he rained hail on the land of Egypt; hail fell, and lightning flashed back and forth. It was the worst storm in all the land of Egypt since it had become a nation.

Throughout Egypt, hail struck everything in the fields, both people and animals; it beat down everything growing in the fields at the time and stripped every tree. The only place it did not hail was the land of Goshen, where the Hebrews were. Then Pharaoh summoned Moses and Aaron. "This time I have sinned," he said to them. "The Lord is in the right, and I and my people are in the wrong. Pray to him, for we have had enough thunder and hail. I will let you go. You don't have to stay any longer."

Moses replied, "When I have gone out of the city, I will spread out my hands in prayer to the Lord. The thunder will stop, and there will be no more hail so you may know that the earth is the Lord's. But I know that you and your officials still do not fear the Lord."

The flax and barley were destroyed since the barley had headed and the flax was in bloom. The wheat and spelt, however, were not destroyed because they ripen later. Then Moses left Pharaoh and went out of the city. He spread out his hands toward the Lord. The thunder and hail stopped, and the rain no longer poured down on the land. When Pharaoh saw that the rain and hail and thunder had stopped, he sinned again. He and his officials hardened their hearts, and he would not let the Hebrews go.

The plague of locusts

Then the Lord said to Moses, "Go to Pharaoh, for I have hardened his heart and the hearts of his officials so that I may perform these signs of mine among them that you may tell your children and grandchildren how I dealt harshly with the Egyptians and how I performed my signs among them, and that you may know that I am the Lord."

So Moses and Aaron went to Pharaoh and said to him, "This is what the Lord of the Hebrews, says: 'How long will you refuse to humble yourself before me? Let my people go so that they may worship me. If you refuse to let them go, I will bring locusts into your country tomorrow. They will cover the face of the ground so that it cannot be seen. They will devour what little you have left after the hail including every tree that is growing in your fields. They will fill your houses and those of all your officials and all the Egyptians— something neither your parents nor your ancestors have ever seen from the day they settled in this land till now.'" Then Moses turned and left Pharaoh.

Pharaoh's officials said to him, "How long will this man be a snare to us? Let the people go so that they may worship their Lord. Do you not yet realize that Egypt is ruined?" To somehow appease his officials, Moses and Aaron were brought back to Pharaoh. "Go, worship your Lord," he said. "But tell me who will be going."

Moses answered, "We will go with our young and our old, with our sons and our daughters, and with our flocks and herds because we are to celebrate a festival to the Lord."

Pharaoh said, "The Lord be with you if I let you go along with your women and children! Clearly you are bent on evil. No! Have only the men go and worship the Lord since that's what you have been asking for." Then Moses and Aaron were driven out of Pharaoh's presence.

And the Lord said to Moses, "Stretch out your hand over Egypt so that locusts swarm over the land." So Moses stretched out his staff over Egypt, and the Lord made an east wind blow across the land all that day and all that night. By morning, the wind had brought the locusts. They invaded all Egypt and settled down in every area of the country in great numbers. Never before had there been such a plague of locusts nor will there ever be again.

They covered all the ground until it was black. They devoured all that was left after the hail, everything growing in the fields, and the fruit on the trees. Nothing green remained on tree or plant in all the land of Egypt.

Pharaoh quickly summoned Moses and Aaron and said, "I have sinned against the Lord your God and against you. Now forgive my sin once more and pray to him to take this deadly plague away from me."

Moses then left Pharaoh and prayed to the Lord, and the Lord changed the wind to a very strong west wind, which caught up the locusts and carried them into the Red Sea. Not a locust was left anywhere in Egypt. But this time, the Lord hardened Pharaoh's heart, and he would not let the Israelites go.

The plague of darkness

As an insult to another Egyptian god, the sun god, the Lord said to Moses, "Stretch out your hand toward the sky so that darkness spreads over Egypt, darkness that can be felt." So Moses stretched out his hand toward the sky, and total darkness covered all Egypt for three days. No one could see anyone else or move about for three days. Yet all the Hebrews had light in the places where they lived.

Then Pharaoh summoned Moses and said, "Go, worship the Lord. Even your women and children may go with you—only leave your flocks and herds behind."

But Moses said, "You must allow us to have sacrifices and burnt offerings to present to the Lord. Our livestock too must go with us—not a hoof is to be left behind. We have to use some of them in worshipping him, and until we get there, we will not know what we are to use to worship him."

But the Lord hardened Pharaoh's heart, and he was not willing to let them go, to the bewilderment of his officials. Pharaoh said to Moses, "Get out of my sight! Make sure you do not appear before me again! The day you see my face, you will die."

"Just as you say," Moses replied. "I will never appear before you again."

The plague on the firstborn

Now the Lord had said to Moses, "I will bring one more plague on Pharaoh and on Egypt. After that, he will let you go from here, and when he does, he will drive you out completely. Tell the people that men and women alike are to ask their Egyptian neighbors for articles of silver and gold." He made the Egyptians favorably disposed toward the people, and Moses himself was highly regarded in Egypt by Pharaoh's officials and by the people. The Lord had predisposed them to give the Israelites whatever they asked for and even more beyond their requests as some saw it as a way to make appeasement before their nation was completely decimated and leaving them with nothing. For others, it was their way of acknowledging the sovereignty of the Creator whom the Hebrews worshipped.

Moses then said to the people, "This is what the Lord says: 'About midnight I will go throughout Egypt. Every firstborn son in Egypt will die—from the firstborn son of Pharaoh, who sits on the throne, to the firstborn son of the female slave, who is at her hand mill, and all the firstborn of the animals as well. There will be loud wailing throughout Egypt worse than there has ever been or ever will be again. But among the Israelites, not a dog will bark at any person or animal. Then you will know that the Lord makes a distinction between Egypt and the Hebrews."

Before this final plague, Moses had warned Pharaoh, saying "All these officials of yours will come to me, bowing down before me and saying, 'Go, you and all the people who follow you!' After that I will leave." Then Moses, hot with anger, had left Pharaoh's court.

The angel of death

In preparation for the last plague, as instructed by the Lord, Moses and Aaron told the whole community of Israel that each man was to take a lamb for his family, one for each household. If any household was too small for a whole lamb, they must share one with their nearest neighbor, having taken into account the number of people there are. They were to determine the amount of lamb needed in accordance with what each person could eat. The animals they chose had to be year-old males without defect and could be from the sheep or the goats.

They were to take care of them until the fourteenth day of the month, when all the members of the community of Israel must slaughter them at twilight. Then they were to take some of the blood and put it on the sides and tops of the doorframes of the houses where they ate the lambs. That same night, they were to eat the meat roasted over the fire along with bitter herbs and bread made without yeast. They were not to eat the meat raw or boiled in water but roast it over a fire with the head, legs, and internal organs. They were not to leave any of it till morning; if some was left till morning, it had to be burnt. They were to eat it with their cloaks tucked into their belts, sandals on their feet, and staff in hand and ready to travel, for they will be heading out of Egypt. They were to eat it in haste because it was the Lord's Passover.

On that same night, the Lord will pass through Egypt and strike down every firstborn of both people and animals, and he will bring judgment on all the gods of Egypt. The blood on the doorposts would be a sign for their houses so that the destructive death plague will not touch them when he struck Egypt, but rather, he would pass over wherever he saw the blood. This was going to be a day to commemorate; for the generations to come, they were to celebrate it as a festival to the Lord as a lasting ordinance.

When the instructions to the elders of Israel were completed, the people bowed down and worshiped and then proceeded to do what they had been commanded to do.

At midnight, as promised, it happened. The death angel struck down all the firstborn in Egypt—from the firstborn of Pharaoh, who sat on the throne, to the firstborn of the prisoner, who was in the dungeon, and the firstborn of all the livestock as well. Pharaoh and all his officials and all the Egyptians got up during the night, and there was loud wailing in Egypt, for there was not a house without someone dead.

It suddenly dawned on Pharaoh and the Egyptians at that moment that the Creator the Hebrews worshiped had the power of life and death all along and could destroy at will. There was no greater power ever heard of or seen before other than foggy memories of creation and the flood which were now just myths to the Egyptians and much of the known world. None of the gods of Egypt was spared humiliation, and none could stand to be counted.

Israel is thrown out by Pharaoh in about 1513 BC

During the night, Pharaoh summoned Moses and Aaron and said, "Up! Leave my people, you and the Hebrews! Go, worship the Lord as you have requested. Take your flocks and herds, as you have said, and go. And bless me," he said after a painful bout of humility.

The Egyptians urged the people to hurry and leave the country, for now it was clear they could all die at a moment's notice when sanctioned by the Lord of the Hebrews.

The Israelites had done as Moses instructed and had asked the Egyptians for whatever they desired. The Egyptians transferred an incredible amount of wealth unto the Hebrews in all manner of costly articles including a lot of gold, silver, and expensive clothing. It was as if they were being paid back wages over generations with interest. It was an incredible event because there was no haggling or attempts of persuasion but rather the Egyptians being overwhelmingly obliging to give whatever they felt the Hebrews would like.

The exodus

Then the Israelites took their journey from Rameses to Sukkoth. There were about six hundred thousand men on foot, besides women and children, for an estimated population of about three million people.

Many other people who were non-Hebrew went up with them and also large droves of livestock, both flocks and herds. With the dough the Israelites had brought from Egypt, they baked loaves of unleavened bread. Now the length of time the Israelite people lived in Egypt was 430 years, and at the end of the 430 years, to the very day, all the Hebrews left Egypt just as the Creator had promised Abraham.

Freedom crossing

When Pharaoh let the people go, the Creator did not lead them on the road through the Philistine country though that was shorter. He was concerned that if they faced war, they might change their minds and return to Egypt. This was because they had not been trained as soldiers and were no match for any serious combat without divine intervention.

In a remarkable show of compassion and divine guidance, the Lord placed a very special pillar of cloud in front of them to lead them on what path to take, and at night, it changed into a pillar of fire to provide illumination, thereby enabling them to travel by day or night. Never was anything like this seen before, but it was the continuation of the Creator showing the Hebrews, Egyptians, and the rest of the neighboring nations the difference between him and other gods.

This was a massive relief to Moses because all he had to do was follow the cloud. So the Creator led the people around by the desert road toward the Red Sea. Neither the pillar of cloud by day nor the pillar of fire by night left its place in front of the people. Moses had taken the bones of Joseph with him because Joseph had made the Hebrews swear an oath.

Then the Lord said to Moses, "Tell the Israelites to turn back and encamp near Pi Hahiroth, between Migdol and the sea. They are to encamp by the sea, directly opposite Baal Zephon." As if to answer the unverbalized question in Moses's mind based on his military training and knowledge, the Lord added, "Pharaoh will think, *The Hebrews are wandering around the land in confusion, hemmed in by the desert.* And I will harden Pharaoh's heart, and he will pursue them. But I will gain glory for myself through Pharaoh and all his army, and the Egyptians will know that I am the Lord." And they did as the Lord had commanded Moses.

When the king of Egypt was told that the people had fled, Pharaoh and his officials changed their minds about them and said, "What have we done? We have let the Israelites go and have lost their services!" He therefore had his chariot made ready and took his powerful army with him.

He took six hundred of the best chariots along with all the other chariots of Egypt with officers over all of them as a massive show of Egypt's military might. The Lord hardened the heart of Pharaoh so that he pursued the Israelites, who were marching out boldly while not being pursued.

The Egyptians, all Pharaoh's horses and chariots, horsemen, and troops pursued the Israelites and overtook them as they camped by the sea near Pi Hahiroth opposite Baal Zephon.

As Pharaoh approached, the Israelites looked up, and there were the Egyptians, marching after them. They were terrified and cried out to the Lord. Suddenly, the bold march quickly fizzled into a bunch of whimpering babies, and cry for divine intervention they did. They knew they were no match to the Egyptian military might, and the Lord knew and had anticipated this. He needed them to understand that this was the Lord's fight and not theirs as long as they looked up to him and followed his guidance.

Lashing out at Moses, they said, "Was it because there were no graves in Egypt that you brought us to the desert to die? What have you done to us by bringing us out of Egypt? Didn't we say to you in Egypt, 'Leave us alone. Let us serve the Egyptians'? It would have been better for us to serve the Egyptians than to die in the desert!"

Moses, answering the people, said, "Do not be afraid. Stand firm, and you will see the deliverance the Lord will bring you today. The Egyptians you see today you will never see again. The Lord will fight for you—you need only to be still."

Then the Lord said to Moses, "Tell the Israelites to move on towards the sea. Raise and stretch out your staff over the sea to divide the water so that the Israelites can go through the sea on dry ground. I will harden the hearts of the Egyptians so that they will go in after them, and I will gain glory through Pharaoh and all his army through his chariots and his horsemen. The Egyptians will know that there is only one true Creator."

Then the invisible angel, who had been traveling in front of Israel's hapless army in the pillar of cloud, withdrew and went behind them. In a very spectacular move, the pillar of cloud also moved from in front and stood behind them, coming between the armies of Egypt and Israel. Throughout the night, the cloud brought darkness to the one side and light to the other side so that neither went near the other all night long, reminiscent of what he did when he created light and separated it from darkness.

Then Moses stretched out his hand over the sea, and all that night, the Lord drove the sea back with a strong east wind. The waters were divided, creating a very dry passageway, and the Israelites went through the sea on dry ground with a wall of water on their right and on their left.

In a bizarre decision, defying normal military or basic human logic, the Egyptians pursued them, riding between two massive vertical walls of liquid water, and all Pharaoh's horses and chariots and horsemen followed them deep into the sea like men possessed. During the last watch of the night, the Lord looked down from the pillar of fire and cloud at the Egyptian army and threw it into confusion.

While in the very midst of the sea with too much distance to be able to flee, the Lord jammed the wheels of their chariots so that they had difficulty driving, thereby giving the Hebrews time to clear out safely and be on the shore. Finally, in exasperation and seeing that they were trapped deep in the sea, the Egyptians cried out, saying, "Let us get away from the Hebrews! Their Lord is fighting for them against Egypt. Let's flee for our lives!"

With all Israel now safely on the other side of the shore, the Lord asked Moses to stretch out his hand over the sea. As soon as he did, the liquid walls folded back in, and the sea went back to its place, covering the chariots and horsemen—the entire army of Pharaoh that had followed the Israelites into the sea—and not one of them survived.

That day the Lord saved Israel from the hands of the Egyptians in a most spectacular way that the world and the Egyptians would remember for generations to come, and the Hebrews saw the Egyptians' dead soldiers washed onto the shore. This concluded the improbable departure of Israel from Egypt, something the Lord had told Abraham hundreds of years earlier.

And when the Israelites saw the mighty hand of the Lord displayed against the Egyptians, the people feared the Lord and put their trust in him and in Moses his servant. The Creator wanted them to know he was their defender and wanted this image engraved in their hearts forever as well as any others who choose to have the Creator of the heavens and the earth as their defense.

Chapter 12

Man's Greatest Problem—The Curable but Fatal Heart-and-Mind Disease

The sheer awe and shock of the plagues and their ensuing devastation were enough to make anyone to be terrified of the Creator. No one had ever seen liquid water stack up into mountainous structures like icebergs. This was too much for a mortal mind to accommodate. In watching the indescribable demise of the Egyptian elite military machine, the Israelites, who had seen their lives flash before their eyes, burst into unrestrained songs of joy at the deliverance.

Though word had travelled around the nations far and wide, the Creator knew the next part of the job was to create intimacy with the Hebrews because he is a personal Lord who loves to interact with those who walk with him.

They had just seen the hand of judgment reflecting a destructive and punitive side of him, but in this next phase of their journey to Canaan, he was to show them the healing, nourishing, providential, and interactive side of himself. This way, the world will have a chance of seeing the different characteristics of the Creator.

This part of the process involved the people believing that he had their best interest at heart. They had to trust him for him to be able to work with them; they would have to trust him even though he was invisible and would walk and obey him of their own free will.

He was the Creator who never compelled anyone and would never violate anyone's free will. Man would have to decide and live with the consequences of the decision.

And so began the process as they headed into the Promised Land.

The waters of Marah and Elim

Then Moses led Israel from the Red Sea, and they went into the Desert of Shur. For three days, led by the mysterious cloud, they traveled in the desert without finding water. When they came to Marah, they found water but could not drink it because it was bitter. The people grumbled against Moses, blaming him for trying to kill them with thirst. Then Moses cried out to the Lord and he showed him an ordinary piece of wood lying by and asked him to toss it into the water in the sight of all the people. He threw it into the water, and the water became fit to drink. Thus continued the mental and spiritual rehabilitation job for the Creator on the nation. His hope is that humanity will understand, looking at this journey, that everyone will go through the rehabilitation phase when they chose to accept the Creator as their Lord.

The heart and head job

A few days later, the people could be heard reminiscing about the meat pots and other foods they missed in Egypt and then angrily complaining and grumbling over unavailability of food. They had totally forgotten about the supernatural healing of the polluted water. Others then voiced agitating cries of despair among the people on the insurmountable challenge of feeding three million people in this desert with bread and meat, seeing that the mysterious cloud and Moses were only leading them through a desert path devoid of food. "The insanity of it all!" they wailed.

The Creator heard their complaints and gripes. He then called Moses and informed him that he would send them bread and meat. All he was trying to do was teach them that he was the source of all things and the creator of the heavens and the earth and all things visible and invisible. He wanted to teach them to ask him so they would understand that he communicated with his creatures and wanted them to understand that he wanted a father-and-children relationship. Prayer was when they made requests directly to him, and he spoke back to them. They needed this understanding to survive life in a fallen world where deceit by the devil was rife among the people.

They had been used to vicious kings and idol gods made of stone, and relating to a loving, living, and protective Creator was a totally new concept. He needed to have their heads work with their hearts. As a result, he patiently put up with the gripes but determined to do what he could to have a nation whose king is the Creator of the heavens and the earth—a nation that would live in peace without evil and detestable practices that brewed corruption, violence, and hate. He wanted them to have a land that flowed with milk and honey, where there was abundance of food and safety, to reflect his heart for humanity.

Then the Lord said to Moses, "Each day, for six days, I will rain down bread and meat from heaven so that the people will go out each day and gather enough for just that day. They are to rest from any kind of work on the seventh day, and so they are authorized to collect twice the amount of food on the sixth day because there would be none on the seventh day. In this way, I will teach them to build their faith on my word and obedience to me for their safety and good. They need to know that I keep my word, and I need them to do the same for things they promise to do."

In addition to providing them manna, which were honey-sweet frosty wafers that were the base of any meal that could be made with a starch base—it could be boiled, baked, fried, and made into any form of meal—he also provided a daily supply of very plump and succulent quail which flew into the camp in hordes for six days.

So it was that in the evening quail came and covered the camp, and in the morning, there was a layer of dew around the camp; and when the dew was gone, the thin manna flakes appeared on the desert floor with health benefits out of this world.

The Creator had given instructions for the people to gather just enough for each day and no one was to keep any of it until morning and the obvious reasons included unavailable preservation means like refrigeration, fresh taste, and a reminder that it came from the Lord. However, some of them paid no attention to Moses; they kept part of it until morning, but it was full of maggots and began to smell. So Moses was angry with them and had to remind them not to do it again.

Never had millions of people been supernaturally fed daily by the Creator for the duration of their journey, and there were no health issues among the people for the corresponding period.

As the cloud moved them across the desert, the food supply was now daily provided miraculously according to the Creator's promise, but the availability of water for them and their cattle was one way they were tested. Each time there was no water to drink, they complained to Moses and threatened to stone him instead of simply asking especially after having seen how many times the Creator had provided water for them—everything else included.

Some of the nations like the Amalekites decided to attack them early in their journey into Canaan, and they found out the hard way that the Creator, who was leading the Hebrews, was their defense—and a very formidable defense at that. It confirmed what they had heard about that happened in Egypt.

The first time ever a whole nation saw a manifestation of the Creator at the same time

On the first day of the third month after the Hebrews left Egypt, they came to the desert of Sinai and camped there in the desert in front of the mountain. Then the Creator called Moses from the mountain and he went up to him and after speaking with him, he sent him down to the people with the following message:

"You yourselves have seen what I did to Egypt and how I carried you on eagles' wings and brought you to myself. Now if you obey me fully and keep my covenant, then out of all nations you will be my treasured possession. Although the whole earth is mine, you will be for me a kingdom of priests and a holy nation."

The people all responded together, stating that they would do everything the Creator had said. So Moses took their answer back to the Lord.

The Creator knew the people needed a code of conduct to properly relate to him, to each other, and to be able to form a civil and moral society in the land of Canaan. This was to set them apart from the rest of the world that had lost its true spiritual and moral moorings and to be the model for others to follow. He was determined to gently lead all of humanity back to himself, and he knew humanity needed some serious handholding, knowing the heart of man.

Even more importantly, he also had no intention of violating their free will but rather leave it to them to make the choice and walk before him in an exemplary way that reflected his love, patience, and merciful judgment standards. He wanted the world to understand that he is the Creator who makes and keeps covenants and never goes back on a promise. He is the Creator who was willing to reason together with mankind, to bridge man's mortal domain and the spiritual world where the invisible Creator dwells in.

Dealing with the incessant complaining and remarkable ingratitude confirmed to the Creator that the job of rehabilitating the heart of man, who is given free will, was turning out to be quite challenging. He loved man, and he was determined to stay gracious and do whatever it took to stay the course to complete the job in love.

The Creator who speaks

Then to Moses's amazement, the Creator informed him that he was going to come to the people so that they could hear him speaking with Moses and the people as a whole in order to validate Moses's position as their leader. First, Moses needed to go and consecrate the people over the next two days mentally and hygienically. He needed then ready by the third day because on that day, he will come down on Mount Sinai in the sight of all the people. However, he needed Moses to put a visible perimeter marker around the mountain for the people and to tell them not to cross it, not approach the mountain or touch the foot of it.

Man in his very sinful state cannot survive the presence of the Creator, and the Hebrews needed to be protected from a premature interaction with him. Only when they heard a long blast of a ram's horn were they then to approach the mountain and only up to the markers. Moses did as was instructed and prepared the people for the visit.

There was incredible excitement and expectation as the people speculated on what the Creator looked like and how they were going to interact with him and they got ready as best as they could ever get.

Then it happened—on the morning of the third day, as scheduled for the visit, there was deafening thunder and blinding lightning as a thick cloud formed over the mountain accompanied by a very loud trumpet blast which set everyone in the camp trembling.

As Moses tried leading them to the foot of the mountain to meet with the Creator, their desire to meet such power as they were witnessing greatly diminished. Mount Sinai was covered with smoke because the Lord began to descend on it in fire and the smoke billowed up from it like smoke from a furnace and the whole mountain convulsed and trembled violently as his presence approached it. This was like nothing anyone had expected, seen, or heard before, and it made everyone look so inconsequential in the presence of such majesty.

As his presence drew closer, the thunder, lightning, the trumpet blasts, and the smoking mountain were just too much for the people, so they fled away from the mountain. From their safe distance, they called out to Moses and told him they did not want any part of the Creator talking to them; they preferred just having Moses talk to him and then he in turn to them. The Creator then called on Moses to approach the thick darkness.

The Creator's post Eden living code for humanity

And in the hearing of everyone, the Creator spoke the following words to them, saying a summary of statutes to live by in a civil society:

"I am the Lord, the creator of the heavens and the earth, who brought you out of Egypt, out of the land of slavery."

1. "You shall have no other gods before me."
2. "You shall not make for yourself an image in the form of anything in heaven above or on the earth beneath or in the waters below. You shall not bow down to them or worship them, for I, the Creator of all things, am a jealous one, meting out deserved punishment to the children for the sin of the parents to the third and fourth generation of those who rebel against me, but showing love to a thousand generations of those who love me and keep my commandments."
3. "You shall not misuse the name of the Lord your Creator, for the Lord will not hold anyone guiltless who misuses his name."
4. "Remember the Sabbath day by keeping it holy. Six days you shall labor and do all your work, but the seventh day is a Sabbath to the Lord your Creator. On it you shall not do any work, neither you nor your son or daughter nor your male or female servant nor your animals nor any foreigner residing in your towns. For in six days the Lord made the heavens and the earth, the sea, and all that is in them, but he rested on the seventh day. Therefore, the Lord blessed the Sabbath day and made it holy."
5. "Honor your father and your mother so that you may live long in the land the Lord your Creator is giving you."
6. "You shall not commit murder."
7. "You shall not commit adultery."
8. "You shall not steal."
9. "You shall not lie or give false testimony against your neighbor."

10. "You shall not covet your neighbor's house. You shall not covet your neighbor's wife or his male or female servant, his ox or donkey, or anything that belongs to your neighbor."

Then the Lord expounded on some of the commandments for clarity so that they would understand these laws were from him and not Moses. It was also vital for them to hear his audible voice and understand the difference between idols and the living Creator. Moses had experienced a little of this in the burning bush encounter when the Creator called him to go to Pharaoh but nothing quite spectacular and terrifying like this.

The guardian angel to prepare the way

As the Creator was concluding, he informed the people that he was sending an angel ahead of them to guard them along the way. They were to pay attention to him and listen to what he said and to not rebel against him. He had been given authority to speak on the Creator's behalf and would therefore not likely forgive any rebellion since his name and authority was in the angel.

He promised that if they listened carefully to what he said and followed his instructions, he would be an enemy to their enemies and will oppose those who opposed them. His angel was to go ahead of them to bring them into the Promised Land with the plan to wipe or drive out those who dwell there now because of their reprehensible acts toward humanity that culminated in continuous violence in the land. They were warned not to bow down before Canaanite gods, worship them, or follow their evil practices. Upon occupying the land, the idols were to be demolished and eradicated. His blessings were also promised on their food and water, eradication of sickness and barrenness from among them, and the granting of the full lifespan for the people.

To pave the way for them into the land, the Creator promised to throw into confusion every evil nation they encountered with plans to harm them, and they would be seen to turn their backs and run. Where necessary, hornets would be unleashed upon the land to drive their enemies ahead of their arrival at a pace that would not leave the land desolate. This was to continue until their populations had grown enough to take possession of all the land.

To confirm the covenant, the Creator asked Moses to come up to him in the mountain including Aaron and two of his sons and seventy of the elders of Israel. To the Israelites, the glory of the Lord looked like a consuming fire on top of the mountain.

Into this, Moses, Aaron, and the seventy elders of Israel went up and saw a manifestation of the Creator similarly as he had revealed himself to Abraham, Isaac, and Jacob though each time in different ways that they could understand. In this manifestation, under the sound of his voice in the place was something like a pavement made of lapis lazuli as bright blue as the sky. Seeing this manifestation of the Creator in the thick darkness, they ate and drank in agreement to the covenant of abiding by his commandments and his lordship.

After the covenant, the elders were sent back down from the mountain, and they were asked to return with the rest of the people to the camp. Moses, on the other hand, was asked to come up to the Creator in the blackness on the mountain and stay there in order to receive tablets of stone with the complete law and commandments written on them by the finger of the Creator.

Moses received the written commandments and was also given the design of a tabernacle (ark) to be built comprising of a rectangular portable wooden box covered in gold that was to be set up inside a tent enclosure. This was to serve as a dedicated place that the Spirit of the Creator could meet with the people corporately. Inside the gold-plated box were to be placed the tablets of stone on which were written the commandments that the Creator gave the people. This set of stones were the covenant agreed on between the Creator, the people, and humanity at large. The large enclosure in which the Ark was placed in was referred to as the tabernacle of congregation. This is where the Spirit of the Creator was to meet with the people in the future after its construction.

Moses was made to understand that all judgment on humanity from the Creator will be based on this covenant because it was given to guide the social interactions between people and their relationship to the Creator. At this time, since the departure of Adam from the garden of Eden, the Spirit of the Creator did not dwell anymore in people, but he could visit, accompany, and dwell among them but not permanently in them. The ark and the tabernacle of congregation, therefore, served as the dedicated symbolic transit lodge of the Creator with instructions on how to handle it and prepare for meetings with his Spirit.

The order on how to formally interact with their Creator involved regular animal sacrifices which were to remind them of the ugliness of sin. It also served in pointing them to the Redeemer and how he intended to deal with the sin problem in order to restore humanity to where he could put his Spirit back into man.

Chapter 13

A Job More Daunting than the Creation of the Universe.

After the unprecedented meeting of the Creator with the children of Israel, Moses built the Ark exactly as he was instructed. After its completion, it was set up inside a portable tent (tabernacle) that was to serve as the place to house the ark when they were not travelling. As it was being dedicated, the pillar of cloud descended and covered the tabernacle, and his glory filled it in the form of the thickened cloud.

In all the travels of the Hebrews, whenever the cloud lifted from above the tabernacle, they would set out, but they stayed put if it did not lift. So it was that the cloud of the Lord was over the tabernacle by day, and fire was in the cloud by night, in the sight of all to see during all their travels. Nothing like this had ever been seen or heard of in the whole world, and it looked like the Creator was pulling off all the stops to reveal himself to this group of people, including the Canaanites and the rest of the world that watched.

However, the process of getting the engrained Egyptian pagan and immoral religious practices out of the Hebrews and getting them to walk trusting the Creator they could not see at will like idols turned out to be quite challenging to Moses and the Creator.

The pillar of cloud by day, pillar of fire by night, the daily provision of quail and manna, water out of dry rocks, shoes and clothes that never wore out but stayed in perfect condition, the absence of sickness among the people, battles against powerful enemies in which they prevailed supernaturally were among the tools the Creator used in the teaching process. All these were capped by the unprecedented manifestation of the Creator on Mount Sinai to the entire millions of the people, and yet only a few took the Creator at his word and were willing to walk before him as guided for their very own good.

The magnitude of unbelief and failure of the people to take the Creator at his word and trust that he meant everything he said was extraordinarily shocking, and it revealed the heart of man. Man apparently has a very ugly heart-and-mind disease that appears to be almost incorrigible and can be safely described as deceitful and desperately wicked.

While there were myriads of incidents that shocked even the angelic host and the devil, two of these incidents summarize the ugliness of the heart disease man possesses. One happened right after the Creator's appearance on Mount Sinai to the whole congregation. Moses had been asked to come up the mountain to receive the tablets of stone of the commandments written by the Creator himself as well as the design details of the ark and tabernacle.

When Moses stayed longer than they had expected, the people demanded that Aaron make them a golden calf (one of the gods of Egypt) to lead them on their journey. They made offerings to the calf and worshipped it with the traditional indecorous revelry associated with very unrestrained sexual perversion in direct disobedience and breaking of the covenant they had just made days before. Not even the devil, who happened to have passed by chance, saw this coming; and when he reported this to the other fallen angels, it sent them into a frenzy of celebratory acrobatic backflips of joy. This behavior was very difficult to explain rationally because during Moses's absence, they still received the daily miraculous supply of manna and quail, the pillar of cloud was present by day, and by night changed to a pillar of fire, implying the Creator was still with them.

The other happened when the Creator asked that Moses select a leader from each tribe for a total of twelve men. These men were to go into Canaan as spies to check out the land and see if it was as good as what he had promised them. The Creator wanted them to see firsthand how good and fertile the land was to encourage the people.

When the spies returned after forty days, the report they gave about the land was exceedingly good. As an example, it took two men to carry one cluster of grapes brought back with them on a pole. They had never seen produce the likes of it. However, ten of the twelve spies told the people that while the land was everything and much more than the Creator had said, there was a problem. They warned that there was no way they could get the land and occupy it because the current occupants were giants.

To make their point, they declared that they looked like grass-hoppers in the sight of the giants. They claimed that they were the equivalent of chopped liver to these giants and, therefore, had a snow-ball chance in hell of getting the land. Psychologically weakened, the people than cried out, weeping wildly, ready to stone Moses, and blaming the Creator for bringing them to become prey to the Canaanite slaughter machines. This, they claimed, would leave their children as unprotected orphans to be enslaved by the Canaanites after they had been slaughtered.

In just a matter of weeks, they had forgotten how they had been delivered from Pharaoh's elite killing machines without them even lifting a finger. This level of unbelief and faithlessness amid contin-ued miracles was just too much even for the longsuffering Creator. This was just one among very numerous incidents of unbelief and rebellion, and so the Creator had no choice but to pass judgment.

He then told Moses to inform the people that only those who were under the age of accountability, as determined by the Creator, were going to be allowed to enter the Promised Land. The rest of the rebellious adults were never going to go into the land. Therefore, a journey that should have taken them just a few weeks from Egypt to Canaan turned into forty years of wandering in the wilderness, with each year matching the forty days the spies were out spying the land of Canaan. All the adults were going to die in this forty-year window, and only then would they be allowed to go in.

During the forty years, the generation of adults that came out of Egypt and chose to rebel and weaken the hands of their children with unbelief in the Creator, with little or no regard for the corporate good and safety of others, all died off except for two men, Joshua, and Caleb. These two men wholeheartedly trusted the Creator and kept the covenant he had made with the people. Even Moses got into trouble with the Creator when he got angry at the people for their terrible unbelief and did something he was not supposed to have done.

The appointed festivals

The Creator, seeing the magnitude of work needed to keep the people's mind focused on the established covenant, decided to appoint festivals, which he declared as sacred assemblies, and told Moses to instruct the people about observing them. Knowing the attention span of man, these were to be observed to serve as a reminder to them of

- the story of what the Creator had done in their exodus from Egypt and travel to Canaan;
- the reality, ugliness, and destructive effects of sin, judgment, and forgiveness;
- the need of drawing the nation together for celebration and fellowship with the Creator;
- the importance and necessity of trusting the Creator in a treacherous and fallen world; and
- a very gentle but firm neon sign pointer to the coming Redeemer.

The festivals the Creator appointed were

- the Sabbath,
- the Passover and the Festival of Unleavened Bread,
- Offering the First Fruits,
- the Festival of Weeks,
- the Festival of Trumpets,
- the Day of Atonement,
- the Festival of Tabernacles.

After the forty years of wandering in the wilderness, when the last of the adults in the rebellious generation had died off, the Creator then commanded Moses to prepare for entry into the land of Canaan.

Moses's farewell and warning to the leaders

As Moses prepared the people to enter the Promised Land and for his death, he gathered them together to remind them of key aspects of what they were to expect of the Creator, what he was expecting of them, and why he was taking the land away from the Canaanites and giving it to them.

He warned them that when they entered the land, they were not to learn of or to imitate the evil and detestable ways of the nations there nor participate in the evil sacrifices of their live children in the fire, practices in divination or sorcery, interpretation of omens, engagement in witchcraft or casting of spells, participating in spiritism, or the practice of consultation of the dead. Anyone who did these things was to be an abomination to the Creator; it was because of these same human-degrading practices that resulted in perpetual violence in society that the Creator was driving out those nations before them.

They were reminded also to follow his decrees and to carefully obey the commands so that he would send them rain in its season and the ground would naturally be exceedingly productive, yielding its crops and the trees their fruit. They were promised to be able to eat all the food they wanted and to live in safety and peace in the land without fear of terror raids from the surrounding nations.

Wild beasts that were human predators were to be restrained from the land, and the sword of battle was going to be kept out of the country. Any enemies who choose to attack them were to fall by the sword before them as five of them would be able to chase a hundred, and a hundred of them will chase ten thousand of their enemies.

All in all, the Creator promised to look favorably on them and make them fruitful and increase their population, and he promised to honor his covenant with them. He promised to walk with and maintain his dwelling among them, whereby he would be their Lord and they his people.

However, if they failed to listen to him and carry out all his commands, which would result in violation of his covenant, thereby resulting in depravity and contemptible behavior toward each other as well as profaning the land, then he would bring judgment in the following ways:

He would bring on them sudden terror, allow wasting diseases in the forms of epidemics that will destroy their sight and sap their strength. They will plant seed in vain because their enemies will eat it, and they will be defeated by their enemies; those who hate them will rule over them, and they will flee even when no one was pursuing them.

If after all this they would not listen to him, he would make the sky above them like iron and the ground beneath them like bronze. Their strength will be spent in vain because the soil will not yield its crops, nor will the trees of their land yield their fruit naturally; they will toil to fertilize and irrigate for any significant yield.

If they stayed unrepentant, he would allow micro and macro beasts against them to reduce their numbers through the death of their cattle and children, thereby making the land desolate. If they still hardened themselves against correction, he was going to allow enemy nations to bring the sword on them, whereby they will be given into enemy hands. With their supply of food cut off, their food will be rationed and will be doled out by weight, whereby they will eat but will not be satisfied.

If despite this they continued to pursue evil ways, then he will be compelled to be hostile toward them, and he will punish them with famine in such a way that they will eat the flesh of their sons and the flesh of their daughters due to lack of food.

As a last act, to be fair to the expelled Canaanites, he will then scatter them among the nations and will draw out his sword and pursue them. Their land will be laid waste, and their cities will lie in ruins. As for those who will be left, he will make their hearts so fearful in the lands of their enemies that the sound of a windblown leaf will put them to flight. They will run and stumble over one another as though fleeing from the sword, even though no one is pursuing them, and they will not be able to stand before their enemies. They will perish among the nations, and the land of their enemies will devour them. Those of them who will be left will waste away in the lands of their enemies because of their sins.

The great antidote

Then Moses reminded them that the plans the Creator had for them were plans to protect and prosper them and not to harm them, plans to give them hope and a future. Therefore, when they found themselves in a fallen state and chose to call on him in prayer, he will listen to them; and if they were to seek him, they will find him when they did so with all their heart.

Moreover, when they ended up in the land of their enemies, he will remember his covenant with Abraham regarding the land. He will not reject them or abhor them to destroy them completely, but for Abraham's sake, he will remember the covenant with their ancestors whom he brought out of Egypt in the sight of the nations to be their Lord and the land he had promised and gave Abraham. They were, therefore, to remember that he is the Creator of the heavens and the earth.

Moses was then informed by the Creator to anoint Joshua before all the people so he could lead them into the Promised Land as their new leader. After his farewell, the Hebrews watched the transfer of authority after having informed them that they would be going into the Promised Land without him and that it was his time to meet the Creator.

Moses's great exit

In the hearing of all the elders, Moses was told to go up the mountain of Nebo to meet his Creator. So at 120 years of age, the elders and Joshua, in tears, walked with him to the foot of the mountain of Nebo. It was a heart-wrenching separation as the people wept openly, knowing it was the end of the road for the great prophet, the meekest human who ever walked the face of the earth; no wonder he was the greatest leader of any nation on earth. No other human other than Adam had been this close to the Creator in obedience and in communication.

He then went up alone to the top of Pisgah, from where the Creator showed him the Promised Land in its entirety. Moses then died there and the Creator buried him there in the land of Moab and no one knows where his grave is to this day. Joshua, Moses's servant, was now in charge as commanded by the Creator to lead the people into the Promised Land.

Never till now did any nation have such an intimate relationship with the Creator who spoke so clearly and made himself as accessible as a human could ever wish. For forty years, under the leadership of Moses, the Creator pulled all the stops to allow the current and future generations of humanity to see the difference between the living Creator and idols claimed to be gods.

Change of the guard—unto the land promised to Abraham

After the death of Moses, the servant of the Lord, the Lord said to Joshua, son of Nun, Moses's aide, "Moses my servant is dead. Now then, you and all these people, get ready to cross the Jordan River into the land I am about to give to the Israelites. I will give you every place where you set your foot, as I promised Moses. Your territory will extend from the desert to Lebanon and from the great river, the Euphrates, all the Hittite country to the Mediterranean Sea in the west. No one will be able to stand against you all the days of your life. As I was with Moses, so I will be with you. I will never leave you nor forsake you. Be strong and courageous because you will lead these people to inherit the land I swore to their ancestors to give them.

"However, you must be strong and very courageous to be very careful to obey all the law my servant Moses gave you. Do not turn from it to the right or to the left, for you to be successful wherever you go. Keep this book of the Law always on your lips. Meditate on it day and night so that you may be careful to do everything written in it. Then you will be prosperous and successful. Have I not commanded you? Be strong and courageous. Do not be afraid. Do not be discouraged, for the Lord your Creator will be with you wherever you go."

Joshua ordered the officers of the people, "Go through the camp and tell the people, 'Get your provisions ready. Three days from now, you will cross the Jordan here to go in and take possession of the land the Lord is giving you for your own.'" Joshua reminded the people of the faithfulness of the Creator in keeping his covenants and that their success depended on them keeping their end of the covenant by abiding by his laws Moses had given them.

As promised, the Creator needed all the people to know he was with Joshua just as he had been with Moses, starting with temporarily stopping the flow of the Jordan River at the height of the flood season to let them cross on dry ground, analogous to the splitting of the Red Sea when they left Egypt. If the people needed a moral and faith boost, this was it. This generation had not seen the likes of this, and they were fired up like never before.

When many of the nations saw and heard that the Creator had dried up a path on the Jordan River for them to walk across on dry ground as he did with the Red Sea, the Canaanites were thrown into a state of confusion and dread. When the impregnable city of Jericho fell decisively within a very short time, their dread was changed into panic and terror. It was up to them to flee the land and save their lives or fight to the death.

The creator adopts a daring prostitute

Prior to the fall of Jericho, the great city, a prostitute in the city who recognized that the Lord of the Hebrews was superior to all Canaanite gods, secretly and earnestly wished he was her Lord. Despite the bravado displayed by the military, the people's confidence and source of protection were really in the strength of the formidable city wall, a product of remarkable engineering ingenuity. However, for the prostitute, she believed that they did not stand a chance against that kind of power they had heard of and seen with respect to the Jordan River.

In fact, she considered the leaders of her nation incredibly stupid and profoundly ignorant in failing to understand the magnitude of that kind of power. The question that needed answering was, who could dam the great Jordan river at the height of the flood season with air, long enough for a great multitude of people to go across on dry ground, and then allow the water to start flowing after they had all crossed over? Could the walls they had stand up to that kind of power? It happened in Egypt years prior, and now right here in their own country.

Any idea that these stories were myths, was dispelled because it was happening right before them in real time. *Now that is the touch of unfeigned Deity*, she mused. "Oh, how I wish I belonged to him," she wailed quietly, wishing she could have an opportunity to speak her desire to this mighty and invisible Creator.

Upon hearing her quiet cry and desire, the Creator immediately called on Joshua and asked him to dispatch spies to go to Jericho with specific directions to a home that was located on a specific section of the wall. This was somewhat confusing to Joshua as to why the Creator needed him to do that and what purpose it served, for that matter. Unknown to him, the Creator had heard the solitary wail of the prostitute and he needed to deliver her, as was always his objective to those who believed and truly wanted his Lordship.

After the Hebrew spies entered the city, they made their way to the home in the exact location they were sent to, and it did not arouse any suspicion because of her profession. After a brief exchange with her, to her utter amazement, she realized that the Creator had heard her quiet request and had sent messengers specifically to prepare her for deliverance.

She was beyond herself in intoxicating and mind-shattering joy and awe. Seeing the graciousness and love of the Creator, she cautiously but boldly asked for a promise, with an oath in the name of the Lord of the Hebrews from the messengers, for the life of her entire family. Her request was accepted on the condition that everyone she wanted to be saved needed to be inside her home at the time of the battle. She was given a scarlet ribbon to tie to a window in the house as a pledge of the Creator's protection over everyone in her home.

The Hebrews were amazed at the faith displayed by the prostitute. Though the city was in a panic for fear of the Hebrews, she now knew that she and her parents, among other relatives, would be delivered from the impending doom, according to the word of the Creator; and she, in turn, pledged her allegiance to the Lord of the Hebrews and then helped the spies escape to safety from the Jericho military patrol units.

The Creator respected her faith, and she and her whole family were the only ones saved in the ensuing battle. She was so honored by the Creator in her conversion from a prostitute to a respectably married woman whom the Creator treated as any other Hebrew, and she became part of the bloodline of the promised Redeemer. The Creator had indeed promised to spare whether an individual or a whole nation that was willing to change from their wicked ways and walk with him. As a bonus, the Creator gave her a front-row seat to see his might, which she had come to believe was beyond human comprehension.

At the exact moment, just before the battle on the day of engagement, there was a long trumpet blast, followed by a great shout by the Hebrew soldiers. Then the unexpected happened; the great walls of Jericho fell flat to the ground, and the only piece of the wall that remained standing was the piece on which the prostitute's house was built. The spectacular collapse of the walls left the city totally discomfited and her family in awe of the Creator, and the words that she kept muttering as she dropped to her knees in reverence to her new invincible Lord were "He is indeed the Creator."

Some nations like the Gibeonites with wise leaders, who also decided that the Creator whom the Hebrews worshiped was above any god they were serving, had heard of or seen and were willing to abandon their own gods and serve him unconditionally. The Creator respected their wish and facilitated a simple peace alliance with the Hebrews, and the Gibeonites ended up being service providers to the house of worship of the Creator in the land. From that day, the Gibeonites came under the protective covering of the Creator, and he defended them just as the Hebrews and punished those who tried to hurt them.

In one of the greatest battles the Hebrews faced, an exceedingly large coalition force of a confederation of the powerful Canaanite kings decided to join forces and attack the Hebrews to stop their advance. These were some of the people the spies were afraid of, and in joining forces, they expected to rout the small ragtag Hebrew army that did not even have iron chariots and body armor. They were decimated and wiped out when the Creator got involved in the battle, and rocks were dropped from the sky like hail with more of the enemies destroyed by the rocks than the hapless Hebrew army. Here the Creator was telling them this was his fight and not theirs and that he was their defender and not a god who needed to be defended or fought for.

The others who decided to fight to the death were soundly defeated and destroyed by Joshua, and the nations were subdued, leaving just enough of the Canaanites to serve to train the new generation of the Israelites in warfare to keep them from being complacent and presumptuous in their relationship with their Lord.

Joshua's farewell to the leaders

Joshua allotted the conquered territories of land to the twelve tribes as had been instructed by Moses and the Creator. After a long time had passed and the Creator had given the Hebrews rest from all their enemies around them, Joshua, by then a very old man, summoned all the people, their elders, leaders, judges, and officials to him.

He reiterated the commands that Moses had given in his farewell speech to them and exhorted them to stay faithful to the covenant they had made with the Creator by obeying all that was written in the book of the Law of Moses without turning aside to the right or to the left. This was the condition for the Creator to maintain his protective covering over them and all that he had promised in the covenant. For as long as he lived, the people kept and obeyed the statutes; every promise the Creator had made in his covenant with them was kept. They lived in peace with the neighboring nations, the land had rain in its seasons, it was fertile, and they had food in abundance and no plagues or diseases. Life was really great.

After these things, Joshua, son of Nun, the servant of the Lord, died at the age of 110, and they buried him in the land of his inheritance, at Timnath Serah in the hill country of Ephraim, north of Mount Gaash.

The Hebrews kept and followed the statutes of the Creator throughout the lifetime of Joshua and of the elders who outlived him and who had experienced everything the Creator had done for them. And Joseph's bones, which they had brought up from Egypt, were buried at Shechem in the tract of land that Jacob bought for a hundred pieces of silver from the sons of Hamor, the father of Shechem.

Chapter 14

A Picture of Humanity and "Modern" Man?

After that whole generation that had walked with Joshua had died off, another generation grew up that had never experienced peril resulting from divine chastisement. They had lived in great comfort, abundance of food, wealth, and safety and therefore became presumptuous and forgot the Creator. They had assumed that they were feared by the surrounding nations because they were very powerful and skilled at fighting.

This new generation of the Israelites abandoned the covenant with the Creator and plunged into idolatry, culminating in serving Baal (a male divinity) and Ashtoreth (a female divinity) whereby they engaged in evil and abominable practices. With violence now spreading in the nation as a result of these detestable practices, the Creator had no choice but to not keep his end of the covenant as he had warned them.

He therefore gave them into the hands of raiders, who plundered them. He sold them into the hands of their enemies all around, whom they were no longer able to resist. Whenever Israel went out to fight, the hand of the Creator was against them to defeat them just as he had warned.

In the hands of their enemies, they were greatly oppressed and very distressed during which they cried out to him for deliverance. He heard their cries, and out of compassion, he gave them deliverers, who rescued them from the hand of their enemies. These deliverers came in the form of judges and prophets.

However, as soon as they were at rest, they went right back into their evil practices, resulting in the Lord abandoning them again to the hand of their enemies so that they ruled over them. And when they cried out again to him, he heard their cries and, in his compassion, delivered them time after time.

During these years, the Creator was no longer considered by the Canaanites as a threat because it was difficult to tell the difference between a Hebrew and a Canaanite since the Hebrews participated in idol worship and the abominable practices the Canaanites were known for. And so continued this vicious cycle over a period of about 410 years till a prophet called Samuel was raised by the Creator among the people, a man who had decided he was going to serve the Creator from his youth, and that is the kind of heart the Creator had been searching for.

Turning point

The Hebrew festivals were now almost meaningless rituals so much so that even the Creator was disgusted by them. During this time, the priest Eli had two sons who ministered in the priestly office, and Eli was quite old now and had no control over his sons. The two sons who officiated the sacrifices and priestly office had become so profane that they gave very little regard to the strict protocols Moses had instituted in the law the Creator gave them. They went as far as sexually assaulting vulnerable women who came in for counsel regarding questions about the law and the covenant of the Lord.

There was a woman called Hannah who had been in great distress by reason of incessant taunts from her husband's other wife because she was barren. One day, while at the temple during one of the festivals, she remembered the greatness of the Creator and how he had dealt with Abraham and Isaac. She decided to challenge him at the end of one of the festivals. She prayed and asked the Creator for a son; in turn, she promised that if he did answer her prayer, she would dedicate the child back to him, and he would serve the Creator for the rest of his life.

The Creator answered her prayer and gave her a son whom she named Samuel, and after she weaned him, she took him to the house of the Lord where he was raised by Eli the priest and was taught the ways of the Lord and the written law of Moses. She paid him regular visits with articles of clothing and other items of affection and the boy grew up and had reverential fear and love for the Creator. The Lord loved the boy and gave his mother more children as a reward for trusting him and being willing to unconditionally sacrifice the one thing she desired above all else in her life. The Creator started guiding his heart at a very early age, seeing he was inclined to know him and follow him wholeheartedly.

It was not very long before all Israel noticed that the young Samuel was a true prophet as he started serving the priest. One was considered a true prophet of the Lord if his prophecies were accurate and in line with the law of Moses. He was given a prophecy to Eli, the priest then, about the annihilation of his family for dishonoring the priestly office. Everyone could tell the Spirit of the Lord operated on him and his prophecies were deadly accurate and this made the people fear him greatly.

The Philistines capture the ark

The Creator had decided that he now had a willing and obedient servant, and it was time he changed the guard and, hopefully, the direction of the nation.

Now the Israelites went out to fight against the powerful Philistines during a period of rebellion and, therefore, no longer under the protective covering of the Creator. The Israelites camped at Ebenezer and the Philistines at Aphek. The Philistines deployed their forces to meet Israel, and as the battle spread, Israel was defeated by the Philistines, who killed about four thousand of them on the battlefield.

When the hapless soldiers returned to camp, the elders of Israel started questioning why the Lord had brought defeat on them that day before the Philistines. In seeing that the young prophet Samuel was beginning to speak the mind of the Creator to them, they assumed he was obligated to protect them.

It was clear to them that they could not physically defeat the Philistines and, therefore, feared that the outcome of the battle will not turn out in their favor. They then decided to bring the ark of the covenant into battle in order to force the hand of the Creator to save them from their enemies; this had never been done before.

The people, therefore, who had failed to keep their end of the covenant, sent for the ark of the covenant of the Lord to be brought to the battlefield; and when the Priest's two rebellious sons, Hophni and Phinehas, entered the camp with the ark, all Israel raised such a great shout that the ground shook.

Hearing the uproar, the Philistines asked what all the shouting in the Hebrew camp was about. When they learned that the ark of the Lord had come into the camp, the Philistines were afraid, remembering their historical encounters and what happened in Egypt. However, they were encouraged when they were reminded that morally the Hebrews were no better as they seemed to worship some of the idols they worshipped. They also considered the fact that the Hebrews were currently subject to them, implying they had the upper hand. Encouraged by this, they set their battle lines.

On the other side, the great shout and self-motivation was void of any power. They were not backed by the Lord, and all they had were two rebels bearing the ark of the covenant, something they had not been keeping.

With battle lines set, they then engaged each other and the Israelites were soundly defeated and those left alive fled to their tents. The slaughter was very great indeed, for Israel lost thirty-thousand foot soldiers; and to make matters worse, the ark of the covenant was captured and Eli's two sons, Hophni and Phinehas, were also slaughtered by the Philistines.

That same day, a man ran from the battle line and went to Shiloh with his clothes torn and dust on his head. When he arrived, there was Eli the priest sitting on his chair by the side of the road, watching, because his heart feared for the ark. When the man entered the town and told what had happened, the whole town sent up a bitter cry. Eli heard the outcry and asked what the meaning of the uproar was.

He then told him that Israel had fled before the Philistines; the army had suffered heavy losses; his two sons, Hophni and Phinehas, were dead; and the ark of the covenant had been captured. When he mentioned the capture of the ark, Eli fell backward off his chair by the side of the gate and broke his neck, and he died, for he was an old man, and he was excessively fat and heavy. He had led Israel forty years.

The land of the Philistines encounters the ark up close

After the Philistines had captured the ark, they took it from battlefield to Ashdod. It was easy to handle because it was attached to poles that made it easy to carry without touching the ark itself. Then they carried the ark by its poles into Dagon's temple and set it beside Dagon, the revered idol god of the Philistines. This was no usual accomplishment; to have been able to capture and be in possession of the ark of the Hebrews was one for the books.

However, when the people of Ashdod rose early the next day, there was Dagon, fallen on his face on the ground before the ark of the Lord! They took Dagon and put him back in his place with plans to show off the great spoil to the Philistine people.

But the following morning when they rose, there was Dagon, fallen on his face on the ground before the ark in a very unbecoming posture for a great god! His head and hands had been broken off and were lying on the threshold; only his body remained. It was obvious that this was no accident, and it made the priests of Dagon very nervous and concerned. The reason for that is because a regular fall could not break him up due to the materials that had been used to make it; it had to be something beyond known architectural technology then known.

Then the Creator decided to give the Philistines an opportunity to know him better and see him up close and personal. Therefore, he brought devastation on them and afflicted them with an explosion of very ugly ulcerating tumors, hemorrhoids, and a bad plague of rats that appeared out of nowhere in Ashdod and its vicinity. The planned celebrations for the capture of the ark turned into unbridled destruction of the revelers.

When the people of Ashdod saw what was happening, they cried out and demanded that the ark be taken away because the hand of the Hebrew Lord was heavy on them and on Dagon, their god. So they called together all the rulers of the Philistines and asked them what they should do with the ark, and it was decided to have it moved to Gath.

But after they had moved it, the Lord's hand was against that city, and the same fate as Ashdod fell on Gath on both the young and old, throwing it into a great panic. So they sent the ark off to Ekron. As the ark was entering Ekron, the people of Ekron cried out, saying that the ark was going to kill them as well. So they called together all the rulers of the Philistines and pleaded with them to send the ark away. They preferred sending it back to its own place before they were all killed because there was no letup in the destruction, for death had joined the plagues, and every city was now in panic and turmoil.

The Creator fights his own battles

When the ark of the Lord had been in Philistine territory seven months, the time was marked by carnage they had never experienced and did not even know what to do. The cry of the Philistines had reached the Creator, and he decided to give them a break. This was because they had had a chance to experience his power and their acknowledgment of their inability to survive the presence of ark and the Lord of the Hebrews while asking for mercy for their god.

So when they finally called for their wise men, the priests and the diviners and asked them what they should do for the Lord's hand to be lifted from them, they recommended the following actions:

- Send the ark of the Lord back with a gift offering comprising of five gold tumors and five gold rats, according to the number of the Philistine rulers, because the same plague had stricken both the people and their rulers.

- Make models of the tumors and of the rats that were destroying the country and give glory to the Creator. Perhaps he would lift his hand from them and their gods and their land.
- They were warned not to harden their hearts as the Egyptians and Pharaoh did when Israel's Lord dealt harshly with them, resulting in they letting go of the Hebrews after unprecedented destruction of their land.
- They recommended getting a new cart ready with two cows that had calved and had never been yoked and to hitch the cows to the cart but take their calves away and pen them up.
- They were to take the ark and put it on the cart and in a chest beside it to put the gold objects they needed to send back to him as a guilt offering. They were to send it on its way but keep watching it. If it went up to its own territory, toward Beth Shemesh, then the Lord had brought this great disaster on them. But if it did not, then they will know that it was not his hand that struck them but that it happened to them by chance.

Following the counsel of the wise men, they placed the ark of the Lord on the cart along with it the chest containing the gold rats and the models of the tumors. Then the cows went straight up toward Beth Shemesh, keeping on the road and lowing all the way; they did not turn to the right or to the left. The rulers of the Philistines followed them as far as the border of Beth Shemesh. This confirmed to the Philistines that it was the hand of the Creator that had unleashed the punishment.

Now the people of Beth Shemesh were harvesting their wheat in the valley, and when they looked up and saw the ark, they rejoiced at the sight. The cart came to the field of Joshua of Beth Shemesh, and there it stopped beside a large rock. The people chopped up the wood of the cart and sacrificed the cows as a burnt offering to the Lord with great joy and amazement.

The Levites took down the ark together with the chest containing the gold objects and placed them on the large rock. On that day, the people of Beth Shemesh offered burnt offerings and made sacrifices to the Lord. The five rulers of the Philistines saw all this and then returned that same day to Ekron. These are the gold tumors the Philistines sent as a guilt offering to the Lord, one each for Ashdod, Gaza, Ashkelon, Gath, and Ekron.

And so the Creator gave the Philistines a chance to see him as the living Lord and his power and to let them know their gods were no match to him and that he had the power of life and death. He sent back his ark to Israel and let Israel understand that he did not need them to accomplish his purposes if they chose not to participate as he had previously covenanted with them.

So continued the confirmation that renewing the heart of man and having him see, believe, and trust in the Creator for who he is and even his very existence was far more daunting than the creation of the universe. The propensity for the love of evil in man's heart and its deceitfulness was just overwhelming, and so it was that men love evil even to their own destruction. No group of people so clearly epitomized the heart of humans everywhere on earth like these Hebrews.

Samuel the prophet and judge

With Samuel the prophet now in charge of mediating between the Creator and the children of Israel in the priestly office, order was restored. This was accomplished by leading the entire nation in a national repentance and a return to obedience to the Creator's statutes. He made the Hebrews put an end to the worship of the foreign idol gods, put away the foreign gods, and return to the worship of the Creator. When they did this, thereby fulfilling their end of the covenant, the Lord restored the protective covering he had promised them, and the menacing Philistines were subdued. Under his watch and directions, peace was restored in the land, just as he had promised them in his covenant. Life was great in the land under the leadership of Samuel during his entire tenure as prophet and judge.

In the later years of Samuel, after having enjoyed a long period of peace and stability, the people of Israel returned to their old ways. The elders came to him and informed him that since he was now old, they wanted him to now appoint a king to lead them just like the other nations. Among other reasons they gave, they wanted a king, their champion, to march ahead of the army into battle in pomp and style, and they were not willing to budge on that request.

They could have asked for another prophet or another faithful judge, but rather, they asked for a king other than the Creator who led and protected them all this while. It was evident though that they clearly wanted a relationship with the Creator, but on their terms and a loose lifestyle with loose moral constraints, where there was no accountability, the prelude to perversion. They believed they were now strong enough to depend on their own abilities and did not have to depend on the Creator.

Therefore, when they asked Samuel to give them a king to lead them, he could see its was a request that was headed in the wrong direction with inevitable undesirable outcomes. He went and prayed to the Lord about the request, and he was told to listen to all that the people were saying and that it was he, the Creator, whom they were rejecting as their king and to grant them their wish.

Before granting them the king, the Creator asked Samuel to solemnly warn them what the king who will reign over them will claim as his rights, and Samuel went to the people and said, as instructed,

> This is what the king who will reign over you will claim as his rights: He will take your sons and make them serve with his chariots and horses, and serve as his personal security detail. Some he will assign to be commanders of thousands and commanders of fifties, and others to plow his ground and reap his harvest. Others he will assign to make weapons of war and equipment for his transportation. He will take your daugh-

ters to be perfumers and cooks and bakers. He will take the best of your fields and vineyards and olive groves and give them to those serving his interests and attendants.

He will levy a tax of at least a tenth of your crops, cattle and of your vintage to support his officials and attendants. Your male and female servants and the best of your cattle and donkeys he will take for his own use and eventually you yourselves will become his slaves. When that day comes, you will cry out for relief from the king you have chosen, decrying his taxation and the burdens, but the Lord will not answer you in that day.

But the people refused to listen to Samuel. "No!" they said. "We want a king over us. Then we will be like all the other nations, with a king to lead us and to go out before us and fight our battles."

With that declaration, Samuel then sent the people and leaders back home to their own towns with the promise to attend to their request after consulting the Creator.

Then the Lord, heeding to their demand, sent Samuel to anoint the tallest and probably the most valiant man they had in the nation, who happened to be quite handsome and looked like he was a born warrior. He was chosen by the Creator himself based on the kind of personality the people had asked for, and he became Israel's first king. The Creator, as gracious as always, provided the king with spiritual guidance through the written law of Moses, Samuel, and other prophets, dreams, visions, and the priests. He was surrounded by a spiritual cloud and a special anointing of the Spirit of the Creator identical to what he gave the prophets. It was entirely up to him whether he wanted the Creator's guidance or not, but the Creator was obligated to give him access to himself, being the leader of his people.

Unfortunately for Israel, not only did Saul, their first king, exercise the rights Samuel had warned them about, but he decided to establish the monarchy on his own terms, with him deciding on his successor. He chose to obey the Creator only when it was favorable to him and relied more on his own ability than divine guidance. His failure to fully trust and depend on the guidance of the Creator resulted in embarrassing battle outcomes for the Hebrews against their enemies.

In the most memorable battle in the history of the Hebrews against one of their greatest nemeses, their choice of leadership was brought full circle to them on a platinum platter. At this point in his kingship, the Hebrews had slipped so far from the Creator to the point where he was hardly consulted for anything by the king. And then it happened.

The mighty Philistines challenged king Saul and Israel, and battle lines were drawn. Then Goliath, a Philistine giant from Gath, showed up to lead his army against the Hebrew soldiers, who took one look at him and fled for their lives in sheer terror at the size of the man. He was not just an ordinary giant, but he was a great and established champion in the land of the Philistines.

He was about 9.6 feet tall (2.9 meters). He had a bronze helmet on his head and wore a coat of scale armor of bronze weighing 125 pounds (57 kilograms), and on his legs, he wore bronze greaves, and a bronze javelin was slung on his back. The shaft of his spear was about 8 feet (2.6 meters), and its iron point weighed 15 pounds (6.8 kilograms). He was a formidable fighting machine, and no wonder why all Israel fled from him. To make matters worse, he had four other brothers who were all giants. Apparently, in asking for a human king leader, the Hebrews forgot that there were giants among the Philistines.

At a very embarrassing moment, King Saul ran into this Philistine champion, who was much taller, bigger, and clearly more powerful than him, and Saul fled for his life and would not dare face him.

When Goliath saw that Israel was afraid to fight, he then offered them a deal to avoid full-fledged fighting. He asked Saul to either come over himself or send over anyone to fight him, one on one, and whichever side lost, that nation will serve the winning nation.

For forty days he begged and taunted Israel to send a man, but none would dare go, for it was humanly impossible for anyone in Israel to defeat him. He then proceeded to mock even the Lord of Israel to the hilarious laughter of the Philistine soldiers.

Then a Hebrew youth who had gone to deliver food at the battle lines happened to hear the giant mock the Creator and, remembering the stories of the glory days when he led Israel, accepted the giant's challenge in the name of the Lord of Israel.

Saul, in an even more embarrassing and shameful display of his cowardice and lack of faith, volunteered the midteenage kid to face the formidable giant. The young man, David, faced him one on one and, knowing he had called out to the Creator in faith, charged and cut down the dreaded and fully armored giant with a slingshot targeted and sunk into the exposed portion of his forehead.

The boy had been taught at home, knew, and believed there was no one like the Creator the nation had always depended on. This was déjà vu for the Philistines as they once again saw the hand of the Hebrew Lord revived. Fled they did when the giant, who led them, was slain with a slingshot by a kid and his head cut off with his own sword. They were cut down and decimated by the ragtag Israelite army, who pursued them as they fled.

On that day, the Hebrews were reminded of the Creator they served as the youth stood on the promise that no battle was won by might or power but by the Spirit of the Creator, which is why he had not been intimidated by the giant.

This miraculous victory in the name of the Lord did not steer Saul in any way back to the Creator. Instead, it created a heart of jealousy toward David. Despite repeated unheeded warnings from the Creator through the prophet Samuel to Saul, he persisted in his disobedience toward the Creator. As a result of disobedience to specific instructions and the hurt of the nation at large, the Creator then decided to end his spiritual guidance to Saul. He also withdrew his protective covering over the nation, thereby allowing the pesky Philistines to wage war again against Israel, having sensed vulnerability in Saul's military ranks.

Part of this was evident in that Saul spent a great amount of his time and resources all over the country trying to kill David, the young man who happened to greatly love the Creator.

In killing Goliath, David established a reputation for himself with a following of a formidable group of warriors. His loyalty to king Saul was unwavering, and he served him in whatever capacity the king requested and was successful in whatever assignment the king gave him.

Based on the stories passed down about his ancestors, he believed he could trust the Creator in complete abandon especially after taking down the formidable Goliath with just a slingshot. Now he knew he could completely rely on the protective covering the nation had enjoyed under the covenant the Creator had with the nation, despite his youth, and that meant living by the statutes Moses had passed down.

He was an admirer of Joseph, whose commitment and faithfulness to the Creator saved the nation of Israel in its formative years in Egypt. Despite his successes, his loyalty to Saul had never wavered, and he never challenged or usurped Saul's authority in any way to the very end.

What Saul feared the most was that David trusted the Creator and was loyal and he feared that David was likely going to be the next king and the only way to stop it was for him to kill David. With David under divine protection, that was an impossible task. When the Creator saw that Saul would not turn to him in repentance or guidance but continued leading the nation down a self-destructive path, he asked Samuel to secretly anoint David to be the next king of Israel. Most importantly of all, David loved and trusted the Lord and had set his mind to walk righteously before him. That was the qualification the Creator needed for his choice of a king—one who would execute justice in righteousness as a leader and lead by example in a walk of righteousness.

A sad exit (about 1007 BC)

Again, with the protective covering around the king and the nation withdrawn, the Philistines laid out battle lines for the mother of wars against Israel. King Saul had some serious problems to contend with, one being that he had ran David out of the country; Samuel had died; and the Creator no longer talked to him either through the prophets or dreams especially after he slaughtered priests whom he felt were disloyal to him.

Upon coming to grips with the reality of his peril and dread of the prancing Philistine slaughter machine, his heart melted. King Saul, seeing the array of the formidable army, tried calling on the Creator out of desperation. Instead of crying to him in repentance and asking for forgiveness for his insubordination, the night before the great battle, he rather sought for sorcerers to get help from the spirit world. This was a practice condemned and forbidden by the Creator; it did not help, so he now had to face the battle without the divine protection he had rejected.

Saul had no choice but to fight the Philistines and, without the privileged divine anointing, looked like a grasshopper on concrete caught in a rainstorm laced with hailstones. His valiant sons and the soldiers of Israel who followed the king they had asked for, who no longer had the Creator's backing because of his rebellion, were all slaughtered like helpless sheep without a shepherd by the Philistines. And so ended the reign of Israel's first designer king demanded by the people.

1055 BC—David becomes King (biblical timeline poster)

In the interim, out of mercy and faithfulness to his covenant, the Creator had chosen himself a king, one everyone knew was a man of very good character. King David, who had defeated the giant as a midteenager, brought Israel together and under the Creator's protective canopy and proper fellowship with him. His faith in the Creator and his righteous leadership was eventually described by the Creator as a benchmark for acceptable kingly leadership in the nation because he was a man after the Creator's heart who executed righteous judgment over the people.

After he had been fully established as king in about 1055 BC, through him the Philistines and all the other hostile neighboring nations were subdued, and Israel flourished and prospered the way the Creator had intended for them. He then set his sight in building a temple to serve as a permanent residence for the ark of the covenant. Till this time, it was still housed in the tabernacle, a foldable tent in the town of Shiloh. This temple was to be built in Jerusalem so the nation could have the appropriate worship center in which the Ark of the covenant could be situated permanently, and they could have national corporate fellowship with the Creator.

The Creator accepted the offer of building a temple for the ark but deferred the construction to his son Solomon. However, he was rewarded with the distinctive honor of being a direct ancestor of the Creator's promised Redeemer for the redemption of humanity, whom he had revealed to Jacob, that he will be in the ancestral line of Judah.

After the death of David, his son Solomon, endowed with extraordinary wisdom, built the temple for the ark of the covenant in Jerusalem. During the dedication, the Creator promised to establish Jerusalem as his symbolic permanent residential capital on earth; it served as the center of worship for the nation.

Solomon maintained the greatness of Israel for a while until his international political alliances got the best of him. He made treaties with nations, married wives who were idol worshippers who subsequently led to a return to their old ways of idolatry and rebellion against the Creator. When this happened, their enemies were allowed to invade their land, starting with the reign of King Solomon's son when the nation was split into a northern and southern kingdom. In the center of this split was whether to worship the Creator and keep his statutes with the nation's capital at Jerusalem or the Canaanite idols with the capital at Samaria.

During the reign of the kings, analogous to the reign of the judges, both good and bad kings, the Creator continued to provide many prophets who delivered continued and special warnings to the people and the kings and served as spiritual watchmen for the nation. The nation prospered and lived in peace when the king kept the covenant, but they suffered when they rejected and failed to keep the covenant. And so continued the same vicious cycle of their relationship with the Creator. No nation on earth had ever been so close to the Creator, a relationship he desires with the whole world.

The sad truth was that the nation he had hoped to be a model for the whole world only tended to call on him when they were in trouble but turned their backs on him when they lived in prosperity, quickly forgetting who made them prosperous.

At a very low point in the history of the kings of the nation, one of the very bad and spiritually dark times in the greater Israel was ruled by king Ahab, son of Omri. He was described as the one king who did more evil in the eyes of the Creator than any of the kings before him. He not only considered it trivial to commit the abominable sins of his predecessors, but he also married Jezebel, daughter of Ethbaal, king of the Sidonians, who were ardent idol worshippers of a god called Baal. He set up an altar for Baal, the idol god, in the temple of Baal that he built in Samaria as well as an Asherah pole, another idol goddess. The position of Baal in Israel was now officially far higher than that of the Creator, forcing the Creator's hand into action as the moral and spiritual decline of the people eclipsed the land.

867 BC—Reawakening

So it happened that in about 867 BC, one of the Creator's prominent prophets, Elijah the Tishbite, was sent by him to confront King Ahab with a message to tell the king that there will be neither dew nor rain in the next few years except at his word, when commanded by the Creator. He left after proclaiming the drought that was to ensue and fled from the presence of the king. This resulted in a punishing drought that caused severe famine in the land. There wasn't even enough grass to support livestock, and there was death everywhere.

By the third year, with the land in dire straits, the Creator sent Elijah to go and present himself to Ahab so that he could send rain on the land and end the drought.

When Ahab saw Elijah, he blamed him for the drought; and he, in turn, blamed Ahab because he and his family had abandoned the Creator's statutes and was now serving Baal. He therefore asked Ahab to summon the people from all over Israel to meet him on Mount Carmel and to bring along the 850 prophets of the idol gods whose chief administrator was Jezebel, Ahab's wife. They both agreed in the presence of the king's officials that this was an opportunity and the time to settle the spiritual leadership matter before the people.

The claimed divine called out to prove themselves on Mount Carmel

Seeing this opportunity to settle scores with Elijah, while he had him within sight, Ahab sent word throughout all Israel and assembled the prophets on Mount Carmel as requested by Elijah.

Elijah went before the people and asked them how long they were willing to waiver between two opinions; he wanted them to follow and serve Baal if he was the true God or just some lifeless and powerless idol. On the other hand, was it the one who had brought them from bondage in Egypt and had given them the land they now dwelled in? All he was offering was to put both to a simple test. Hearing this challenge, the people said nothing, some being afraid to express their opinions for fear of unfavorable political reprisals and the others just no longer sure of who was the right Lord of the land.

Then Elijah proposed that the 850 prophets of Baal and Ashtoreth be given one bull and he one bull as well. Each party was to cut up the bull and prepare it for an offering by fire on an altar; however, they were not to set fire to the offering. Each party was to pray and call out to their god and let the god answer by sending fire to consume the offering. The god who answered by fire would be the true God, and they were to serve and worship him.

The Creator, in his mercy, desired just to bring his people home and deliver them from the self-destructive and detestable practices the idol worship subjected them to. He guided Elijah to make this offer that did not put anyone in harm's way and make the outcome obvious, fair, and just so there would be no confusion of any sort.

Then all the people agreed that it was a very fair request. Elijah then asked the prophets of Baal to choose one of the bulls and prepare it first since they were many. He asked them to call on the name of their gods but warned them to not light the fire themselves but leave it to their gods to do it.

They then took the bull given them and prepared it, laid it out on the alter, and then called on the name of Baal, praying and chanting from morning till noon. "Baal, answer us!" they shouted. But there was no response, and they danced around the altar they had made for hours with nothing happening. At noon, Elijah began to taunt them. "Shout louder!" he said. "Surely he is a god! Perhaps he is deep in thought or busy or traveling. Maybe he is sleeping and must be awakened."

So they shouted louder and slashed themselves with swords and spears, as was their custom, until their blood flowed. Midday passed, and they continued their frantic prophesying until the time for the evening sacrifice. But there was no response, no one answered, no one paid attention as the people, including the king, stood by and watched. As evening came, the exhausted, bleeding, and weeping prophets were then ushered to the side, weeping because Baal had not answered their call. They looked like people who were sincere but terribly wrong, and a bunch never looked so wretched and pitiful. Many who had been born and raised as Baal worshippers could not understand why he did not respond, and they wept in dismay.

Then Elijah set up his altar, using twelve stones, one for each of the tribes of Israel, and then dug a large trench around it. He arranged the wood, cut the bull into pieces, and laid it on the wood.

Then he asked the people to fill four large jars with water and pour it on the offering and on the wood. He asked them to do it three times until the water ran down around the altar and even filled the trench. Then he stepped forward and prayed, "The sovereign Lord of Abraham, Isaac, and Israel, the creator of the heavens and the earth, let it be known today that you are Lord in Israel and that I am your servant and have done all these things at your command.

Answer me, Lord, answer me, so these people will know that you are their Lord and leader and that you are turning their hearts back again." At the end of the very simple prayer, the fire of the Lord fell and burned up the sacrifice, the wood, the stones, the soil, and licked up the water in the trench.

When all the people saw this, they fell prostrate and cried, "The Lord, he is God! The Lord, he is God!" as they were reminded of past stories about their Lord. Many wept for joy as they remembered stories of good kings who had been obedient to the Creator and the people had seen great and prosperous times and lived in safety even though surrounded by enemies.

Then Elijah commanded them to seize the prophets of Baal who had been misleading the people, and he had them brought down to the Kishon where they were punished according to the law to which even the king consented.

And so on that day, the Creator reminded the people who was the true Lord and gave them the opportunity to turn back to him so he could take care of them as in the past. And to make his point, he sent rain on the same day to bring an end to the drought. Many went home happy, singing in the beautiful life-giving rain to see the hand of the Creator back in their lives. King Ahab, despite witnessing a remarkable trigger to a spiritual revival, did not take it to heart, instead focused on describing to his wife about the punishment meted out to her prophets. She in turn sent the prophet Elijah a message promising the same punishment to him to be sanctioned by her.

And so it was that over the hundreds of years of different kings, the Creator worked closely with the ones who invited him in their reign, thereby blessing the people, or left them to their own devices when the kings chose not to get him involved.

During the reign of these kings, he sent many prophets with messages about the coming Redeemer with a lot of additional details. This included confirmation of his ancestral lineage, his conception and birth by a virgin girl, exact place and time of birth, the exact date of the start of his ministry, the nature of his ministry, his rejection by the nation's leaders, his betrayal and the nature of his death, his resurrection and ascension, and a myriad of other things describing his life.

These prophecies were given across hundreds of years by different prophets to ensure that there will not be any confusion in identifying him when he appeared on the scene since he was to come as a human. The details became clearer as the time drew closer. This being the greatest event on planet earth after creation of the universe, and knowing the nature of the fallen man, the Creator wanted the whole world to know who the Redeemer was and to easily identify him. He had ensured that there was good written record keeping, advances in science and knowledge, and therefore easy for man to understand the significance of the advent of the Redeemer.

Accurately identifying him was crucial for the entire humanity. That knowledge had implications on the quality of human life of the living and as well as to allow humanity to decide whether to spend eternity with the Creator or away from him after they die, and for such high stakes, the Creator pulled off all the stops.

The decision by the Creator in sending the Redeemer as a human instead of as an angel or some form of another being was significant. The critical decision in having him come as a simple human was to give humanity a chance to relate to him and see him do things impossible by an ordinary human especially power over man's biggest problem—physical death.

In effect, a human who had full control of all the laws of nature had to be whoever he claimed to be because only the one who created nature could control it at will by a word. In addition, there is nothing less intimidating than a helpless newborn baby. The Creator had decided he had to go as low as humanly possible so man would not be intimidated in any way. The love the Creator has for man is beyond human comprehension, and it is a great marvel to the angels in heaven and even Satan's demonic host of fallen angels.

854 BC—another Syrian opportunity

Being stuck with a continuously rebellious people led by rebellious kings, in order to keep his promise to Abraham, the Creator continued to look for opportunities to bring his people and the neighboring nations to a better knowledge of him. And so it was that in about 854 BC, the great and brilliant Syrian general, commander of the king's army, had distinguished himself in the field and in loyalty to his master, the king of Aram. He was a valiant soldier, very wealthy from his share of the loot brought back from the many successful battles; and so he was highly regarded, and the king trusted him with his life.

Some of these battles had been against Israel during periods when the Creator had lifted the protective covering over the nation. In one of those battles, they carried away captives back into Syria from Israel. In effect, the Creator was using Syria at this point to chastise Israel and wake them up from their fallen state and was using the tools that usually got the attention of the people and its king as well as an opportunity to reach the Assyrians.

In public, the general was a Syrian symbol of might; but at home during his bath, he and his family knew he was living on borrowed time. He had leprosy, and as far as he knew, it was incurable, and none of the Syrian physicians or gods of all the neighboring nations could do anything about it. He was a dead man walking.

A little Jewish captive whom the general had brought home from one of the raids found the general to be a very pleasant and compassionate man, though very proud, and she loved him. She saw that he went through periods of depression often, and so during one of those occasions, she mentioned to her mistress that if her master would see the prophet who was in Samaria, he would cure him of his leprosy.

Word got to the general, and after some reflection, he remembered that the Lord of Israel had a track record and usually punished Israel when they strayed from his statutes. At this time, the Syrian army was much stronger and could attack Israel at will and indeed had control over Israel. The general, seeing that he had nothing to lose, therefore decided to give the Lord of Israel a try, and he communicated this to his master the king.

The king, on his part, decided to make this official and demanded the healing as an official and diplomatic request, and so he asked his general to go accompanied by a letter to the king of Israel. So Naaman left, taking with him 750 pounds of silver, 150 pounds of gold, and ten sets of very expensive clothing of exquisite beauty. The letter that he took to the king of Israel read,

> With this letter I am sending my servant Naaman
> to you so that you may cure him of his leprosy.

When Naaman arrived at the palace, he presented the letter to the king. As soon as the king of Israel read the letter in his private chamber, he tore his robes in dismay and said, "Am I the Creator? Can I kill and bring back to life? Why does this fellow send someone to me to be cured of his leprosy? See how he is trying to pick a quarrel and another unprovoked war with me!"

When Elisha the Creator's prophet heard that the king of Israel had torn his robes, he prayed about the situation to the Creator, and after receiving instructions from him, he sent the king this message:

> Why have you torn your robes? Have the man
> come to me, and he will know that there is a
> prophet of the true Creator of the heavens and
> the earth in Israel.

With great relief, the king sent Naaman to Elisha the prophet. So the great general proceeded with his entourage and chariots, which came to a stop at the door of Elisha's house. It was a big and impressive entourage.

Per the specific instructions from the Creator, Elisha the prophet stayed inside the house but sent a messenger to him with a very simple statement and command that said,

> Go dip yourself seven times in the Jordan River
> and your flesh will be healed and you will be
> cleansed of your leprosy.

But Naaman was furious and stormed away very angry, saying, "I thought that he would surely come out of the house to me and stand and call on the name of the Lord, wave his hand over the infection, and cure me of my leprosy. Are not the rivers of Damascus better than all the waters of Israel? Couldn't I wash in them and be cleansed?" So he turned and stormed off in a red-faced rage and embarrassment.

However, his servants were a little more familiar with the ways of the Lord of Israel because most of the time when he did things, it was always above human explanation and comprehension. They knew how often he had done things to the Assyrians that were still in their history books that could not be explained. He was like no other god, and so with some very gentle but firm and respectful persuasion, they succeeded in persuading him to do as the prophet had instructed.

So, somewhat reluctantly, he went down to the Jordan River, stripped off his military outfit, and started dipping himself while they counted. After each dip, he checked his body to see if the leprosy was gone, and up to the count of six, there was absolutely no change.

He had expected to see a decrease in the size of the disease during every count, but absolutely nothing visible happened when he checked. Fuming and shaking with anger, he decided he might as well finish making a complete fool of himself and dipped in for the full count. As he rose out of the water after the seventh dip, as Elisha the prophet had told him, as they all looked at his body, his flesh was restored and became clean like that of a young baby.

Members of his entourage hugged each other in great joy and relief but also of fear of the power behind the healing, and they felt as though they were on holy ground and needed to tread carefully. They had never seen anything like it ever!

He stood there, stunned for a while, to allow the whole thing to sink in. Fortunately for him, the tears running down his cheeks were masked by the dripping water, but the emotional heaving of his hairy chest gave him away. In utter amazement, his head bowed low, he dressed up, and he and all his attendants went back to the house of the prophet. This time, the prophet came out to see him and with his head still bowed in humility said, "Now I know that there is no God in all the world except in Israel. So please accept the small gift from your servant that I brought you."

The prophet answered, "As surely as the Lord lives, whom I serve, I will not accept a thing." And even though the general urged him and pleaded, he refused. The general remembered that all the priests and prophets of the other gods worked for pay and demanded gifts and was therefore amazed that neither the Creator nor the prophet would accept a penny. His life had been literally given back to him for free in exchange for simple obedience.

Then the general continued, "If you will not take anything, please let me, your servant, be given as much earth as a pair of mules can carry, for your servant will never again make burnt offerings and sacrifices to any other god but the Lord, your God, who has healed me, absolutely free of charge, and I am not even a Hebrew—all he had asked for was just obedience to a simple command.

"But may the Lord forgive your servant for this one thing: When my master, the king, enters the Temple of Rimmon (his god) to bow down and he is leaning on my arm and I must bow there also, when I bow down in the temple of Rimmon, may the Lord forgive your servant for this."

Seeing that Naaman the general now understood the difference between an idol and the power of the living Creator and that walking with the Creator required a change of heart, he said to Naaman, "Go in peace." Naaman had never had such a spectacular homecoming, and Naaman's house became a witness for the power and love of the Creator.

So that day, as the Creator has done over time, he revealed himself to Naaman and had his heart converted. The king of Aram reminded the king of Israel that he loved the people of Syria who chose to follow him just as much as those of Israel who did, and this applied to every nation on the planet.

Chapter 15

Nebuchadnezzar and the Last Four World Empires

The last straw

Over time, the newer generations of the people of Israel became more like the Canaanites to the point where they and their leaders served and worshiped the gods in the land and even had some of the idols placed inside the temple that was built for the worship of the Creator and to house the ark of the covenant.

This depravity resulted in corrupt leadership, and the strong, rich, and powerful took advantage of its weak and poor. The nation had sunken so low spiritually and morally to a point of absolute flagrant rebellion to the Creator and the worship of idols. This resulted in the people slipping deeper and deeper into depravity and despicable morals and vile practices just as bad as the Canaanites. They not only mocked and scoffed at his prophets, but they despised his words and had no desire to see any written laws of the Creator. Despite allowing punishing sieges like that of King Ben-Hadad of Syria (885 BC and 865 BC) over their Israeli cities like Samaria, where people ate their children due to starvation as he had warned, the people remained self-destructively unfaced. With the land covered in violence, they gave the Creator no other choice but to act as he had warned them.

He had promised that he would send them into captivity and scatter them abroad. So in about 721 BC, the Assyrian army attacked and captured the Israelite capital at Samaria and carried away the citizens of the northern kingdom of Israel into captivity. The virtual destruction of Israel left the southern kingdom, Judah, to fend for itself among warring near-eastern kingdoms.

He brought up against the remaining tribe and Jerusalem Nebuchadnezzar, the king of the Babylonians, whose soldiers slaughtered their young men with the sword in the temple and did not spare young men or women, the elderly, or the infirm. The Creator gave them all into the hands of Nebuchadnezzar by withdrawing his protection from around them.

So in about 602 BC, he carried to Babylon all the articles from the temple in Jerusalem, both large and small, and the treasures of the Lord's temple and the treasures of the king and his officials, and these he carried off to the temple of his god in Babylon and put them in the treasure house except for the ark of the covenant, which had been hidden and was, therefore, not among the things carried into Babylon.

They set fire to the Lord's temple and broke down the wall of Jerusalem, burning down all the palaces, and destroyed everything of value there. Their exile to Babylon was to last for seventy years according to the word of the Lord spoken by one of the Creator's prophets called Jeremiah, whose word the king and the people refused to accept. They had become so demented to think that because they were known as the Creator's covenanted people, they would be spared regardless of their lifestyles, and he would not allow his temple to be destroyed. They were wrong because that is exactly what he had promised he would do if they disobeyed his statutes of their covenant.

And so it came to pass that the nation of Israel was carried into captivity, and so began the desolation of the land just as the Creator had warned he would do. In his mercy, he gave a timeline on their return after seventy years in captivity. Because he had sworn to Abraham to give him the land forever, he was going to maintain a remnant and a means to preserve the nation to the end of time and could, therefore, never be completely annihilated by any nation on earth.

Then the king of Babylon ordered Ashpenaz, chief of his court officials, to bring into the king's service some of the exiled Israelites from the royal family and the nobility. These were to be individuals observed to be talented young men without any physical defects, handsome, showing aptitude for every kind of learning, well-informed, quick to understand, and qualified to serve in the king's palace. He was to teach them the language and literature of the Babylonians, among other things, and then bring them into service.

Among those who were chosen were four young men: Daniel, Hananiah, Mishael, and Azariah. The chief official gave them new Babylonian names: to Daniel the name Belteshazzar, to Hananiah Shadrach, to Mishael Meshach, and to Azariah Abednego.

But Daniel was very versed and well taught on the law of Moses and had resolved in his heart along with his three friends not to defile themselves with the Babylonian idolatrous practices but to stay in obedience to his Creator. He knew they were in exile because of national rebellion and sin but had resolved in setting a righteous standard in his lifestyle to honor the Creator at any cost.

The Creator loved that, as he always does with anyone who is willing to walk with him. He decided he would use Daniel's resolve to bring Babylon, the current world empire then, to the knowledge of him and his ways. Now with Daniel and his friends having decided to be his witness, the Creator then stirred the heart of the overseeing official to show favor and compassion to them.

In addition to these four young men, the Creator gave knowledge and understanding of all kinds of literature and learning, and Daniel could understand and interpret visions and dreams of all kinds.

At the end of the time set by the king to bring them into his service, the chief official presented them to Nebuchadnezzar. The king talked with them, and he found none equal to Daniel and his three friends. In every matter of wisdom and understanding about which the king questioned them, he found them ten times better than all the magicians and enchanters in his whole kingdom, and it pleased the king greatly to have them in his service.

Nebuchadnezzar's introduction to the Creator

In the second year of his reign, Nebuchadnezzar had dreams; his mind was troubled, and he could not sleep. The king, therefore, summoned the magicians, enchanters, sorcerers, and astrologers to tell him what he had dreamed and what it meant. A key problem was that the king could not remember the dream itself, but he knew it was very important.

Then the astrologers answered the king, asking him to tell them the dream so that they could interpret it. Then the king got angry and warned the astrologers that if they did not tell him what his dream was and interpret it, he will have them cut into pieces and their houses turned into piles of rubble. But if they told him the dream and interpret it, they would receive from him gifts and rewards and great honor. So it was that they were commanded to tell him the dream and interpret it immediately.

Once more they pleaded with the king to tell them about the dream, for only then could they interpret it. Then the king answered, "I am certain that you are trying to gain time because you realize that this is what I have firmly decided: If you do not tell me the dream, there is only one penalty for you. You have conspired to tell me misleading and wicked things, hoping the situation will change. So then, tell me the dream, and I will know that you can interpret it for me."

The astrologers, now dismayed and in a panic, answered the king, saying, "There is no one on earth who can do what the king asks! No king, however great and mighty, has ever asked such a thing of any magician or enchanter, sorcerer, or astrologer. What the king asks is too difficult. No one can reveal it to the king except the gods, and they do not live among humans."

True to form, by this truthful statement, the wise men and astrologers laid the bridge and foundation for the revelation of the Creator to the entire Babylonian kingdom and its leadership.

This made the king so angry and furious that he ordered the execution of all the wise men of Babylon. The decree was issued to put them to death, and men were sent to look for Daniel and his friends as well because they were not present there at the time. Then the commander of the king's guard went out to conduct the execution. When he met Daniel, upon learning of the king's edict, he went in to see the king and asked for time so that he might interpret the dream for him, to which the king happily agreed.

Then Daniel returned to his house and explained the matter to his three friends. They then prayed to the Creator in heaven concerning this mystery so that he and his friends might not be executed with the rest of the wise men of Babylon. The Creator happily obliged, being the one who had set this up, and heartened that Daniel and his friends called out to him. During the night, the mystery was therefore revealed to Daniel in a vision.

A challenge only the Creator can handle

Then Daniel went to the commander of the king's guard and asked him not to execute the wise men of Babylon but to take him now to the king so that he could interpret his dream for him. He joyfully took Daniel to the king after rounding up the officials and informed them that he had found a man among the exiles from Judah who could tell the king what his dream meant.

The king, knowing deep inside him that this was an exceedingly difficult task, if not impossible from a human standpoint, asked Daniel pointedly, "Are you able to tell me what I saw in my dream and interpret it?"

Daniel replied, "No wise man, enchanter, magician, sorcerer, or diviner can explain to the king the mystery he has asked about but the Lord alone who is in heaven who is the creator of the heavens and the earth who reveals mysteries. He has shown king Nebuchadnezzar what will happen in days to come. Your dream and the visions that passed through your mind as you were lying in bed are these:

"As Your Majesty was lying there, your mind turned to things to come, and the Creator of the universe, who is the revealer of mysteries, showed you what is going to happen. As for me, this mystery has been revealed to me not because I have greater wisdom than anyone else alive but so that Your Majesty may know the interpretation and that you may understand what went through your mind.

"Your Majesty looked, and there before you stood a large statue—an enormous dazzling statue, awesome in appearance. The head of the statue was made of pure gold, its chest and arms of silver, its belly and thighs of bronze, its legs of iron, its feet partly of iron and partly of baked clay. While you were watching, a rock was cut out but not by human hands. It struck the statue on its feet of iron and clay and smashed them.

"Then the iron, the clay, the bronze, the silver, and the gold were all broken to pieces and became like chaff on a threshing floor in the summer. The wind swept them away without leaving a trace. But the rock that struck the statue became a huge mountain and filled the whole earth. This was the dream, and now we will interpret it to the king.

"Your Majesty, you are the king of kings. The Creator has given you dominion, power, might, and glory. In your hands he has placed all mankind and the beasts of the field and the birds in the sky. Wherever they live, he has made you ruler over them all. Your kingdom, the Babylonian kingdom, is that head of gold.

"After you, another kingdom, represented by silver, will arise, inferior to yours. Next, a third kingdom, represented by bronze, will rule over the whole earth. Finally, there will be a fourth kingdom, strong as iron, for iron breaks and smashes everything, and as iron breaks things to pieces, so it will crush and break all the others.

"Just as you saw that the feet and toes were partly of baked clay and partly of iron, so this will be a divided kingdom, yet it will have some of the strength of iron in it even as you saw iron mixed with clay. As the toes were partly iron and partly clay, so this kingdom will be partly strong and partly brittle. And just as you saw the iron mixed with baked clay, so the people will be a mixture and will not remain united any more than iron mixes with clay.

"In the time of those kings, the Creator will set up a kingdom that will never be destroyed nor will it be left to another people. It will crush all those kingdoms and bring their fallible ways to an end, but it will itself endure forever.

"This is the meaning of the vision of the rock cut out of a mountain but not by human hands, a rock that broke the iron, the bronze, the clay, the silver, and the gold to pieces. The Creator has shown the king what will take place in the future. The dream is true, and its interpretation is trustworthy because history will verify and validate it."

In a move no one had ever seen in the great Babylonian empire, the king Nebuchadnezzar, overwhelmed by the disclosure, fell prostrate before Daniel, paying him homage and honor, and ordered that an offering and incense be presented to him, the kind of reverence only bestowed on a deity. The king's officials and the wise men of Babylon could not help but admire the one who had just saved all their lives with their families, their dignity, and bowed to him just as the king had done.

The king said to Daniel, "Surely your God, the Creator is the God of gods and the Lord of kings and a revealer of mysteries, for you were able to reveal this mystery."

Then the king placed Daniel in a high position and lavished many gifts on him. He made him ruler over the entire province of Babylon and placed him in charge of all its wise men. Moreover, at Daniel's request, the king appointed Shadrach, Meshach, and Abednego as administrators over the province of Babylon, while Daniel himself remained at the royal court.

In this sweeping display of the Creator's mercy and love for humanity, the greatest empire on earth then was given a front-row seat at a display of his power through Daniel and his companions as well as show the world how many world empires were to rule the earth before the rule of human governments come to an end as it is known today.

The only Utopian earthly kingdom the world will ever have

Additional details revealed to Daniel about the kingdom set up after that of the iron and clay indicate that it will be the only time of peaceful coexistence among people, people with animals, climate, and the environment. In the time of this kingdom, carnivores like the lion will eat grass just like the ox, venomous snakes will be harmless and will play with children, the earth will produce crops in great abundance, thus eliminating famine everywhere on earth. It will be the only time the whole world will see true peace on earth because fallible humans will no longer rule but rather the Redeemer himself, ruling from Jerusalem. This kingdom will last only for one thousand years, and human lifespan will be such that those who die at one hundred years of age will be considered children. This is the kingdom that will transition into eternity after it is purged of the devil and his fallen angles and those who choose to reject the Redeemer's offer of life with the Creator.

Summary of the last five empires

- *Babylonian* empire (head of gold) 606 BC to 538 BC
- Cyrus of the *Medo-Persian* empire (breast and arms of silver) did conquer Babylon in 538 BC to 333 BC
- Alexander the Great of the *Grecian* empire (belly and thighs of bronze) did conquer the Persian empire in 333 BC to 146 BC
- Augustus Caesar of the *Roman* empire (legs of iron and clay) came into play in 44 BC to AD 455 which has not been replaced by any other world empire.
- The *kingdom* of the Creator will be an earthly kingdom for one thousand years before transitioning into eternity.

Daniel was given more revelations by the Creator regarding the details of the world empires after Babylon and about the end times of human governments. Most importantly, the honor of disclosing to the world the exact number of years to the day when the Redeemer, promised as far back as in the days of Adam, will be unveiled in the nation of Israel.

Through him and his companions, the Creator performed miracles in Babylon that impacted the leadership of Babylon, and he achieved a great reward—the acknowledgment and acceptance of the Creator of the universe by Nebuchadnezzar as his Lord. This happened after his final but personal one-on-one encounter with the Creator, with a front-row seat in seeing his power and graciousness, whereby the king Nebuchadnezzar made the following declaration:

> At the end of the time of my indoctrination when I was made to understand the difference between the Almighty and little helpless man, I, Nebuchadnezzar, raised my eyes toward heaven, and my sanity was restored. Then I praised the Most High; I honored and glorified him who lives forever. His dominion is an eternal dominion; his kingdom endures from generation to generation.
>
> All the peoples of the earth are really nothing. He could do as he pleases with the powers of heaven and the peoples of the earth. No one can hold back his hand or say to him: "What have you done?"
>
> At the same time that my sanity was restored, my honor and splendor were returned to me for the glory of my kingdom. My advisers and nobles sought me out, and I was restored to my throne and became even greater than before.
>
> Now I, Nebuchadnezzar, praise and exalt and glorify the King of heaven, because everything he does is right, and all his ways are just. And those who walk in pride he is able to humble.

Like the other succeeding empires, the Creator made provision for their leaders to know and experience him, and it was up to them to decide on what to do with that knowledge. The Creator ensured that records were kept for the entire humanity to have access to and to be reminded of truth.

The errand with an appeal from the heart of the Creator

During the time of the kings in Israel when the Creator was containing the kings of Israel and its people, in about *760 BC*, a report on the wickedness of the people in Nineveh was presented to the Creator. The people were indeed exceedingly wicked and very despised even by their neighboring nations including the children of Israel.

He looked down at the Ninevites and decided the situation warranted judgment. They were very prosperous and their dwelling was quite fortified and they, therefore, felt quite secure and did as they pleased with no regard for the Creator. His decision was to give them a chance to determine their own fate, as is always his pattern. However, unlike the case for Sodom and Gomorrah when he sent angels to do the job, the Creator decided to call on one of his prophets in Israel by name Jonah, son of Amittai, and asked him to go to the great city of Nineveh and deliver a message to it because its wickedness had come up before him, and he gave him the message to declare to the people of Nineveh.

Jonah could not believe what the Creator of the heavens and the earth was asking him to do. Everyone knew how vile and evil the people were—a people who had invented some of the cruelest torture techniques on its war victims and were immensely proud of their art.

He believed the Creator of heaven had overstepped his boundaries of mercy and justice at the very thought of even considering giving these wicked terrorists a chance for redemption. The thought of live humans impaled in upright positions and left on the poles to slowly die as a warning to their adversaries, among other horrendous inhumane atrocities, was too much for Jonah.

Jonah, not being able to stand the thought of these people being considered for forgiveness, decided to run away from the Creator and headed for Tarshish thousands of miles away in the opposite direction to Nineveh. He went down to Joppa, where he found a ship bound for that port; and after paying the fare, he went aboard and sailed for Tarshish to flee from his assignment. The Creator considered Jonah's decision and, being gracious and never one to violate a human's free will, said nothing to Jonah when he fled to Tarshish.

A perfect day to ride the waves

It was an exceptionally beautiful day to sail—a blue sky, calm waters, and a gentle breeze. After Jonah's ship had set sail and was well on its way in the deep waters of the Mediterranean Sea on its way toward the Atlantic, the Creator sent a great gale on the sea, creating a violent and tempestuous storm that appeared as though the ship was its primary target.

The seasoned sailors quickly realized this was no ordinary storm and were terribly afraid, and each cried out to his own god because they were certain unless there was some divine intervention, they were absolutely doomed to drown.

The massive waves tossed the ship around like a little toy as it rode the massive waves up the crests and then plunged down into dreadful wave valleys that spelled death by drowning. They feverishly dumped all their cargo into the sea to lighten the ship, but the vessel still looked imperiled because there was no letup by the mighty waves.

Circling deep below the ship was a monster of a fish that had been tailing the ship for a while. At least two of the sailors thought they may have seen a monstrous fin under the depths but quickly dismissed the thought as being a trick of the light on the tossed-out cargo floating and sinking all around them.

However, with Jonah sensing this was definitely an incident having to do something with him, he snuck down below deck, where he lay down and fell into a deep sleep. The captain doing his rounds by clinging to railings followed the distinct sound of the echo of someone snoring below deck. To his amazement, he found Jonah asleep, and waking him up, he said, "How can you sleep at a time like this? Get up, come up deck with me, and call on your god! Maybe he will take notice of us so that we will not perish. We all worship a plurality of gods, and one of them is bound to hear us."

After he had been brought up and there was still no letup in the battering of the ship, the sailors decided to cast lots to find out who or what was responsible for this calamity. They cast lots, and the lot fell on Jonah. With that, they all turned to him and asked if he was indeed responsible for this trouble for them, what kind of work he did, where he came from, his country of origin, and his people.

"I am a Hebrew," he answered. "And I worship the Lord of heaven, who created the sea and the dry land. I am a prophet of the Creator and serve as a messenger when he has specific messages to be delivered." He spoke with such calmness and confidence that they were even more terrified, and they asked him what he had done. He then told them he was running away from the Lord. Upon telling them this, the sea got even rougher and violently shook the structure of the ship with such force that it threatened to break up even at the very joints. They then cried out in sheer terror, and not knowing what else to do, they turned and asked him, "Could you talk to him and then let us know what we should do to make the sea calm down for us?"

"Pick me up and throw me into the sea," he replied with that terrifying calmness and uncanny confidence. "And it will become calm. As I have told you already, I know that it is my fault that this great storm has come upon you." The men could not bring themselves to throw him into the sea. Instead, they did their best to try and row back to land. But they could not, for the sea grew even the more violent.

Seeing that their gods were no help and their demise was now certain, they cried out to Jonah's God, saying, "Please, Lord, Creator of the earth and sea, do not let us die for taking this man's life. Do not hold us accountable for killing an innocent man, for you, Lord, have done as you pleased, and we would do as he has instructed us."

With great sadness, free flowing tears in their eyes and trembling in fear, they took Jonah, who looked as calm as a cucumber with a somewhat faint wry smile on his face, and tossed him overboard with his luggage. As soon as his body hit the water, as if a switch had been turned off, the raging sea immediately grew calm.

At this, the men greatly feared the Lord, and they offered a sacrifice to him and made life-changing vows to him. These men during adversity came to the knowledge of the true and mighty Creator who created all things, and they did not need anyone to explain anything to them; they had seen it with their very own eyes, and that was enough. Now having lost all their cargo, they headed back for land for fresh supplies and recounted the memorable experience. They were changed for life and vowed never to forget the Lord of Jonah.

Divine transport and a wise king

Unknown to the sailors, tailing and shadowing them the whole time under the waves was an enormous fish prepared by the Creator to swallow Jonah. Upon landing in the water, he sank down to the waiting fish, which took just one gulp to swallow him and then headed for Nineveh. Jonah was kept in the belly of the fish for three days and three nights.

Upon seeing that he was not yet sliced up by the teeth of the fish nor yet digested before losing consciousness, his prophet in him voluntarily prayed and called to the Lord from inside the fish from whatever consciousness he had, and the Lord heard and answered him. And the Lord commanded the fish, and it took him to and vomited Jonah onto dry land.

A couple of fishermen working on their fishing gear a good distance away but within viewing range of the beach saw the unimaginable. They saw the biggest fish they had never seen or imagined existed in the great deep emerge from the waves on this sandy beach and regurgitate what looked like a bald man, whole, and a carry-on unto the sand, clear off the breaking waves. With mouths wide open, they watched the enormous fish slowly wiggle and slide backward with the help of its powerful and monstrous tail into the water and like a submarine slowly disappeared under the waves.

As they watched, the next scene was even more uncanny; they saw the strange-colored man crawl forward, roll on his back; and that was as much as they could handle before they fled, with the last image they could remember being that of the man's bald head reflecting the sun. This definitely could not be human or a good omen, and they had to flee for their lives before some terrible evil befell them—and fled they did, making sure the being did not see them.

As Jonah lay on the sand and looked up at the beautiful blue sky, happy to be alive after the great fish had retreated and vanished beneath the waves, the word of the Lord came to him a second time, saying, "Go to the great city of Nineveh and proclaim to it the message I gave you."

This time Jonah obeyed and after he washed himself up headed for Nineveh. Other than his purple tan, there were no acid burns on him, and neither was his luggage damaged in any way. Looking around him, he saw a path leading up into land from the beach, and he followed it to try and determine where he was. It was not long before he saw some of the hallmarks of the people of Nineveh.

Now Nineveh was an exceptionally large city; it took three days to go through it. Jonah began by going a day's journey into the city, proclaiming the message the Creator had given him, which simply stated that "In forty days, Nineveh will be overthrown if it did not turn from its evil ways and seek the Creator of heavens and the earth."

The purple bald man walked with a confident step, proclaimed his message fearlessly, and seemed to enjoy the prospect of the city coming under judgment. When Jonah's warning reached the king of Nineveh, he was quite intrigued and summoned his wise men and ruling council for consultation. He had the scribes and scholars investigate the records about the Creator that the strange purple man was referring to.

The archived information was quite substantial and very discomforting.

This was the One who destroyed the cities of Sodom, Gomorrah, Admah, and Zeboiim for their wicked practices by raining down fire and brimstone in which only three souls who heeded to the warning were saved.

This was the One who decimated the nation of Egypt with horrible plagues to force Pharaoh to let the Hebrews leave Egypt. Pharaoh finally relented only after every firstborn human and animals died in one night, including Pharaoh's son. He then opened the

Red Sea to allow the Hebrews to cross it on dry ground but drowned Pharaoh's formidable elite army when they tried chasing after them.

This was the One who used just air to dam up the Jordan River during flood season to allow the Hebrews to cross over into the land of Canaan, during which he caused the mighty walls of Jericho to fall flat, leading to the easy extermination of all its wicked inhabitants.

The strangest of all is this One spoke audibly and supposedly led the Hebrews by a pillar of fire by night and a pillar of cloud by day in their travel to the land of Canaan from Egypt. He also chastised them often when they strayed from his commandments and laws, and this took the form of pestilences, famine, or invasion and plunder by other armies. They were restored when they repented of their wickedness.

In one of those cases when the Hebrews were in rebellion against him, the Philistines attacked them and captured the ark, the symbolic place where his Spirit met with the Hebrews when he visited them. The Philistines were badly punished for touching the ark and taking it to their land. While it was there, the Philistines began dying by the tens of thousands while plagued with very painful and bleeding hemorrhoids in every Philistine city the ark was taken to until their wise men decided to try and send it back to the Hebrews.

By this time, the lawmakers and the king of Nineveh realized that they were in trouble, and they trembled in fear. They acknowledged that they practiced a lot of the evil for which the other nations had been destroyed, and when they looked at the moral code of the Hebrews handed down by the Creator, they were absolutely certain that they were doomed.

As the deliberations continued to determine how to respond to the message, two men were brought into the assembly with a message for the king. They bowed themselves to the ground before the king and asked for permission to recount what they had seen the previous day at the beach, having recognized Jonah as the baldheaded man they had seen regurgitated on the beach by the monstrous fish. They came only because they knew this was no ordinary man and that he was either from a true God or from the devil.

Based on the information in the records about the ways of the Creator who had demonstrated his power in all the land, the king and his council knew very clearly that they were in violation and by his standards, they were indeed violent and wicked.

After the deliberations, the king of Nineveh issued the following proclamation:

> By the decree of the king and his nobles: Do not let people or animals, herds or flocks, taste anything; do not let them eat or drink for the time set by the king. But let people and animals be covered with sackcloth. Let everyone call urgently on the Creator. Let them give up their evil ways and their violence. Who knows? He may yet relent and with compassion turn from his fierce anger so that we will not perish.

The king immediately rose from his throne, took off his royal robes, covered himself with sackcloth, and sat down in the dust as he too fasted and prayed along with the rest of the people and animals.

Many Ninevites were familiar with the Creator and were very knowledgeable of his track record and believed Jonah's message. Not wanting the fate of the cities of Jericho, Sodom and Gomorrah, Egypt, the Philistines, all of them, from the greatest to the least, put on sackcloth and participated in the fast. When the Creator saw what they did and how they turned from their evil ways, he relented and did not bring on them the destruction he had threatened.

After declaring his message, Jonah had gone out and sat down at a place east of the city. There he made himself a shelter, sat in its shade a good and safe distance away, and waited to see what would happen to the city. At the end of the fortieth day, looking down, Jonah could see that the Creator had called off the destruction of Nineveh.

To Jonah this seemed very wrong, and he became angry. He prayed to the Lord, saying, "Isn't this what I said, Lord, when I was still at home? That is what I tried to forestall by fleeing to Tarshish. I knew that you are a gracious and compassionate Lord, slow to anger and abounding in love, the Lord who relents from sending calamity. Now, Lord, take away my life, for it is better for me to die than to live."

But the Lord replied, "Jonah, you know that as surely as I live, I take no pleasure in the death of the wicked but rather that they turn from their wicked ways and live. Is it right for you to be angry with me?"

But Jonah was burning with anger, and the Lord, seeing that Jonah was in no state to reason with him at this time, came up with a plan to enlighten him further. Then the Creator provided a leafy plant and made it grow unnaturally fast overnight over Jonah's shelter to give shade for his head to ease his discomfort, and Jonah was very happy about the plant.

But at dawn the next day, the Lord made and sent a special worm, which chewed the plant's root system so that it withered. When the sun rose, the Creator then directed a scorching east wind at Jonah, and the sun blazed on Jonah's head so that he grew faint and he was livid with anger at the death of the beautiful, leafy, and shade-providing plant.

He wanted to die and, praying aloud, said, "It would be better for me to die than to live." But the Creator then asked Jonah a question: "Is it right for you to be angry about the plant?"

"It is," he said. "And I'm so angry I wish I were dead."

But the Creator said, "You have been concerned about this plant though you did not tend it or make it grow. It sprang up overnight and died overnight. And should I not have concern for the great city of Nineveh, in which there are more than 120 thousand people who cannot tell their right hand from their left and as well as the animals? I take no pleasure in suffering, pain, and the death of the wicked. Man has my Spirit, and that makes his life eternal from the womb. I must give everyone who is in danger of eternal separation from me a chance for redemption. He must choose the eternal life I offer or the eternal death that sin offers.

"As long as man lives till the moment of his last breath, he will have the opportunity to make that choice because I created him with free will within his domain, and I will never violate that. No human is created and preordained for destruction, but every human being will be given an equal opportunity for redemption regardless of his line of human ancestry with a measure ideal for his environment and upbringing. However, once man crosses the threshold of life into death, there is no longer a choice, for there is no repentance in the grave. I am the Almighty, and my judgment is fair and just.

"Remember your ancestor Abraham. He was an idol worshiper, but when I visited and called him, he turned to me and walked away from idolatry. I love the Ninevites just like you and Abraham, and whosoever hears my voice and accepts me will spend eternity with me, and man will always have to make that choice, not me. Remember, I will never violate man's freedom to choose—never!"

Chapter 16

Then Came the Redeemer

As the Father, Son, and Spirit had agreed, the Redeemer was to come into the world as a human, a second Adam with a genetic constitution of man but to be empowered having the Spirit of the Creator at the start of his mission. This meant growing up with very limited divine power, with access to only what the Father was to make available as needed. This was also to enable man to easily relate to the Redeemer, considering the obvious challenges that had been previously discussed.

The Redeemer had never been separated from the Father and Spirit. It was also totally perplexing to the devil and his goons as they looked at the prophecies regarding the Redeemer. They could not understand why the Creator of the universe would humble and humiliate himself for a creature so broken. The devil felt the human was beyond repair and that even he and his minions had no use for except to attempt to destroy out of spite—with needed human cooperation, of course. The devil then decided on a strategy to derail the mission because as a human, the Redeemer was fair game just like the first Adam.

The great desire of the Hebrew maiden

With a significant portion of Israel now returned from captivity and under the Roman empire and rule, a certain young virgin girl called Mary, a descendant of King David, engaged to be married, was chosen as the mother of the Redeemer. Her consent was sought by the special angelic messenger called Gabriel. He visited her while she was alone and informed her that she had been chosen to be the mother of the Redeemer if she so wished. This was the desire and dream of the women of Israel as they had been taught for generations about this prophesied event.

Upon consenting, she was told by the angel that the baby's embryo will be placed in her womb by the Holy Spirit, requiring no sexual relations for her conception. This was the equivalent of the first created man, Adam, before he was sent out of the garden of Eden. She was told what to name the baby, and her life was never the same after that.

In selecting Mary, the Creator showed the most remarkable act of inclusiveness to demonstrate that he loved the Canaanites who were willing to walk away from their evil ways and accept his lordship and live by his statutes. Between Joseph, her husband, and Mary, their ancestry included Canaanites like Rahab the former prostitute in Jericho to Ruth, a Moabite, both of whom had chosen to walk away from idol worship and to have the Creator as their Lord and embrace his covenant.

The send-off

With the heavenly host all standing in reverence and great wonder, the Creator of the universe had to step out of his deity and descend into the earth as an embryonic entity to redeem the creature and universe he greatly loved. A divine angelic security detail was put in place on the earth for the child's family as the Spirit took over the reins of managing the universe and all creation and the placement of the embryo in Mary's womb.

As soon as the development of the embryo became big enough to impact the physiological and anatomic changes in Mary, Joseph, whom she was engaged to, received an angelic visitor to clarify an obvious problem. He was informed by the angel that his wife was pregnant and the child was the promised Redeemer of mankind, as had been prophesied in the Scriptures.

Joseph, shaken, and seeing the presence of the powerful angel, believed that the Creator was involved in this. He was then commanded not to put away his wife, as he had planned to do because their marriage had not yet been sexually consummated, and that the pregnancy was not because she had had any sexual relationship with anyone. The name of the child was confirmed to him, and that was the beginning of angelic visits for instructions on how to handle the child. Being a Mosaic-covenant-believing man, having been taught the statutes, it was not overwhelmingly challenging to him except for the embarrassment of his wife being pregnant before their official marriage. It left many wondering privately as to who the father was.

The child was born at the time and place to the day as prophesied thousands of years before. Mary and Joseph, the parents of the baby, saw and heard things that left absolutely no shadow of a doubt that this was indeed no ordinary child but the promised Messiah. His mental aptitude was extraordinary, reminiscent of Adam in the garden of Eden, because before being a teenager, he baffled even the teachers and doctors at the temple with his knowledge of the Scriptures.

However, he had to be contained by the Creator, as previously arranged, to live as an ordinary human until the appointed time when his ministry was to begin, and only then could he tap into his divine ability as needed. This arrangement created problems for him at home because his family and those who lived in the same village and community with him, other than his parents, saw nothing overtly divine about him while he grew up. But he lived and grew up like every other child in the family, subject to his parents' instructions, and grew in knowledge.

At the age of thirty years old and having grown up as a carpenter's son who now had naturally conceived siblings, he selected twelve disciples whom he taught and prepared with a message for three years. These twelve apostles were given the responsibility of carrying his teaching to the rest of the world with the manifest power as proof of the authority from the Creator himself. Even more importantly, his message was meant to further reveal the heart of the Creator to humanity.

Key highlights of the Redeemer's teachings

First highlight was that the kingdom of the Creator was finally imminent. This would represent the last global empire on earth after the Roman empire, as revealed to Nebuchadnezzar and Daniel by the Creator during his reign in 606 BC to 538 BC of Babylon. This kingdom was to transition into eternity after its one-thousand-year earthly span. It was man's final opportunity to choose whether to live with his Creator, as was intended for Adam, or choose to live eternally separated from him with the consequences of how he lived his life with his fellow humans.

Qualifications to enter the Creator's eternal kingdom

Only *two* paths into the eternal kingdom of the Creator exist.

Path one absolutely and automatically guaranteed for anyone who has successfully lived a perfect life from birth with no sin toward the Creator (breaking of a divine law or a legitimate human law of conduct, directly or indirectly) in thought, word, or deed. This also includes having perfectly righteous motives for everything the person ever did through his or her entire life. Entry for such into the kingdom is direct.

Path two is through the Redeemer. This path is for any human being who realizes he or she cannot make it into the Creator's eternal kingdom on his own merit because that person has broken the Creator's laws (sin) or a legitimate human law of conduct at one time or another, cannot undo wrongs already committed and, therefore, not perfect, seeing that only an absolutely perfect human can enter the Creator's eternal kingdom.

All a human must do then to enter the Creator's kingdom is to believe in the Redeemer by accepting the free offer of the payment already made by him. This was accomplished by the Redeemer dying on the cross in judgment for the sins of all humanity, whereby the Creator no longer holds the eternal death penalty over humanity. The person who believes, accepts this offer, and declares it personally to the Creator directly in a simple personal prayer is forgiven of all sin, and the proof of his acceptance is the refraining from intentionally living in sin going forward. Only two people are involved in this transaction—the individual and the Creator—it requires no organization or religion and applies to every human being alive except for children under the age of accountability as determined by the Creator alone. In many circles, this is referred to as repentance and accepting the Lordship of the Creator to one's life.

The second highlight was that he was the Creator's Son; the Redeemer came down from heaven, and his coming had been prophesied many centuries before by multiple prophets in great details. Even the magi in Persia were aware of his coming, and King Herod's officials and many still alive in Israel were also aware based on the written prophecies. Miracles performed by him during his mission demonstrated that he operated outside of nature's laws because he created nature and those laws. To prove his point, he was here to destroy the world's greatest enemy, physical death. He further expounded that after his death, he would be resurrected bodily after three days and three nights following his burial. This was to be proof that the power of death was finally broken and as a perpetual witness for every human being on earth from that point and into eternity and not to be minimized, to validate the existence of life after death of humans.

The third highlight was that after a human dies, the spirit of the human has two final destinations—heaven and hell—and they were as real as the sun in the sky. Anyone who accepts the redemptive offer will live and interact with the Creator after the physical death in eternal bliss.

On the other hand, those who reject the redemptive offer of the Creator would be separated from him eternally and would spend eternity with the devil, who, incidentally, will also be separated eternally from the Creator.

Man must choose, and the Creator has no intention of forcing anyone to himself; but everyone on earth will have the opportunity to make that choice before death, and it will be recorded by the Creator. He warned gravely that eternal separation from the Creator would offer nothing but unnecessary and unfathomable pain and suffering garnished with profound regret, a thing that could burn even hotter than a flame. Regardless of the circumstances, the Creator will never violate the offer of free will given to man, and so no one will be forced into either destination.

In the fourth highlight, he summarized all the commandments of the Creator to humanity into just two, which are the basis for very peaceful and gratifying human coexistence in society. *The first being*

> For man to love the Creator (to love the Creator is to keep his commandment which is simply loving everything that is good and hating everything that is evil as defined by the creator and easily understood by humanity)

And the second being

> For humans to love each other as they love themselves.

He then defined love as follows:

> Love is when one cares about the happiness, safety, and health of others, just as oneself. Love being patient, kind, and envying no one. Love is never boastful, nor conceited, nor rude; never selfish, not quick to take offence. Love keeps no score of wrongs; does not gloat over another's faults or demise but delights in the truth as stated by the Creator himself.

His teaching further explained that the human being is the Creator's most valuable earthly creation and treasure; and in his eyes, all the riches in the whole earth are not worth the life and soul of one human. Since the Creator has given mankind free will, any decision a man makes on earth, in man's fallen state, has consequences and will affect others directly or indirectly and, therefore, mandate a system for justice and its enforcement.

The fifth highlight was that, after his ascension back to heaven, the Father would send the Holy Spirit, who will now be able to indwell everyone who chooses the redemption offer. The Spirit, whom Adam and Eve lost, will be restored to them, and they will now have the life of the Creator and be able to communicate directly with him. The Spirit will also serve as a truth guide, a comforter to help man handle life's challenges and assaults of deception from the devil, and to empower the redeemed man to overcome expected temptations from the devil. He will strengthen the human to live victoriously over sin and be able to love as commanded by the Creator.

The sixth highlight was that humans were considered the Creator's children and were greatly loved. Humans were created for a father-child relationship with a bond of love. Those who accepted his lordship could talk to him at will through prayer, and they automatically became the responsibility of the Creator. He held his word above his name, making it easy for humanity to test and verify his promises.

The seventh highlight and inarguably the greatest covenant in the Creator's relationship to man—the Creator irreversibly declared the following to those who were willing to accept his Lordship upon appropriating the offer of redemption:

> I am the true vine, you are the branches, and my father is the gardener, making the vine his absolute responsibility. He is responsible for fertilizing and watering the vine and controlling of its climatic conditions and environment to ensure the fruitfulness of the vine. He will cut off every branch that bears no fruit, but every branch that does bear fruit he will prune so that it will be even more fruitful. If you choose to remain in me, I will remain in you because for a branch to bear any fruit it must remain in the vine. So, you

cannot bear fruit unless you remain in me and apart from me, you can do nothing.

If you do not remain in me, you are like a branch that is thrown away and withers; such branches are picked up, thrown into the fire and burned. If you remain in me and my words remain in you, ask the father whatever you wish in my name (Redeemer) and it will be done for you. This is to my father's glory, that you bear much fruit, showing yourselves to be my disciples and me, your Lord. This is my command: Love each other.

Human religious leader tested

The world had never heard a teaching like that before, and the miracles he performed openly before the people clearly put him as a man who really walked outside the laws of nature. For those who were willing to admit the truth, the control of nature was at his command, and he clearly demonstrated his manifested power over life and death.

Now the idea of the Creator being a loving father to man was not only revolutionary, but it also did not exist in any religious circles on earth. In the past, gods have always been dreaded; and in many religions, the thought of the Creator as a father was not even conceivable.

The forgiveness of sin extended to humans through the punishing death of the Redeemer was meant to emphasize this point. To make matters even more complicated for religious sects, he taught that religion or religious groups were not what ensured people's acceptance into the Creator's eternal kingdom but rather a very simple personal one-on-one relationship with the Creator. It got even worse for the leaders; though the Redeemer had come to the world through the nation of Israel, Israel was not guaranteed automatic entrance into the Creator's kingdom. The same requirement applied to all humans, Hebrews or not, who chose to believe and accept the Creator's offer.

The religious leaders had a problem with his teaching because his teaching implied that even they were at the same level in the eyes of the Creator as everyone else. Also, they believed they had established rules to live by which made it impossible for the leaders to sin, which clearly conflicted with his teaching.

Becoming a child of the Creator meant giving up their corrupt and pretentious lifestyles with implications that could mean loss of political power, social status, and ill-gotten wealth, among other issues. They seemed to have forgotten that their primary job as religious leaders was to teach the people the true statutes of the Creator.

Like modern-day politicians, for fear of the losses, they conspired to destroy his mission and kill him if they could. However, a few of the religious leaders knew this was the Redeemer from writings of the prophets; but for fear of being ostracized by the other leaders, as seems to be the case in all corrupt political circles, they only acknowledged him in secret.

Eventually the religious leaders succeeded in a betrayal plot with one of the disciples, Judas Iscariot, for a fee of thirty pieces of silver, for which they happily paid. While Judas had been looking for just some quick cash and possibly a way to force the overthrow of the Roman rule, unknown to him was a more sinister plan to kill the Redeemer. They had reasoned that if they could pin the charge of sedition on him, by Roman law, the penalty was death by the cruelest format the Romans had introduced to stamp out sedition and rebellion from their empire.

Happy with this plan, the religious leaders had him arrested, handed him over to the occupying Roman ruler, Pilate, to whom they stated that they found him subverting their nation. They claimed that he opposed payment of taxes to Caesar and claimed to be the Messiah, a king. They then declared that they had no other king but Caesar and that they considered his claims to be seditious, which had to be punished by the full authority of the law—death by crucifixion—for the crime.

Though Pilate knew this charge was entirely bogus, to get this behind him quickly and maintain peace, he acquiesced while claiming indemnity from guilt for the act and sentenced the Redeemer to death. He was to be crucified as requested by the religious leaders along with two other criminals. Unaware to them, they were spectacularly fulfilling a series of prophecies given by the prophets many centuries before.

To try and pacify his conscience, Pilate asked for a bowl of water with which he washed his hands to symbolically declare his innocence over the death sentence. He had an opportunity to do what was right, but for political reasons, he looked the other way and allowed an injustice. When Judas realized that the Redeemer had been sentenced to death, he was sorry he had betrayed him and returned the money to the religious leaders, who simply brushed him aside.

Terribly embarrassed by the outcome, his pride and humiliation got the best of him; and instead of asking for forgiveness from the Creator, as he had been taught by the Redeemer, he went and hung himself to death. The name *Judas* has remained in history as synonymous to irrational betrayal of a very close and loyal friend for selfish gain.

Man passes the death sentence and method on the Redeemer

Unknown to man and not quite clear to the devil, the Creator had made provision for the human and the devil to decide how the Redeemer was to pay for man's very ugly and painful sin problem. Fueled by the devil, man's jealousy, rage, greed, pride, and a pretentious stand for law and order for the good of humanity, they decided the crime was sedition and the punishment death—slow and painful.

In one stroke, the Jewish spiritual leaders and ruling council affirmed that sedition and rebellion, like other legitimate societal wrongs, had to be punished by the law. The implication was that it would be absolutely wrong to allow rebellion against legitimate governments and laws to go unpunished. In this simple act, the devil and man justified the Creator's decision in meting out the punishment to both man and the devil for their transgressions. Man asked for the penalty, and the Creator paid it in full without a complaint. He was not guilty, but he paid it for the sake of his love for humanity, the crown jewel of his creation of love.

The Execution

To teach a lesson to any other insurrectionists who called themselves kings instead of Caesar, the Redeemer was openly mocked, humiliated, and whipped almost to a pulp by skilled Roman soldiers. And like a lamb, he took the punishment quietly without protesting but doing all he could to hang on to the end. Two other men, both criminals, were also led out with him to be crucified, one on his right, the other on his left.

As the people stood watching them slowly die, the rulers, incensed and blinded by anger, hate, and jealousy, continued to sneer at him, mocking him for saving others but not being able to save himself. They dared him to get off the cross if he was indeed the Messiah or Redeemer or whatever he called himself.

Then in the midst of all of this madness, with a voice quivering from pain and fatigue, the Redeemer prayed to the Father, saying, "Father, forgive these people, for they do not know what they are doing." This stunned the soldiers and those standing by watching, including his weeping mother, considering how badly he had been beaten and unjustly humiliated, and hanging there is such agony.

The criminals who hung there with him, trying to look like very tough outlaws unbroken by Roman cruelty, hurled insults at him too, saying: "Aren't you the Messiah? Save yourself and us!" But the Redeemer said not a word but just groaned under the pain with an expression of pity for them.

Then as if struck by a thunderbolt, one of the criminals suddenly had a change of heart and rebuked his companion. "Don't you fear the Creator," he said. "Since you are under the same sentence? We are punished justly, for we are getting what our deeds deserve. But this man has done nothing wrong."

He suddenly remembered the things the Redeemer had done over the past three years quite openly—the miracles, his strange teaching, and especially the teaching on life after death. He knew he was certain to die in a manner of hours, and there was nothing he could do about that. But he could do something about where his spirit and soul were going after his death. *This man had to be the Messiah, no doubt about it,* he thought, and as far as he was concerned, he was taking no chances of getting out of this life in pain just to enter another form of pain worse than this.

In the bravest stance he had ever taken in his life, turning to the Redeemer, in tears, he acknowledged the fact that he was a sinner who needed a redeemer, and this redeemer was hanging on this cross to die for his sin. In accepting the lordship of the Creator over his life and, therefore, asking to enter the Creator's kingdom, he said, "Lord, remember me when you come into your kingdom."

And the Redeemer, seeing his sincerity and trying as hard as he could to form a weak smile of joy through the agony, answered him, "Truly I tell you, today when you die, you will be with me in paradise."

It was as if a low-energy light bulb had been lit in the forgiven criminal because other than the pain expressed on his face, there now was a very peaceful expression on it that seemed to declare the message, "This is one criminal who would be dying happy, knowing what his eternal destination is."

No amount of name calling of "coward" or the like, from his partner or those standing by, fazed him. And so it happened that those two criminals at death took opposite paths into the afterlife, one dying in his sins and the other accepting the Creator's offer of forgiveness for his sins. With all his sins forgiven, he died happy, and the expression on his face was like nothing the executioners had ever seen—peace, confident joy as if he was expecting a spectacular reception as he passed over the threshold of mortal life into eternity.

Chapter 17

The Redemption of the Creator's Masterpiece

The Spirit of the Creator then decided to give the Roman soldiers, the Jews, the religious leaders, and all of humanity a chance for redemption in the midst of the pain and agony of the Creator of the universe. They were now to find out this was no mere man and confirm for those who were willing to consider his claim that he was the Redeemer, the very only begotten Son of the Creator, and he had indeed created the heavens and the earth at the direction of his father.

The resolution to the sin problem

Up in heaven, before the throne of the Father, was gathered a very great but solemn assembly of the angelic host as an enormously powerful archangel brought forward a scroll written on both sides. Bowing before the father, the angel began reading every sin humans had committed—from Adam through to those that would be committed at the end of time before the ushering in of eternity. These were named one at a time deliberately and pinned on the shoulders of the Redeemer. So ugly were the sins that even the heavenly angelic host cringed at man's wickedness and collaboration with the devil and the fallen angels who followed him.

It was just about noon when he started reading, and in a symbolic indication of the ugliness of sin, a thick darkness was cast over the whole land down on earth. The darkness stayed until three in the afternoon, when the reading was completed. Instead of each human paying a penalty for his own sin, the Redeemer took the punishment and paid the price for humanity's sin problem for the entire human race. The forgiveness was to be meted out only to those who believed and asked for it. Those who rejected the Redeemer's offer will die in their sins and face the consequences thereof.

At the end of the readout, the darkness was lifted, and the Redeemer, seeing his strength to stay alive had totally depleted and that his job was done, called out with a loud voice, "Father, into your hands I commit my Spirit." When he had said this, he breathed his last and died, and his death was followed by an earthquake as his Spirit left his physical body.

The Roman centurion, never having seen or heard the likes of what had happened, mystified by all that had transpired, could not help himself from declaring, "Surely this was a righteous man, the Son of the Creator as he had claimed." When all the people who had gathered to witness this sight saw what took place, they beat their breasts and went away, very confused by the unexplainable occurrences. There was just nothing logical about what was going on in human reasoning.

The redeemed criminal had the biggest smile of all as he watched and saw the confusion on the faces regarding the unexplainable phenomena that had just unfolded. In his pain, upon hearing the declaration of the centurion, his smile got even bigger because he knew, as painful as it was, dying on this cross at this moment with the Redeemer literally cemented his place in the glories of the afterlife. He was striding into eternity clean, leaving his sins on that cross borne by the Messiah. "Oh, what a way and time to die," he mused.

The burial

Joseph, a member of the religious Jewish ruling council, a good and upright man who had not consented to the leaders' decision and action to condemn the Redeemer, went to Pilate and asked for his body. Pilate consented, surprised that he was already dead. Then hurrying, he took it down, wrapped it in linen cloth, and placed it in a tomb cut in the rock, one that had been prepared for Joseph, and no one had yet been laid there since he was still alive. He felt honored to give it to the Redeemer.

They were all in a hurry to bury him because it was Preparation Day, and the Sabbath was about to begin when no work was allowed by law. A great stone was rolled to close the entrance to the tomb. There had been no time to prepare his body for burial because of the Sabbath preparations, so the women who had come with the Redeemer from Galilee followed Joseph to see the location of the tomb. They then went home and prepared spices and perfumes so that after the Sabbath, which was to end in three days, they could go back and prepare the body properly for burial.

The ruling council and the religious leaders persuaded Pilate to deploy a Roman security detail around the tomb until after the third day. This, they explained, was because he had promised that after he died, he will rise again on the third day. They explained that the very presence of the feared Roman guard serving as the security detail would clearly prevent the followers of the Redeemer from stealing his body and then claiming that he had resurrected. Pilate consented and gave them the soldiers who stood guard around the clock for the entire three days and nights.

The devil's last stand

The devil had deployed everything he had in trying to dissuade the Redeemer from carrying out his mission but failed. He knew the resurrection was to happen after three days and three nights of the burial. If the Redeemer successfully resurrected on time, man's enemy, death, would be defeated forever, and the devil will no longer hold the ace card of fear over man.

The devil, therefore, marshalled all his most powerful followers for one last stand to try and disrupt the resurrection process. It was a very powerful army brought in from every corner of the earth and interplanetary locations. The angelic security detail around the tomb was such that the devil and his fallen angelic followers could not get close to it and had, therefore, to watch from a long distance for their own safety.

Then it happened. At the very moment the three days and nights arrived with divine precision, the spirit world lit up from the Creator's throne to the tomb where the Redeemer's body lay. So mighty was the power that the devil and his army were blasted far from the vicinity like electromagnetic radiation from an exploding supernova.

They did not even know what hit them nor did they see it coming. When they stopped rolling and were trying to recover their stance, the devil found himself in a choke hold of a mighty and powerful archangel and he knew he was outclassed and no other of his fallen followers dared come to his assistance. As the devil cowered, he was summarily tossed aside like a filthy rag doll; and though he tried to protest his disrespectful treatment, the look from the angel told him to keep his silence because it was known why he was there.

At the same time, an intense radiation blasted the tomb like what emanates from the combination of all the biggest black holes in the universe and radiated out and across the entire universe in a moment of time. In the transition process, as the dead body was being processed, it was lifted and suspended in midair—linen and all—in its lying position, stretched out in full length as it was converted into a resurrection body.

The radiation penetrated the fabric of the burial cloth, likely leaving in it evidence of how the Creator converts the mortal body into the kind humans will have after the resurrection of the dead. This whole episode seemed like an indication that the curse of sin and death had been destroyed across the entire universe and creation as well as acknowledged and approved by the Father; it all happened in the twinkling of an eye.

This incident was accompanied by an earthquake that knocked the soldiers on guard to the ground. They were paralyzed with terror as they watched two powerful angels step into view and the great stone guarding the cave rolled away like a tiny marble.

The Redeemer no longer had a normal physical mortal body, and the devil knew it was over; death had been defeated. As the devil flanked by his demons covered in dirt looked on, he knew his days were numbered for his final incarceration, and his followers did not look too favorably at their fate. With the dying dignity of a vanquished villain, he ordered his demonic rulers back to their positions all over the world with the order to continue the lies that the Redeemer never visited the earth and that he was not real, but just a fable.

As the Redeemer stepped out of the tomb, the entire angelic host bowed in worship and beamed with adoration at the love he had demonstrated for his creation and the lengths at which he went to do it. They now fully understood what love was in action. He needed to present himself to the Father for a divine acceptance of the sacrifice, to which the Father enthusiastically approved. He then headed back down to present himself to the disciples.

The validation of the redemption process (the first flesh-and-bone resurrected body)

After the Sabbath, at dawn on the first day of the week, which coincided with the resurrection day of the Redeemer, the women went to look at the tomb to complete the preservation process of the Redeemer's body.

They were met by an angel who, seeing they were frightened upon seeing him, said to them, "Do not be afraid, for I know that you are looking for the Messiah, who was crucified. He is not here. He has risen, just as he said. Come and see the place where he lay," as he showed them the empty tomb. He then told them to go quickly and tell his disciples that he was risen from the dead and was going ahead of them into Galilee. There they were to find him.

The women hurried away from the tomb, afraid yet filled with joy, and ran to tell his disciples. Suddenly, as if materializing out of thin air, he met them. "Greetings," he said. Recognizing that voice anywhere and at any time, they came to him, clasped his feet, and worshiped him. Then sensing their fear and bewilderment, he said to them, "Do not be afraid. Go and tell my brothers, the disciples, to go to Galilee. There they will see me." With that, he urged them off, being ecstatic at the turn of events. What a difference three days and three nights had made, and now they had their Lord back in the flesh.

Chaos in the world of religious and political leaders

The guards knew they were in mortal danger because losing a prisoner under their guard meant death by Roman law. Well, they had to choose whether to die by the hands of the Roman law or by the hands of the much more dreaded supernatural force they had had to contend with. After having discussed this among themselves, totally bewildered, they went into the city and reported to the chief priests everything that had happened.

The chief priests, in turn, met with the elders and, instead of admitting their error, devised a public relations plan in which they gave the soldiers a large sum of money, telling them to say that his disciples came during the night and stole him away while they were asleep. They solemnly swore to the soldiers that if this report got to the governor, they would satisfy him appropriately and keep the guards out of trouble—something which they successfully accomplished.

So the soldiers took the money and did as they were instructed. They preferred not having to deal with that experience and were willing to put it behind them even more so than the elders and chief priest. And this improbable story that the disciples stole his body from the formidable Roman guard has been widely circulated among the Jews to this very day.

The soldiers wanted no part of the terrifying experiences from when the man was nailed to the cross to when the body seemed to have reemerged from death in the presence of those two terrifying men with faces like lightning. The darkness, the earthquakes, and all else in a space of three days was more than these very tough and rugged soldiers could handle. There were two ruling council members who knew they had made the right choice in siding with the Redeemer, and it was so gratifying to them, to say the least, and these were Joseph of Arimathea and Nicodemus.

The Great Commission

Then the eleven disciples (with Judas Iscariot now dead) went to Galilee to the mountain where the Redeemer had told them to go after hearing the report from the women. The whole experience had left them with mixed emotions. When they saw him, they were overwhelmed and could not help themselves but worship him. He then comforted them like little children and addressed the questions they fired at him. Then looking at them, he said, "All authority in heaven and on earth has been given to me. Therefore, go and make disciples of all nations, baptizing them in the name of the Father and of the Son and of the Holy Spirit and teaching them to obey everything I have commanded you. And surely, I am with you always to the very end of the age."

He appeared to them over a period of forty days and spoke about the eternal kingdom. On one occasion, while he was eating with them, he commanded them not to leave Jerusalem but to wait for the gift his father promised, which they had heard him speak about. For John baptized with water, but in a few days, they would be baptized with the Holy Spirit.

Gathering around, they asked him whether he was now going to restore the kingdom to Israel, to which he replied that it was not for them to know the times or dates the Father had set by his own authority, but they were going to receive power when the Holy Spirit came on them, for then they would be empowered to be his witnesses or ambassadors in Jerusalem and in all Judea and Samaria and to the ends of the earth.

On his last day with them, after further encouragement and insisting they wait in Jerusalem till they received the gift of the Spirit, something they did not quite understand yet, they watched him suddenly rise and ascend physically. They watched him go with tears in their eyes as he ascended into the clouds and then was gone with a promise to return bodily in his second coming to set up the promised kingdom.

The Holy Spirit

Forty days after the ascension of the Redeemer to heaven, a day when all the disciples were gathered in one place as they had been instructed to do, and the Lord seeing that they were all there, it happened. Suddenly a sound like the blowing of a violent wind came from heaven and filled the whole house where they were sitting. They saw what seemed to be tongues of fire that separated and came to rest on each of them. All of them were filled with the Holy Spirit and began to speak in other languages as the Spirit enabled them. "So this is what it meant to be baptized by the Holy Spirit," they reasoned, and they knew and felt it.

It so happened that at this very particular time, there were visitors from many nations visiting in Jerusalem from far and wide, and they all heard this spectacular sound. As they rushed to the source of the sound, they were bewildered when they heard the lowly Galilean disciples speaking in all the different languages of the visitors, extolling the Creator's majesty.

It turned out that this was just the beginning of what the Creator had in mind. In bearing witness of what the Redeemer had taught, the Spirit performed great miracles through those disciples who had received him. They prayed, and dead people were raised back to life, the lame could walk, blind could see, healings of myriads of diseases, and casting out of demons from those possessed.

The same men who had lived like cowards since the arrest and crucifixion of their master had suddenly become so bold that they were willing to die for what they were teaching without fear. Thousands embraced the redemption offer and accepted the Creator as their Lord and started a life like nothing they ever knew before. It was like taking blinders off their eyes so that they could easily and clearly see what was so obvious that any fool could see and understand. Contrary to the lies of the religious leaders, the Redeemer had indeed resurrected, and the power of death had been broken. The incredible power of the Creator was manifested in the simple disciples, and everyone could see it.

However, the religious leaders and the ruling council fought back to stamp out the wave of conversions; and unable to fight the truth, they resorted to severe persecution of the many who had accepted the redemption offer. They killed and jailed any they could and paid huge sums of money to hunt and kill any ruling council members who changed ranks. However, even some key members of the council and teachers of the law, upon seeing what had transpired, not willing to fight their consciences anymore, decided to accept the Redeemer as their Lord, and one of those was a man called Saul, a Pharisee, who later became known as Paul. He was a very learned man who had been spiritually blinded until he encountered the Redeemer himself in a vision with others on a trip, and he became a great witness to Europe, the near East, and Caesar of the Roman empire.

These new disciples, in addition to the eleven apostles, carried the teachings across the world as they travelled and significantly impacted the Roman empire. The world now had a chance to see the power of the Creator manifested through ordinary people, a process that is meant to continue through to the very end when the kingdom of heaven is finally established on earth. The Roman empire's advanced rule of law and relative peaceful stability at the time helped the spread of the new teaching, and the Creator saw to it that Rome had an opportunity for a front-row seat of exposure to the Redeemer and his teachings just as he did with the previous empires.

Chapter 18

The Most Powerful Transformer in the Universe

A human without the Spirit of the Creator

Before the Creator steps into the lordship position of the life of a human being, his typical behavioral tendencies, in various degrees, usually include

- sexual immorality,
- impurity and debauchery,
- idolatry and witchcraft,
- hatred,
- discord,
- jealousy,
- fits of rage,
- selfish ambitions,
- dissensions,
- factions and envy,
- drunkenness,
- orgies,
- wanton pride,
- and the like, all being part of the hallmark of the sinful nature of the fallen man.

Humans may brand themselves with religious affiliations of any type, and if they have any of the above behavioral tendencies, they are unregenerated and not the human product the Creator wanted them to be. These tendencies in man generally led to a society full of violence, and the Creator detests a violent society because it hurts his creatures.

A human with the Spirit of the Creator

As it turns out, the Spirit of the Creator, sent into man when man chooses to appropriate the offer of redemption, brings with him the most potent force in the universe. The Spirit provides the transforming power to regenerated man into the great masterpiece which lets humans see the beauty the Creator had intended for man. This is only done if the human is willing and asks the Creator to do it. No mediator is needed and that is one of the ways humans begin to interact with the Creator one on one. His method of interaction is clearly laid out in how he dealt with those who chose to walk with him in the past. He always reveals himself in a way every individual will recognize it is him, and it is different from one to the other.

There is no normal human being who does not love the regenerated man. The Creator's Spirit, if allowed, will transform an unregenerated human into one who becomes

- loving,
- joyful,
- peaceful,
- forbearing,
- kind,
- good,
- faithful,
- gentle, and
- having great self-control.

This is what the Creator intends for man to be, and the Spirit of the Creator is sent to empower humans to experience this transformation process. It is the Creator's offer to humanity and is available on demand.

From the looks of it, it appears that humans have a simple choice based on their lifestyle preference—one with the behavioral tendencies of the unregenerated person or one the Creator offers to those who choose to walk with him and, therefore, are guided by his Spirit. As far as the Creator is concerned, it could be one individual or a whole nation. Imagine a nation with only regenerated people. Talk about a bunch who would live life on earth loving others as they themselves want to be loved. That is what the Creator has in his heart and in store for humanity in his kingdom.

Between the resurrection and the return of the Redeemer

When the disciples asked the Redeemer when he would return to earth as well as fully establish his kingdom on earth, he told them that his Father's house had many mansions and that he was going back there to the Father to prepare a place for them, after which he will come back and take them to be with him perpetually. He explained that this will happen in two stages as follows:

1. The message of the forgiveness for the sins of humans must first be preached by them and their followers to the entire world for a witness and an opportunity for all humanity. By then, the city prepared will be ready for them to occupy. He explained that he needed to give the world a chance to exhaust all available options to hear and understand the message for them to decide if they wanted to spend eternity with him or not.

2. Secondly, at the appointed time set by the Father, after the message had reached the entire earth, those who at the given time had decided to be part of the kingdom, known as the redeemed, will all be taken off the earth. The departure sequence was scheduled in stages and determined by the Father alone. For those who would be alive, their departure will occur in a moment of time without any warning, just

like in the days of Noah when the flood came suddenly. The world will know that a sizable population of living humanity had suddenly vanished, and the rest of the world will remember this incident and will try explaining it away as some kind of alien abduction of some sort, among other conspiracy theories.

The Holy Spirit, who currently restrains wickedness from totally engulfing all humanity, will also leave the earth and return to the Father with this mixed multitude of redeemed Arabs, Jews, Asians, Africans, Americans, Europeans, and people from all parts of the earth; and it will be a mixed multitude indeed. The people left behind will include those who had not made up their minds to that point, had rejected the offer, or just pretended to live like they were true followers of the Creator or those who may have trusted their religions and institutions instead of the Creator. Those who are left behind at that time will include Arabs, Jews, Asians, Africans, Americans, Europeans, and people from all parts of the earth.

With the departure of the Holy Spirit from the earth, evil will explode, and the world will be awash in violence and unprecedented suffering and anarchy like never before. For then, there will be great distress unequaled from the beginning of the world until then as the earth will convulse from natural, intentional, and unintended man-made disasters and never to be equaled again. The world will cry out for a deliverer especially the promised Messiah.

> During this period, false messiahs and false prophets will increase in number and some will perform great signs and wonders to deceive, if possible, even those determined to live by the statutes of the Creator in order to enter the eternal kingdom of heaven. At that time some will say, "Look, here is the Messiah!" or "There he is!"

This is not to be believed because his next return will not be in secret or a secret.

Most of the global religious groups will coalesce into a one-world religious system that will be formed to replace the departed true followers of the Creator, and it will have a lot of influence over people left on earth. As a result of the ensuing relentless chaos and calamities that will rock the world, the most dreadful war machines yet will be created, deployed, and utilized as nations battle each other for resources, dominance, and just because they can for the fun of it.

As a result of the explosion of violence and wickedness, those attempting to live by the statutes of the Creator at this time will go through great persecution and pain. The wickedness of man will also be judged by the creator through

- pandemics,
- periods of global scorching heat like never before experienced,
- contaminated water,
- famines.

Death will be temporarily suspended for a period of time when humanity is subjected to certain calamities to taste for themselves the pain of what they had created. During these specific calamities, people will try killing themselves to flee the pain but will not be able and will ask to die, but death will flee until when allowed back. Humanity will be given front-row seats to have a taste of pain they helped create for others just like the chickens coming home to roost.

Revelation of the devil's post-Rapture conference

As only the Creator can, in his mercy and grace, he has chosen to reveal to humanity key activities through time all the way to the one-thousand-year kingdom and what the devil will be involved in and do. Like he said, he declares the end of things from the beginning so that when they happen, those who listen to him will know and remember that he told them ahead of time. He wants humanity prewarned in order not to be needlessly swept into unnecessary suffering. In the next phase of the post-Rapture life, he therefore reveals what is to happen.

The Creator then reveals that during this post-Rapture period, the devil finally finds someone more narcissistic than himself, relinquishes power to him—a man who ventured where not even the devil himself would dare to. While there have been evil and vile men in the history of the world, no one will come close to what the devil's followers will uncover, and word will be passed along to the devil, who will call a meeting to discuss the developments. Just as the Creator revealed the last empires the world will see before the end of time, he has also, as only he can, revealed exactly what the devil will do in order to give all humanity advanced warning. Those who heed the warning will deliver their souls, but those who choose not to will have no excuse when they are swept in the devil's deception.

Excerpts from the devil's post-Rapture conference

LUCIFER. With the true followers of the Creator raptured out of the earth, it is now a matter of moments before the end comes for us. We have all been judged, and we are guilty of sedition against the Creator and a host of numerous grave and even far worse crimes.

AGAG. It is obvious we are no match for the army of the Creator's angels. We must admit that he has been merciful and patient with us even when we passed the point of no return.

BELZE. In helping the religious rulers sentence the Redeemer to death for sedition, we sort of confirmed in the eyes of the angels and humanity that we are guilty and deserve our punishment. Our strategy of making the Creator look like a vengeful and angry oligarch who is intent on punishing angels and humans for trivial infractions of no consequences totally imploded, and we are seen for who we really are.

AGAG. I suppose we were caught in the madness of the moment, and we did not think things through. At the end of the day, there's more to make us look disgusting and well deserving of our fate anyway.

LUCIFER. Anyway, we must move on. It won't be the first time we have majorly messed up. Based on the communication through the grapevines, word has it that there is a man who is possibly the vilest human ever to walk the earth. I have investigated and followed his profile, and as such, I intend to transfer my power, throne, and great authority to him. We can call him the beast.

BELZE. Why do you want to do this?

LUCIFER. Deflection.

AGAG. Could you expound on that?

LUCIFER. Out of frustration of the global turmoil, global roiling calamities, and incessant unrest we have been instrumental in masterminding, a global savior or messiah is being desperately sorted for. We all know the Messiah himself is expected as men investigate fulfilled prophecies regardless of how hard we try deceiving them from believing in the true prophecies and Creator. We need a man on whom we can transfer power to who will mesmerize the whole world and keep them from the truth. Hopefully with almost unlimited power, his ego will be blasted into the stratosphere especially when he sees that his power and authority give him a slight edge above other humans. We shall give him a mouth to blaspheme the Creator and to slander his name, his dwelling place, and those who live in heaven. The whole world will need to be filled with wonder, like the sci-fi movies in order to follow him especially if they are made to believe he can blaspheme the Creator and get away with it unscathed even though just for a season.

BELZE. Based on the Creator's revelations to the entire world, it means he will be a ruthless man of war who implements brilliant economic marvels and short-lived peace treaties that he would break at his convenience. He will destroy and take over the post-Rapture one-world religious system and subsequently declare himself as god and demanding all humans to worship him. He will destroy all who oppose him, and he will drag the world to the precipice of annihilation.

AGAG. If I read this correctly, he will actually declare war against the true Messiah when he appears in the clouds with his angelic army.

LUCIFER. That is our man. Imagine giving him all the power I can. Being human, that will put him almost in par with the preresurrection Messiah, who though human was able to exercise some of his divine attributes. This will be a huge deception tool, and humans are more likely to accept and worship him with little or no help from us.

BELZE. What is the angle with the power play? You understand the implications of power transfer.

LUCIFER. The power is useless to me or any of us. We are doomed anyway, and if this fellow is crazy enough to challenge the Creator in battle, he and any accomplices he has will certainly be the first occupants of the lake of fire, and we should avoid that residence for as long as we can. I may have been the biggest fool to think I could outsmart my Creator, but I might be meeting my match or a greater fool than I am in this beast.

AGAG. We did challenge the Creator's army in battle, thanks to you, Luc!

LUCIFER. The proposal did look good to you all at the time.

BELZE. It did not turn out the way we had thought—just dreadful! I will still never understand how we could have challenged the Creator in battle, one who speaks things into existence, including us, for crying out loud!

AGAG. The firepower we thought we had turned out to be more like cotton balls going against the power in a blazing volcanic eruption, for lack of a better analogy, and that is only the lowest level of angelic defense line.

LUCIFER. I cringe at the thought looking back. What hurts more than anything is the haunting of the thought of never ever going back to live in heaven—the joy, the beauty, the exciting activities, the food, the peace, the music, and the mirth resulting from the presence of the Creator. The thoughts of loss burn deeply.

BELZE. Get a grip on yourself! It is too late for that.

The Messiah shows up as the king

Then without warning, on the day and time only the Father knows and has set will appear the sign of the Messiah. And then all the peoples of the earth will cry out, mourning when they see him coming on the clouds of heaven with power and great glory. For as lightning that comes from the east is visible even in the west, so will his coming be. It will be sudden and without warning, and everyone will see him. His appearing will be to put an end to the global carnage and the ushering in of the start of a thousand-year reign on earth with a rod of iron. The first time the Messiah came as the redeemer, he came as a little born baby, but this time he comes as the King of kings.

Seeing the appearance of the Messiah, the devil and all his followers flee into hiding as far away as they could get. But true to form, the beast, who will have a false prophet also empowered by the devil, will rally the world armies under his command and set battle lines to challenge him and his armies in the skies. Armed with the very advanced ultrahypersonic thermonuclear warheads missiles able to destroy the earth multiple times over, he makes the world believe an evil alien nation is invading earth. At his command, these warheads are unleashed at the Messiah and his armies.

With just a word from the Messiah's mouth, the armies of the earth are eviscerated while the beast and his false prophet are seized and dragged off, screaming into the lake of fire, prepared for the devil and his followers, making these two humans the very first occupants of the residence that terrifies even the devil and his followers.

With the armies crushed, an angel seizes the devil from his hiding place, chains him up, throws him into a pit, and shuts him up for the duration of a thousand years so that he will have no interaction or influence on any humans during this time. The rest of the devil's followers will also be incarcerated and shut up, thereby clearing out all satanic and demonic influence and deception on the earth.

The Messiah then sets up the raptured humans and those persecuted to death, among others, during the post-Rapture rule by the beast in administrative roles to rule the earth for a thousand years of the kingdom of heaven. The Jewish disciples will also be set to judge the Jewish people with David, one who was after the Creator's heart, brought in as their king.

For the first time since the fall of Adam and Eve, the world will be at peace even with the animals. Men get a chance to see life in the absence of the devil and his followers, and this will be the only time when there will be peace on earth when swords and other weapons of war will be repurposed and converted into plowshares and other farming equipment and machinery, and life on earth will be very good.

This will be the only time when the Jews will fully occupy the land given to Abraham by the Creator who keeps his covenant even to the end. David will be brought back to be the reigning monarch of the nation of Israel because he earned the privilege as a man determined to do what the Creator had in his heart—righteous leadership while he lived. For the first time, all highways and other travel channels will link the Arab nations directly with Israel, and they shall all celebrate the festivals the Creator gave Israel as a memorial.

At the end of the thousand years, those who had been born during this time would be given a chance to make a choice whether they want to be part of the kingdom of the Creator or not, for the Father had declared that none will be forced to be a part of his kingdom. To this end, the devil will be loosed from his prison for a short while and allowed to test those dwelling on the earth at this time.

Time folds into eternity

After all these things, as the world moves into the edge of timeless eternity, the devil and his fellow fallen angels will reach the end of their existence. This is a time they had all dreaded but know and accept their punishment as being more than justified and fully deserved.

In a flash, a single powerful archangel dispatched from heaven seizes a whimpering devil in one scoop and chains him while the rest of his fallen angels are rounded up in parallel and tossed into the lake of fire where they would spend eternity for their rebellion in heaven and the carnage perpetrated on humanity and creation. This is the second death.

All humans on earth then will be ushered over the threshold of life then into the world of the dead to be judged by the Creator based on whether they accepted to be part of his kingdom or not. Those who rejected it would be separated eternally from the Creator and will spend eternity away from him.

This will be one of the saddest points in human history—when men are given what they chose in life after seeing the impact their lives had on other humans on earth through to the end of time.

It will open up a state of anguish and torment that will make the flames of hell look like a child's picnic as people look back at what they had rejected in exchange of what they were getting just like the devil.

While the lake of fire has multiple levels, it is not a place anyone would want to wish on their worst enemy; and while it was made as the abode for the devil, those who condoned his ways and rejected the Creator will spend eternity with him in isolation and darkness. There are only two destinations for humanity—heaven or the lake of fire—and it is by choice and no one would be forced to either place, but the choice must be made while one is alive; this is because there is no repentance in the grave or beyond the grave. Most important of all, the Creator seeks no one's opinion which will not be necessary after evidence in the jumbotron is presented during the final judgment!

Prerecreation conference

FATHER. The devil, his followers, and humanity have spoken and made their choices and are now in their chosen destinations.

SON. The redeemed have indeed made their choice, and hence, you have eliminated the tree of knowledge of good and evil and only the tree of life is in the city.

SPIRIT. With man now fully restored to the perfect spiritual state, we have unity.

FATHER. Look! My dwelling place is now among the people, and I will dwell with them. They will be my people and I will be with them and be their God and I will wipe every tear from their eyes. There will be no more death or mourning or crying or pain, for the old order of things has passed away. I am the beginning and the end, and I am making everything new! A new earth and a new heaven.

SON. Man is endowed with so many gifts, and he gets a chance to exercise them to their fullest capacity. Men getting to work for fun instead of toiling and looking forward to live and wallow in true love, which they will give and receive in abandon. To live a life where they are loved as they desire to be and love as they desire to be loved freely.

FATHER. Behold the blueprints of the new heavens and the new earth.

Chapter 19

The Creator's Tested-and-Guaranteed Solution for a Lasting Peace between Israel, the Arabian Nations, and the World at Large

Remember his everlasting and unchanging covenant to Abraham regarding Hagar and Ishmael as well as the part regarding Isaac and the land of Canaan—does history bear this out?

Israel's unconditional terms for revival playbook

After being plagued by spiritual darkness and the ensuing suffering, all Israel came crying to Samuel to cry out to the Creator on their behalf and remind him of his everlasting covenant with them as a people. He knew why they were currently in bondage, and so his message to them was very simple:

He said to all the Israelites, "The Lord's covenant is unchanging. If you are willing to return to the Lord with all your hearts, then rid yourselves first of the foreign gods and the Ashtoreths and commit yourselves to the Lord and serve him only, and he will deliver you out of the hand of the Philistines and your other enemies." This they proceeded to do, and all the Israelites put away their Baals, Ashtoreths, and all the other idols and served the Lord only.

Then Samuel said to them, "Assemble all Israel at Mizpah, and I will intercede with the Lord for you." When they had assembled at Mizpah, they drew water and poured it out before the Lord. On that day, they fasted, and there they confessed their sins to the Lord with the promise to abide by his word.

After Samuel prayed, the Creator unleashed on the enemies, particularly the Philistines, so much so that the Philistines were subdued, and they stopped invading Israel's territory. Throughout Samuel's lifetime, while they kept the statutes of the Creator, the hand of the Lord was against the Philistines. The towns from Ekron to Gath that the Philistines had captured from Israel were restored to Israel, and Israel delivered the neighboring territory from the hands of the Philistines. And there was peace between Israel and the Amorites as well.

Between *913–910 BC and 873–869 BCE*, Asa, the third king of the kingdom of Judah in Israel, ruled in Jerusalem. Taking his cue from the records on the prophet Samuel, King Asa did what was good and right in the eyes of the Creator. He removed the abominable altars of idolatrous worship and cut down all the idols that had been erected and were being worshipped. He commanded the people of Judah to seek the Creator, the Lord of their ancestors, and to obey his laws and commands. He removed the high places and the abominable incense altars in every town in Judah, and in keeping the covenant, the kingdom was at peace under him. He built up the fortified cities of Judah since the land was at peace. No one was at war with him during those years, for the Creator gave him rest.

"Let us build up these towns," he said to Judah. "And put walls around them with towers, gates, and bars. The land is still ours because we have sought the Lord our God. We sought him, and he has given us rest on every side." So they built and prospered.

Seeing that King Asa of Judah was not aligned with the rest of the nation of Israel, it therefore looked like fair game to a great army because he had an army of only three hundred thousand men from Judah equipped with large shields and with spears and 280 thousand from Benjamin armed with small shields and with bows. Attracted by the abundance of wealth in the region, Zerah the Cushite therefore marched out against them with an army of a million very seasoned fighting men and three hundred chariots. King Asa, encouraging himself in the Creator's divine protective covering, even though vastly outnumbered, outclassed, and without a natural chance of surviving the battle, went out to meet him, and they took up battle positions in the Valley of Zephathah near Mareshah.

Then King Asa called to the Creator and said, "Lord, there is no one like you to help the powerless against the mighty. Help us, Lord, for we rely on you and in your name and your covenant, and we have come against this vast army. Lord, you are our leader. Do not let mere mortals prevail against you because we are standing on your name and covenant."

The Creator, heeding to Asa's humble prayer, unleashed a supernatural terror on the enemy and struck down the invading Cushites before Asa's little army. This was reminiscent of the days when the Creator led them in battle when they were attacked. The Cushites fled, and Asa and his army pursued them as far as Gerar. Such a great number of Cushites fell that they could not recover; they were crushed irreparably by the small defending army of the men of Judah. They then carried off an enormous amount of plunder of droves of sheep, goats, and camels brought in as supplies by the invading army and then headed back to Jerusalem in great triumph and rejoicing.

Asa reactivates the everlasting covenant with the Creator

Being the all-seeing and interactive Creator toward humanity, he sent a message through one of his prophets called Azariah, the son of Oded, as he was returning from the battle, saying, "Listen to me, Asa and all the people of the tribes of Judah and Benjamin. The Lord is with you when you are with him. If you seek him, he will be found by you, but if you forsake him, he will forsake you. For a long time, Israel was without the true God, without a priest to teach my statutes, and they operated without my law. But in their distress, they turned to me and sought me, and I was found by them as I had always promised. In those days when the nation operated without my statutes, it was not safe to travel about, for all the inhabitants of the lands were in great turmoil. One nation was being crushed by another and one city by another because the Creator allowed them to be troubled with every kind of distress of their own making. But as for you, be strong and do not give up, for your work will be rewarded."

When Asa heard these words and the prophecy of Azariah, son of Oded, the prophet, he took courage. He undertook the task of removing the detestable idols from the whole land of Judah and Benjamin and from the towns he had captured in the hills of Ephraim. He repaired the altar of the Lord that was in front of the portico of the Lord's temple.

Then he assembled all the people of Judah and Benjamin and those from Ephraim, Manasseh, and Simeon, who had settled among them, for large numbers had come over to him from the idolatrous parts of the greater Israel when they saw that the Lord was with him.

They assembled at Jerusalem in the third month of the fifteenth year of Asa's reign. At that time, they sacrificed to the Lord and this time not just as a mindless and mundane ceremony but remembered his goodness to them and, therefore, entered into a covenant to seek the Lord of their ancestors with all their heart and soul. The king and all the people decided that whoever would not seek after the ways of the Lord was to be removed from their midst, whether small or great, man or woman. They took an oath to the Lord with loud acclamation, with shouting and with trumpets and horns. All the people rejoiced about the oath because they had sworn it wholeheartedly. They sought the Creator eagerly, and he was found by them. Therefore, the Lord gave them rest on every side.

King Asa also deposed his grandmother Maakah from her position as queen mother because she had made a repulsive idolatrous statue for the worship of Asherah. Asa cut it down, broke it up, and burned it in the Kidron Valley. Although he did not remove all the high places from the entire Israel, Asa's heart was fully committed to the Lord all his life. There was no more war until the thirty-fifth year of his reign, and they enjoyed the peace only the Creator could bring between Israel and the surrounding nations.

Other kings of Judah who ruled honoring the covenant of the Creator lived in peace with the Arab nations and throughout their history, but when they abandoned the Creator and ignored his covenant, the protective covering was withdrawn, and it was always suffering.

It was simply a matter of returning to the everlasting covenant the Creator had made with them as recorded by Moses and handed down, and it will be in effect into the millennium in the earthly kingdom of the Creator. Israel needs to do this if they want peace with the other Arab nations or ignore it and have to wait till the millennium. The chronicles of the kings of Israel and Judah attest to this. The Creator stands on his word and will never go back on it, for it is an everlasting covenant.

Epilogue

"For I know the plans I have for you, plans to prosper you and not to harm you, plans to give you hope and a future. Come and let us reason together. When you call on me and reach out to me, I will listen to you. However, when you seek me, you will find me when you seek me with all your heart. I am easy to find. I have no pleasure in the demise of the wicked but to see him or her come to repentance from the wicked ways and live, for why would you want to perish?

"Seek me while I may be found. Call on me while I am near, for there is no repentance in the grave, and you know not when death will come. Be absolutely certain you determine where you intend to spend eternity before you die. It is an irreversible trip, so be careful in your judgment, for there is a way that seems right to a man, but it ends in the way of death. The Redeemer has paid the full price for your free passage into my kingdom. It is free, but you must appropriate it.

"You may still not fully understand, but I will state it to make it clear to you: For my thoughts are not your thoughts, neither are your ways my ways. As the heavens are higher than the earth, so are my ways higher than your ways and my thoughts than your thoughts.

"Hear the conclusion of the whole matter: Remember me, your Creator, in the days of your youth, before the evil days come. Be very careful to honor and keep my statutes, for this is the whole duty of man for righteous living. For at the end of age, I will bring every work into judgment with every secret thing, whether it be good or whether it be evil, for I am a righteous judge. There is more hope for a fool than a human who is wise in his or her own eyes, so please choose life," declares the Creator.

About the Author

The author, who is married with children and a world traveler, greatly loves life. He is an analytical chemist and an inventor of medical products for monitoring life-threatening health conditions. His nature of work in applied science mandates operating in the realm of absolute truth and accuracy for these products that monitor the bridge between life and death.

Milton Keynes UK
Ingram Content Group UK Ltd.
UKHW010833271023
431440UK00001B/98